CORPORATE ASSETS

ONI
PRESS

AN ONI PRESS PUBLICATION

[adult swim]

Rick and Morty™

CORPORATE ASSETS

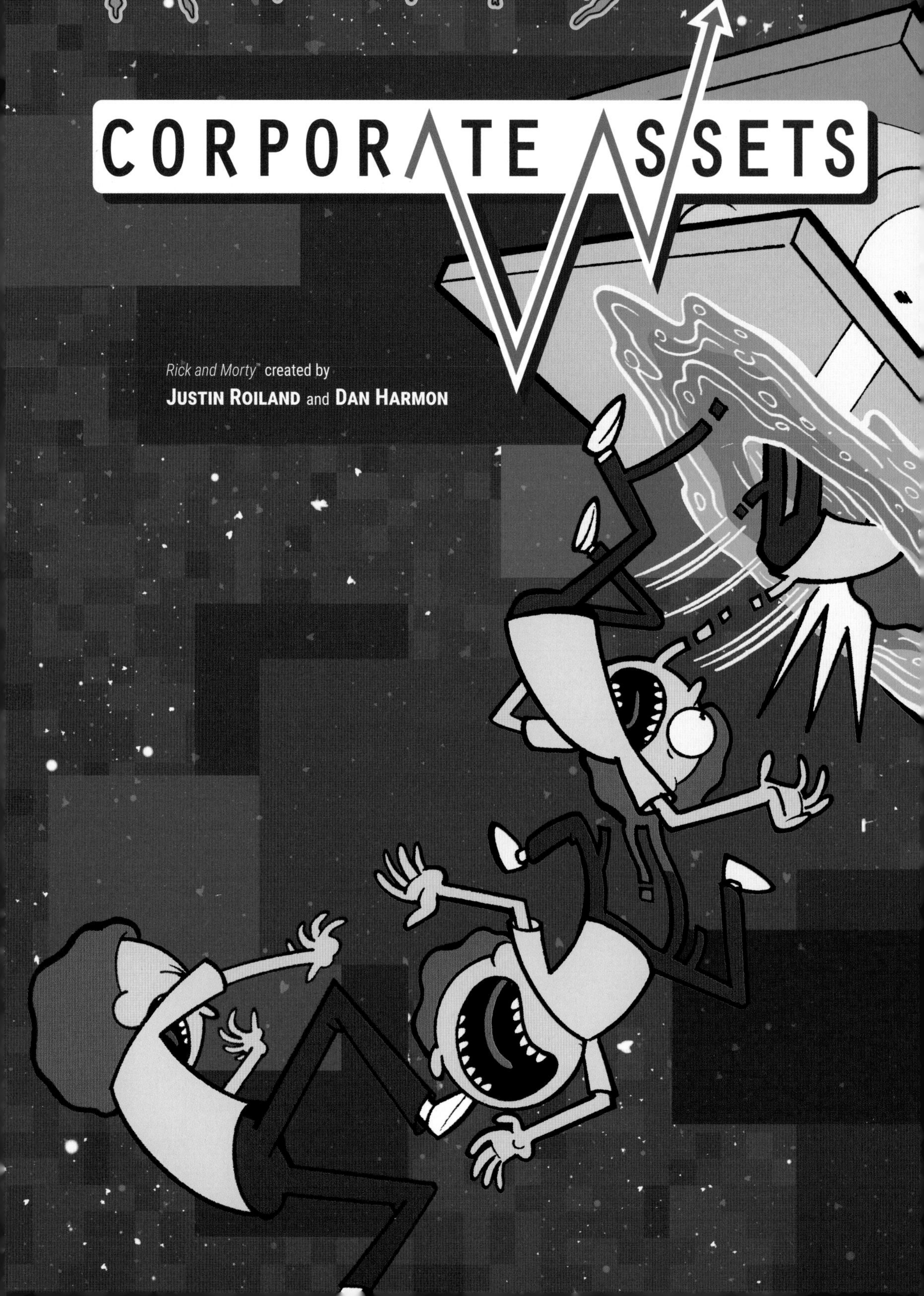

Rick and Morty™ created by
Justin Roiland and **Dan Harmon**

Written by **JAMES ASMUS**

Illustrated by **JARRETT WILLIAMS**

Colored by **JEREMY LAWSON**

Lettered by **CRANK!**

Cover by **JARRETT WILLIAMS** and **JEREMY LAWSON**

Edited by **ROBERT MEYERS**

Designed by **SARAH ROCKWELL**

PUBLISHED BY ONI-LION FORGE PUBLISHING GROUP, LLC.

JAMES LUCAS JONES, PRESIDENT & PUBLISHER

CHARLIE CHU, E.V.P. OF CREATIVE & BUSINESS DEVELOPMENT

STEVE ELLIS, S.V.P. OF GAMES & OPERATIONS

ALEX SEGURA, S.V.P. OF MARKETING & SALES

MICHELLE NGUYEN, ASSOCIATE PUBLISHER

BRAD ROOKS, DIRECTOR OF OPERATIONS

AMBER O'NEILL, SPECIAL PROJECTS MANAGER

KATIE SAINZ, DIRECTOR OF MARKETING

TARA LEHMANN, PUBLICITY DIRECTOR

HENRY BARAJAS, SALES MANAGER

HOLLY AITCHISON, CONSUMER MARKETING MANAGER

TROY LOOK, DIRECTOR OF DESIGN & PRODUCTION

ANGIE KNOWLES, PRODUCTION MANAGER

KATE Z. STONE, SENIOR GRAPHIC DESIGNER

CAREY HALL, GRAPHIC DESIGNER

SARAH ROCKWELL, GRAPHIC DESIGNER

HILARY THOMPSON, GRAPHIC DESIGNER

VINCENT KUKUA, DIGITAL PREPRESS TECHNICIAN

CHRIS CERASI, MANAGING EDITOR

JASMINE AMIRI, SENIOR EDITOR

AMANDA MEADOWS, SENIOR EDITOR

DESIREE RODRIGUEZ, EDITOR

GRACE SCHEIPETER, EDITOR

ZACK SOTO, EDITOR

GABRIEL GRANILLO, EDITORIAL ASSISTANT

BEN EISNER, GAME DEVELOPER

SARA HARDING, ENTERTAINMENT EXECUTIVE ASSISTANT

JUNG LEE, LOGISTICS COORDINATOR

KUIAN KELLUM, WAREHOUSE ASSISTANT

JOE NOZEMACK, PUBLISHER EMERITUS

ONIPRESS.COM

ADULTSWIM.COM /RICKANDMORTY

[adult swim]

THIS VOLUME COLLECTS #1–4 OF THE ONI PRESS SERIES
RICK AND MORTY™: CORPORATE ASSETS

FIRST EDITION: SEPTEMBER 2022
ISBN: 978-1-63715-085-6
EISBN: 978-1-63715-105-1
LIBRARY OF CONGRESS CONTROL NUMBER: 2022932151

1 2 3 4 5 6 7 8 9 10

SPECIAL THANKS TO Justin Roiland, Dan Harmon, Josh Anderson, Victoria Selover, and Kurtis Estes.

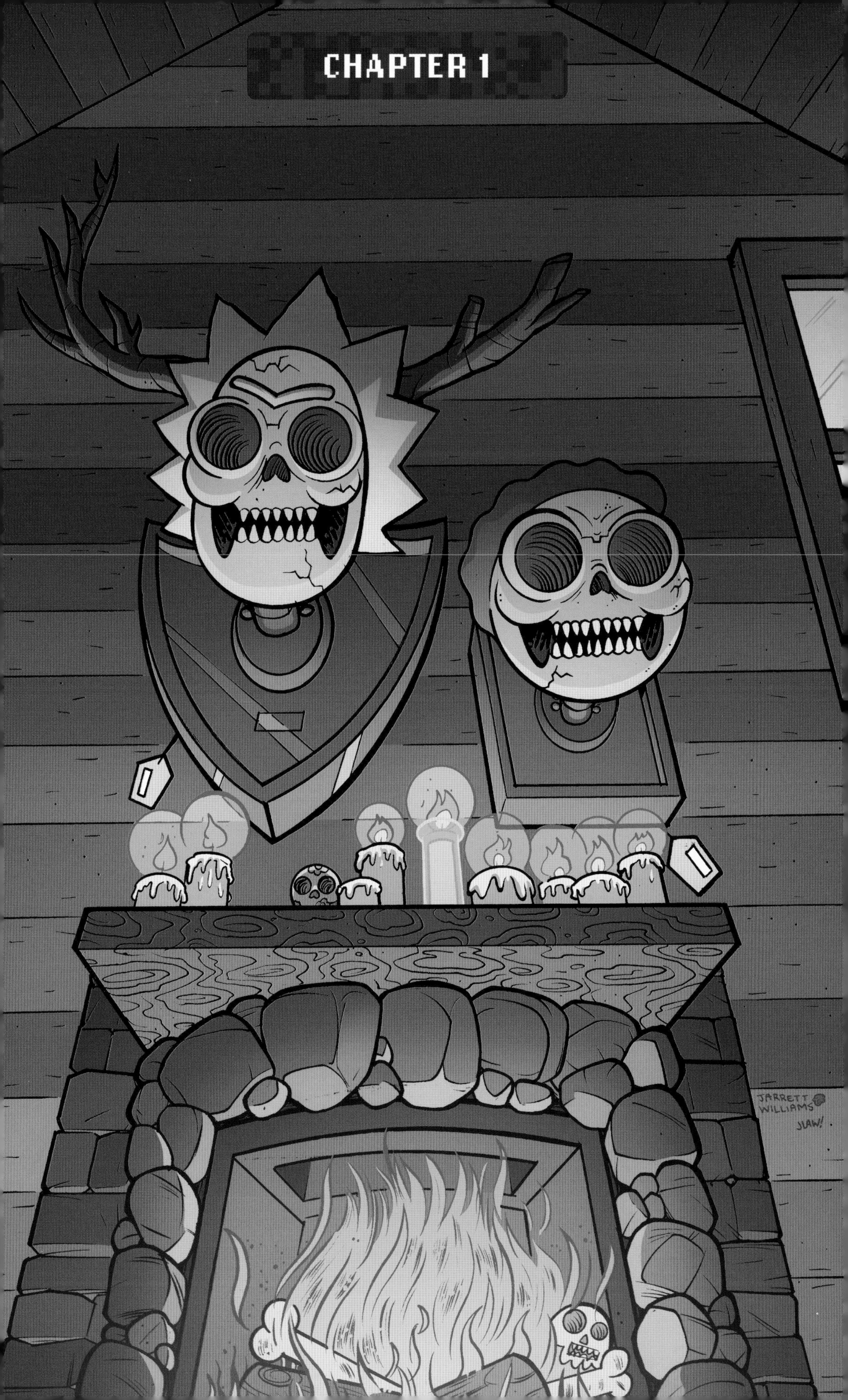
CHAPTER 1
JARRETT WILLIAMS
JLAW!

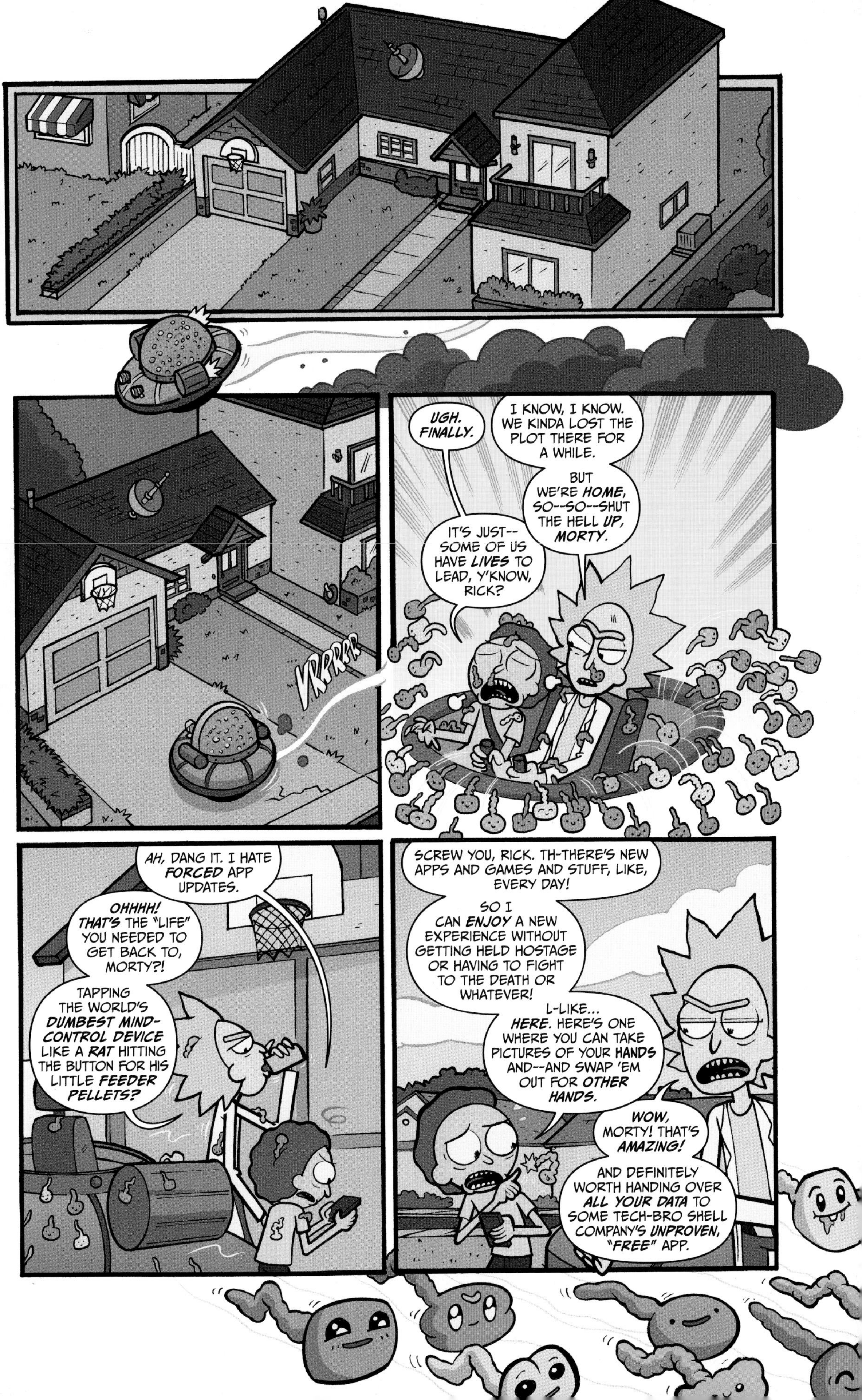

UGH. FINALLY.
I KNOW, I KNOW. WE KINDA LOST THE PLOT THERE FOR A WHILE.
BUT WE'RE HOME, SO--SO--SHUT THE HELL UP, MORTY.
IT'S JUST-- SOME OF US HAVE LIVES TO LEAD, Y'KNOW, RICK?
VRPRPR
AH, DANG IT. I HATE FORCED APP UPDATES.
OHHHH! THAT'S THE "LIFE" YOU NEEDED TO GET BACK TO, MORTY?!
TAPPING THE WORLD'S DUMBEST MIND-CONTROL DEVICE LIKE A RAT HITTING THE BUTTON FOR HIS LITTLE FEEDER PELLETS?
SCREW YOU, RICK. TH-THERE'S NEW APPS AND GAMES AND STUFF, LIKE, EVERY DAY!
SO I CAN ENJOY A NEW EXPERIENCE WITHOUT GETTING HELD HOSTAGE OR HAVING TO FIGHT TO THE DEATH OR WHATEVER!
L-LIKE... HERE. HERE'S ONE WHERE YOU CAN TAKE PICTURES OF YOUR HANDS AND--AND SWAP 'EM OUT FOR OTHER HANDS.
WOW, MORTY! THAT'S AMAZING!
AND DEFINITELY WORTH HANDING OVER ALL YOUR DATA TO SOME TECH-BRO SHELL COMPANY'S UNPROVEN, "FREE" APP.

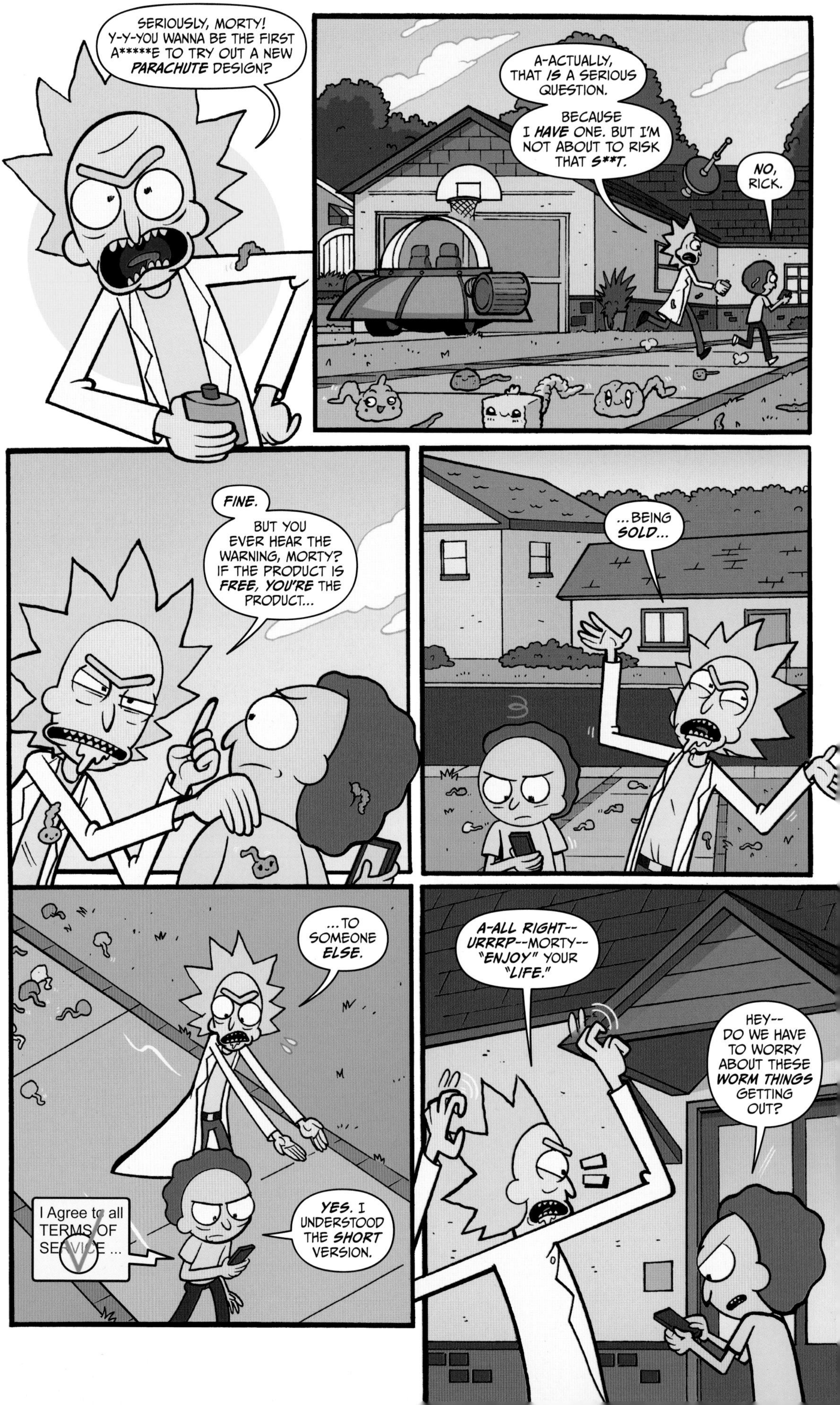

SERIOUSLY, MORTY! Y-Y-YOU WANNA BE THE FIRST A*****E TO TRY OUT A NEW PARACHUTE DESIGN?
A-ACTUALLY, THAT IS A SERIOUS QUESTION.
BECAUSE I HAVE ONE. BUT I'M NOT ABOUT TO RISK THAT S**T.
NO, RICK.
FINE.
BUT YOU EVER HEAR THE WARNING, MORTY? IF THE PRODUCT IS FREE, YOU'RE THE PRODUCT...
...BEING SOLD...
...TO SOMEONE ELSE.
I Agree to all TERMS OF SERVICE ...
YES. I UNDERSTOOD THE SHORT VERSION.
A-ALL RIGHT-- URRRP--MORTY-- "ENJOY" YOUR "LIFE."
HEY-- DO WE HAVE TO WORRY ABOUT THESE WORM THINGS GETTING OUT?

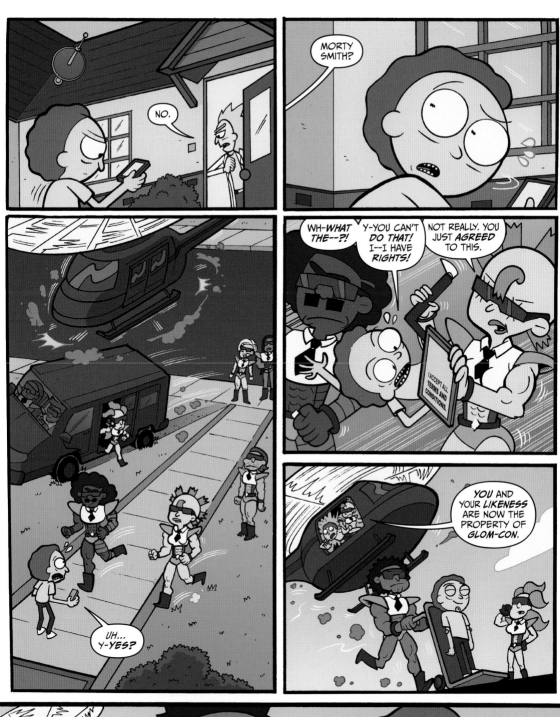

NO.

MORTY SMITH?

WH-*WHAT THE--?!*

Y-YOU CAN'T *DO THAT!* I--I HAVE *RIGHTS!*

NOT REALLY. YOU JUST *AGREED* TO THIS.

I ACCEPT ALL TERMS AND CONDITIONS.

UH... Y-YES?

YOU AND YOUR *LIKENESS* ARE NOW THE PROPERTY OF *GLOM-CON.*

IN *PERPETUITY.*

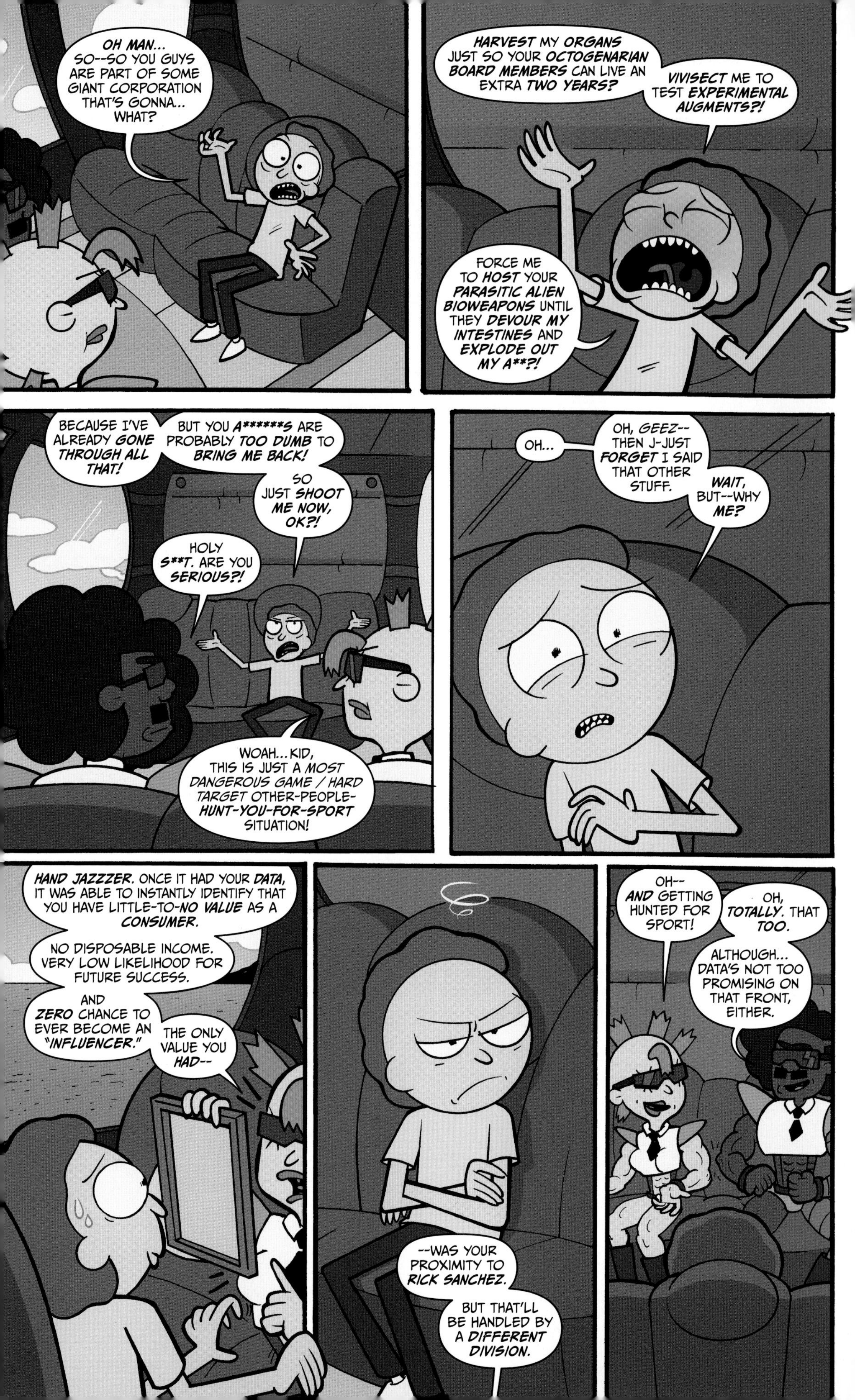
OH MAN... SO--SO YOU GUYS ARE PART OF SOME GIANT CORPORATION THAT'S GONNA... WHAT?
HARVEST MY ORGANS JUST SO YOUR OCTOGENARIAN BOARD MEMBERS CAN LIVE AN EXTRA TWO YEARS?
VIVISECT ME TO TEST EXPERIMENTAL AUGMENTS?!
FORCE ME TO HOST YOUR PARASITIC ALIEN BIOWEAPONS UNTIL THEY DEVOUR MY INTESTINES AND EXPLODE OUT MY A**?!
BECAUSE I'VE ALREADY GONE THROUGH ALL THAT!
BUT YOU A******S ARE PROBABLY TOO DUMB TO BRING ME BACK!
SO JUST SHOOT ME NOW, OK?!
HOLY S**T. ARE YOU SERIOUS?!
WOAH... KID, THIS IS JUST A MOST DANGEROUS GAME / HARD TARGET OTHER-PEOPLE-HUNT-YOU-FOR-SPORT SITUATION!
OH...
OH, GEEZ-- THEN J-JUST FORGET I SAID THAT OTHER STUFF.
WAIT, BUT--WHY ME?
HAND JAZZZER. ONCE IT HAD YOUR DATA, IT WAS ABLE TO INSTANTLY IDENTIFY THAT YOU HAVE LITTLE-TO-NO VALUE AS A CONSUMER.
NO DISPOSABLE INCOME. VERY LOW LIKELIHOOD FOR FUTURE SUCCESS.
AND ZERO CHANCE TO EVER BECOME AN "INFLUENCER."
THE ONLY VALUE YOU HAD--
--WAS YOUR PROXIMITY TO RICK SANCHEZ.
BUT THAT'LL BE HANDLED BY A DIFFERENT DIVISION.
OH-- AND GETTING HUNTED FOR SPORT!
OH, TOTALLY. THAT TOO.
ALTHOUGH... DATA'S NOT TOO PROMISING ON THAT FRONT, EITHER.

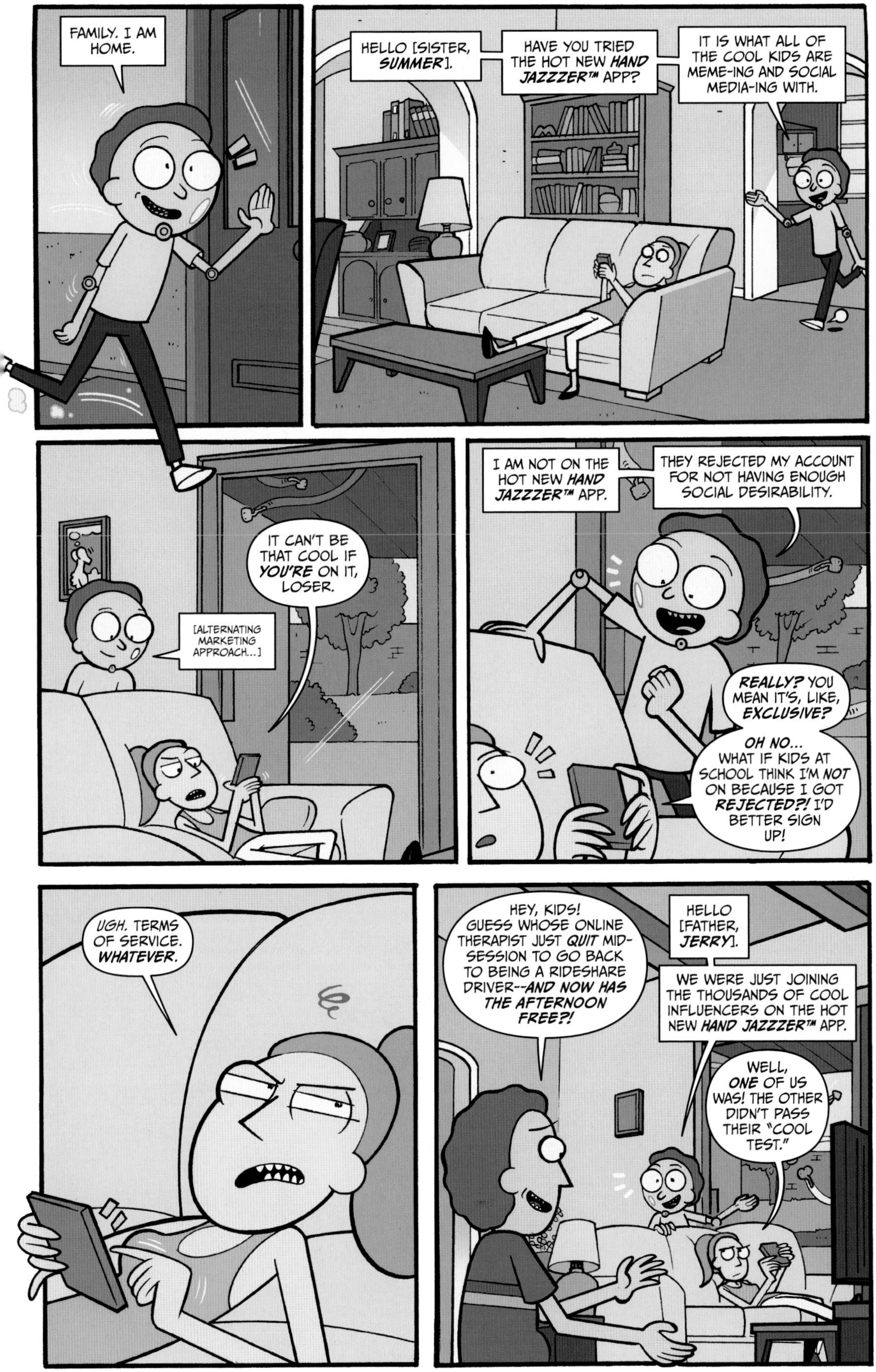

FAMILY. I AM HOME.
HELLO [SISTER, SUMMER].
HAVE YOU TRIED THE HOT NEW HAND JAZZZER™ APP?
IT IS WHAT ALL OF THE COOL KIDS ARE MEME-ING AND SOCIAL MEDIA-ING WITH.
IT CAN'T BE THAT COOL IF YOU'RE ON IT, LOSER.
[ALTERNATING MARKETING APPROACH...]
I AM NOT ON THE HOT NEW HAND JAZZZER™ APP.
THEY REJECTED MY ACCOUNT FOR NOT HAVING ENOUGH SOCIAL DESIRABILITY.
REALLY? YOU MEAN IT'S, LIKE, EXCLUSIVE?
OH NO... WHAT IF KIDS AT SCHOOL THINK I'M NOT ON BECAUSE I GOT REJECTED?! I'D BETTER SIGN UP!
UGH. TERMS OF SERVICE. WHATEVER.
HEY, KIDS! GUESS WHOSE ONLINE THERAPIST JUST QUIT MID-SESSION TO GO BACK TO BEING A RIDESHARE DRIVER--AND NOW HAS THE AFTERNOON FREE?!
HELLO [FATHER, JERRY].
WE WERE JUST JOINING THE THOUSANDS OF COOL INFLUENCERS ON THE HOT NEW HAND JAZZZER™ APP.
WELL, ONE OF US WAS! THE OTHER DIDN'T PASS THEIR "COOL TEST."

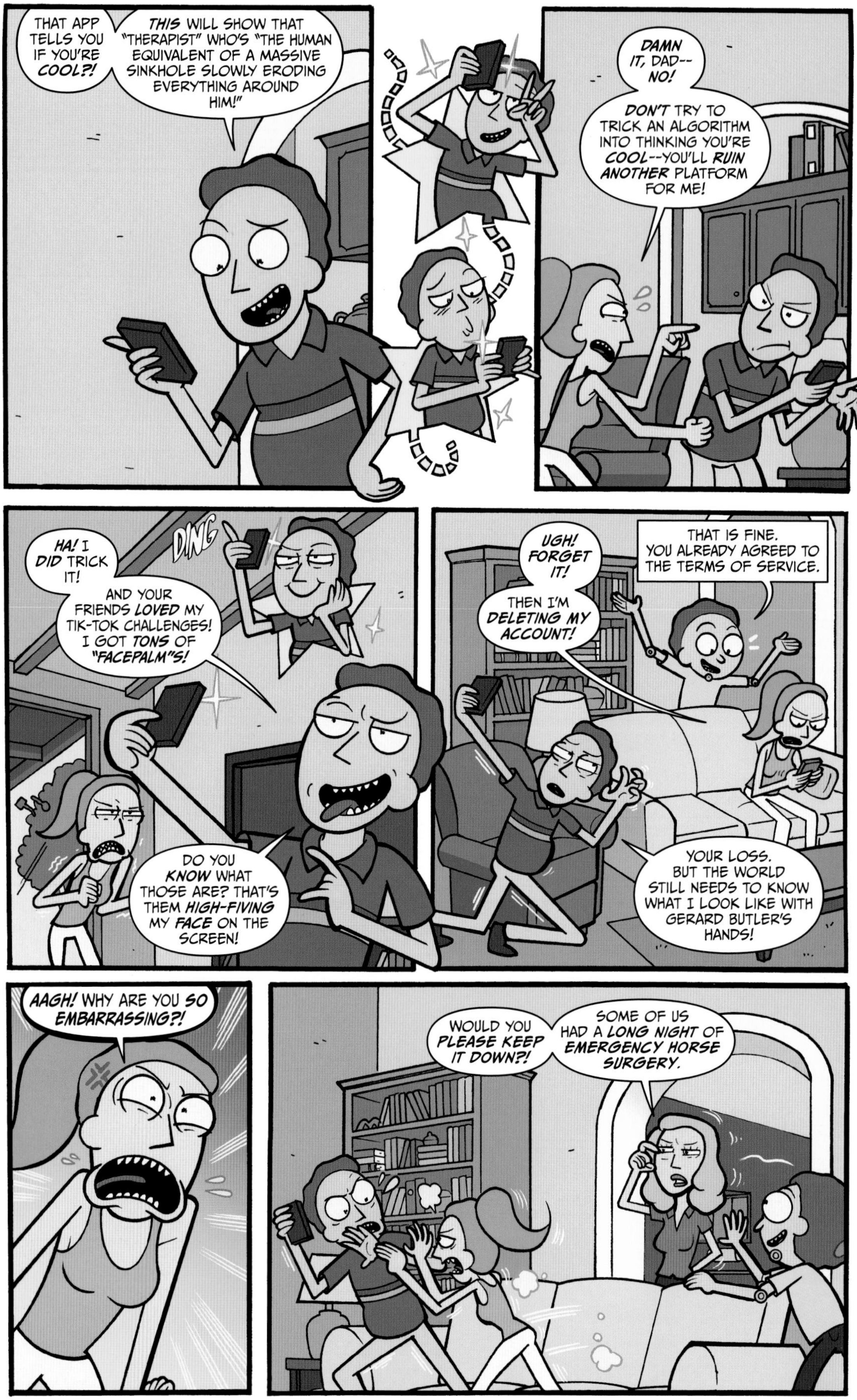
THAT APP TELLS YOU IF YOU'RE COOL?!
THIS WILL SHOW THAT "THERAPIST" WHO'S "THE HUMAN EQUIVALENT OF A MASSIVE SINKHOLE SLOWLY ERODING EVERYTHING AROUND HIM!"
DAMN IT, DAD-- NO!
DON'T TRY TO TRICK AN ALGORITHM INTO THINKING YOU'RE COOL--YOU'LL RUIN ANOTHER PLATFORM FOR ME!
DING
HA! I DID TRICK IT!
AND YOUR FRIENDS LOVED MY TIK-TOK CHALLENGES! I GOT TONS OF "FACEPALM"S!
DO YOU KNOW WHAT THOSE ARE? THAT'S THEM HIGH-FIVING MY FACE ON THE SCREEN!
UGH! FORGET IT!
THEN I'M DELETING MY ACCOUNT!
THAT IS FINE. YOU ALREADY AGREED TO THE TERMS OF SERVICE.
YOUR LOSS. BUT THE WORLD STILL NEEDS TO KNOW WHAT I LOOK LIKE WITH GERARD BUTLER'S HANDS!
AAGH! WHY ARE YOU SO EMBARRASSING?!
WOULD YOU PLEASE KEEP IT DOWN?!
SOME OF US HAD A LONG NIGHT OF EMERGENCY HORSE SURGERY.

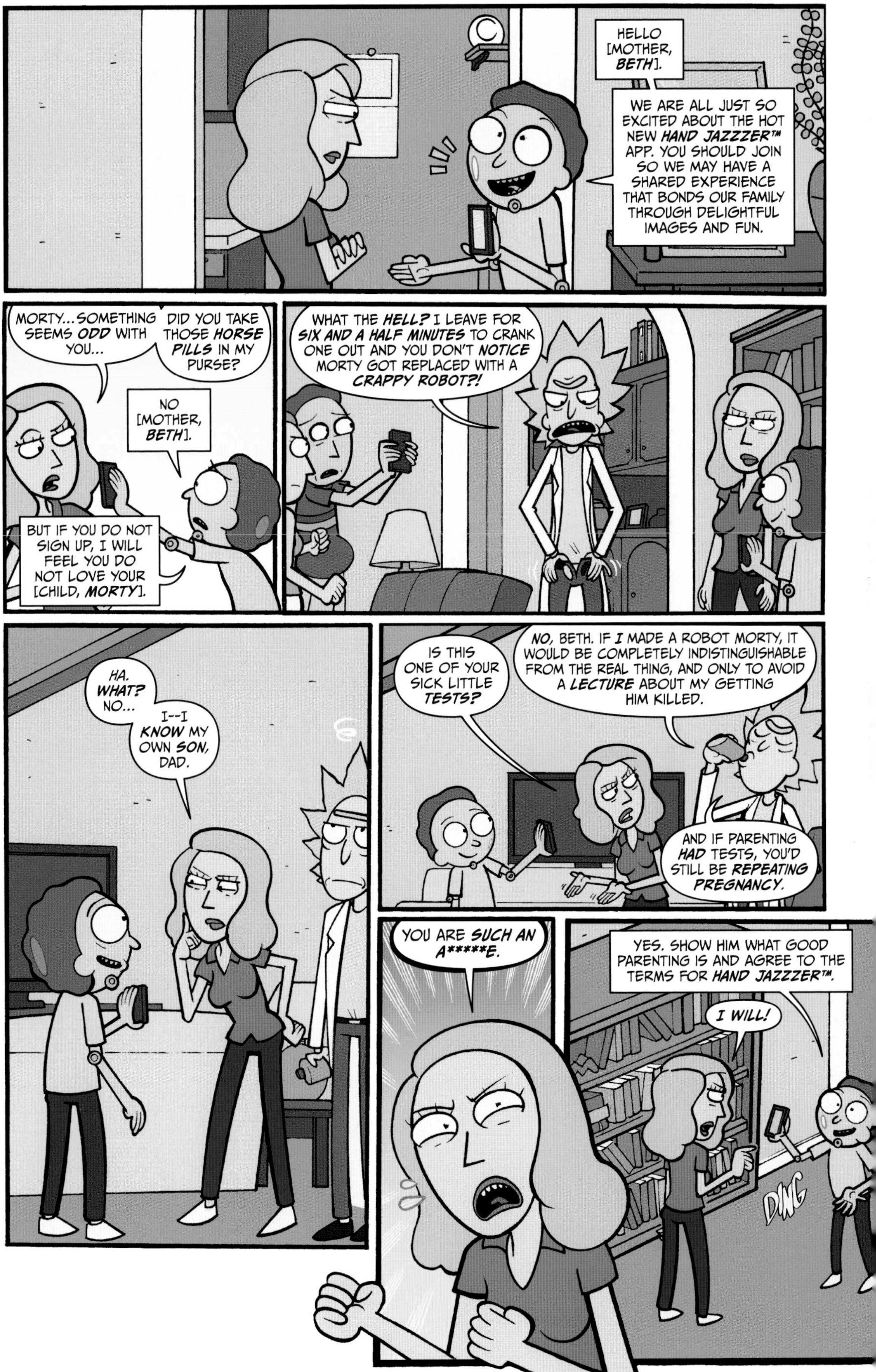
HELLO [MOTHER, BETH].
WE ARE ALL JUST SO EXCITED ABOUT THE HOT NEW HAND JAZZZER™ APP. YOU SHOULD JOIN SO WE MAY HAVE A SHARED EXPERIENCE THAT BONDS OUR FAMILY THROUGH DELIGHTFUL IMAGES AND FUN.
MORTY...SOMETHING SEEMS ODD WITH YOU...
DID YOU TAKE THOSE HORSE PILLS IN MY PURSE?
NO [MOTHER, BETH].
BUT IF YOU DO NOT SIGN UP, I WILL FEEL YOU DO NOT LOVE YOUR [CHILD, MORTY].
WHAT THE HELL? I LEAVE FOR SIX AND A HALF MINUTES TO CRANK ONE OUT AND YOU DON'T NOTICE MORTY GOT REPLACED WITH A CRAPPY ROBOT?!
HA. WHAT? NO...
I--I KNOW MY OWN SON, DAD.
IS THIS ONE OF YOUR SICK LITTLE TESTS?
NO, BETH. IF I MADE A ROBOT MORTY, IT WOULD BE COMPLETELY INDISTINGUISHABLE FROM THE REAL THING, AND ONLY TO AVOID A LECTURE ABOUT MY GETTING HIM KILLED.
AND IF PARENTING HAD TESTS, YOU'D STILL BE REPEATING PREGNANCY.
YOU ARE SUCH AN A*****E.
YES. SHOW HIM WHAT GOOD PARENTING IS AND AGREE TO THE TERMS FOR HAND JAZZZER™.
I WILL!
DING

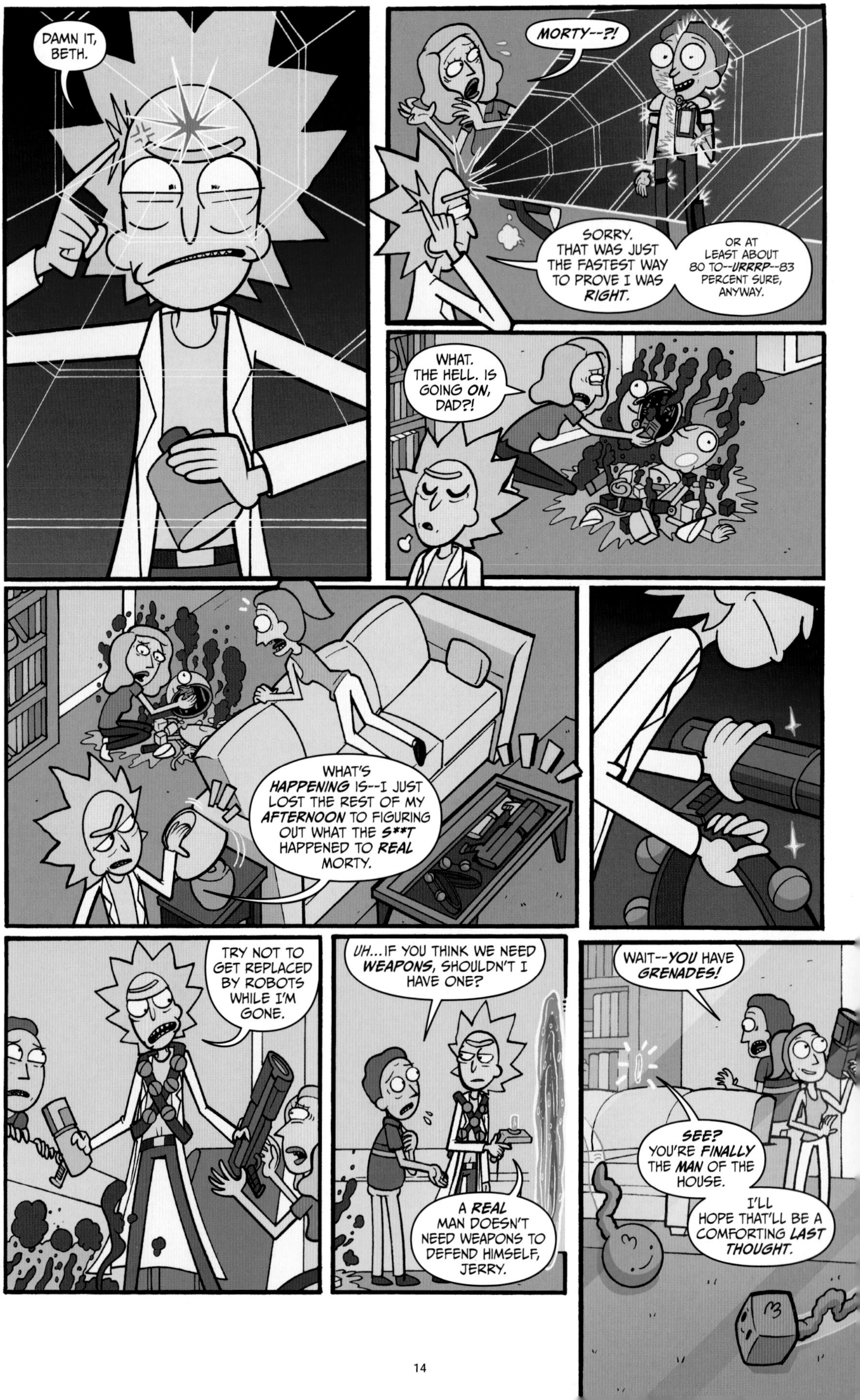
DAMN IT, BETH.
MORTY--?!
SORRY. THAT WAS JUST THE FASTEST WAY TO PROVE I WAS RIGHT.
OR AT LEAST ABOUT 80 TO--URRRP--83 PERCENT SURE, ANYWAY.
WHAT. THE HELL. IS GOING ON, DAD?!
WHAT'S HAPPENING IS--I JUST LOST THE REST OF MY AFTERNOON TO FIGURING OUT WHAT THE S**T HAPPENED TO REAL MORTY.
TRY NOT TO GET REPLACED BY ROBOTS WHILE I'M GONE.
UH...IF YOU THINK WE NEED WEAPONS, SHOULDN'T I HAVE ONE?
A REAL MAN DOESN'T NEED WEAPONS TO DEFEND HIMSELF, JERRY.
WAIT--YOU HAVE GRENADES!
SEE? YOU'RE FINALLY THE MAN OF THE HOUSE.
I'LL HOPE THAT'LL BE A COMFORTING LAST THOUGHT.

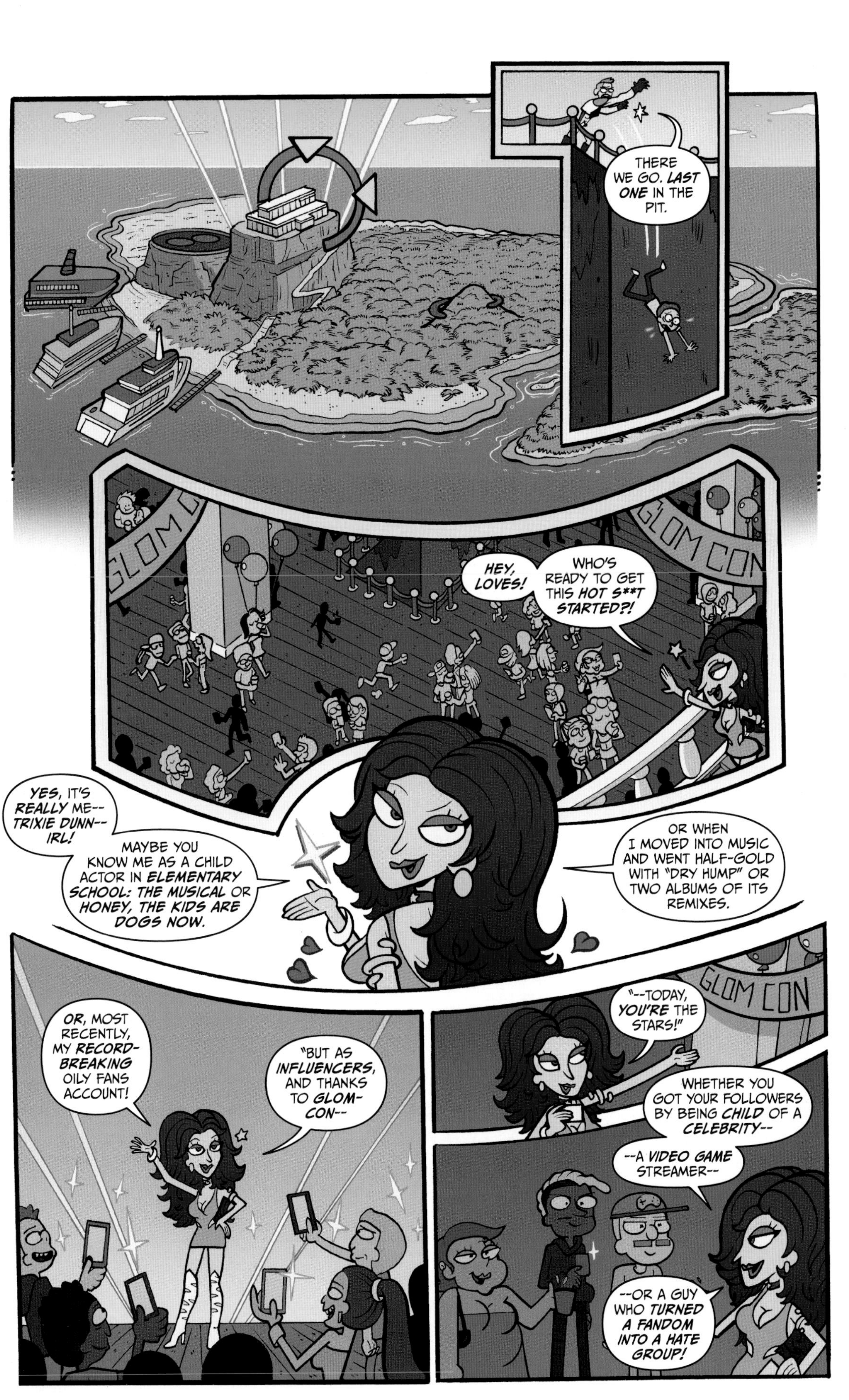

THERE WE GO. LAST ONE IN THE PIT.
GLOM CON
HEY, LOVES!
WHO'S READY TO GET THIS HOT S**T STARTED?!
YES, IT'S REALLY ME--TRIXIE DUNN--IRL!
MAYBE YOU KNOW ME AS A CHILD ACTOR IN ELEMENTARY SCHOOL: THE MUSICAL OR HONEY, THE KIDS ARE DOGS NOW.
OR WHEN I MOVED INTO MUSIC AND WENT HALF-GOLD WITH "DRY HUMP" OR TWO ALBUMS OF ITS REMIXES.
OR, MOST RECENTLY, MY RECORD-BREAKING OILY FANS ACCOUNT!
"BUT AS INFLUENCERS, AND THANKS TO GLOM-CON--
"--TODAY, YOU'RE THE STARS!"
WHETHER YOU GOT YOUR FOLLOWERS BY BEING CHILD OF A CELEBRITY--
--A VIDEO GAME STREAMER--
--OR A GUY WHO TURNED A FANDOM INTO A HATE GROUP!

HEY! THIS IS BULL***T!

TH-THERE'S NO WAY YOU CAN SAY IT'S LEGAL TO KILL US JUST BECAUSE WE CLICKED A STUPID TERMS OF SERVICE!

YOU'RE RIGHT.

TECHNICALLY YOU AGREED TO HAVE ANY SPECIFIC LEGAL DISAGREEMENTS SETTLED BY AN ARBITER, SO--

OKAY! TH-THEN WE DEMAND OUR RIGHTS!

WE DEMAND AN ARBITER!

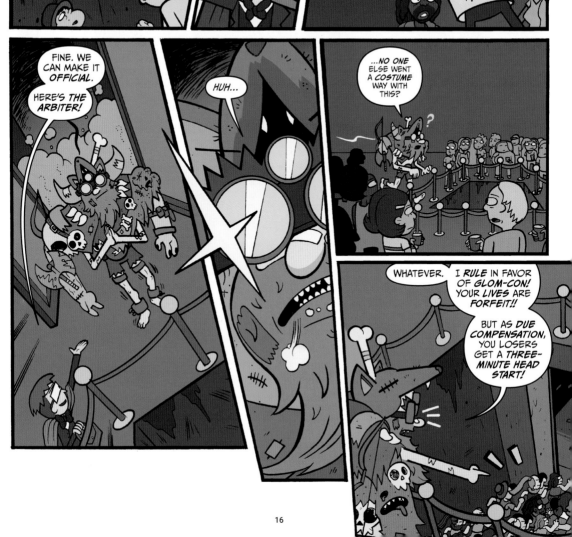

FINE. WE CAN MAKE IT OFFICIAL.

HERE'S THE ARBITER!

HUH...

...NO ONE ELSE WENT A COSTUME WAY WITH THIS?

WHATEVER. I RULE IN FAVOR OF GLOM-CON! YOUR LIVES ARE FORFEIT!!

BUT AS DUE COMPENSATION, YOU LOSERS GET A THREE-MINUTE HEAD START!

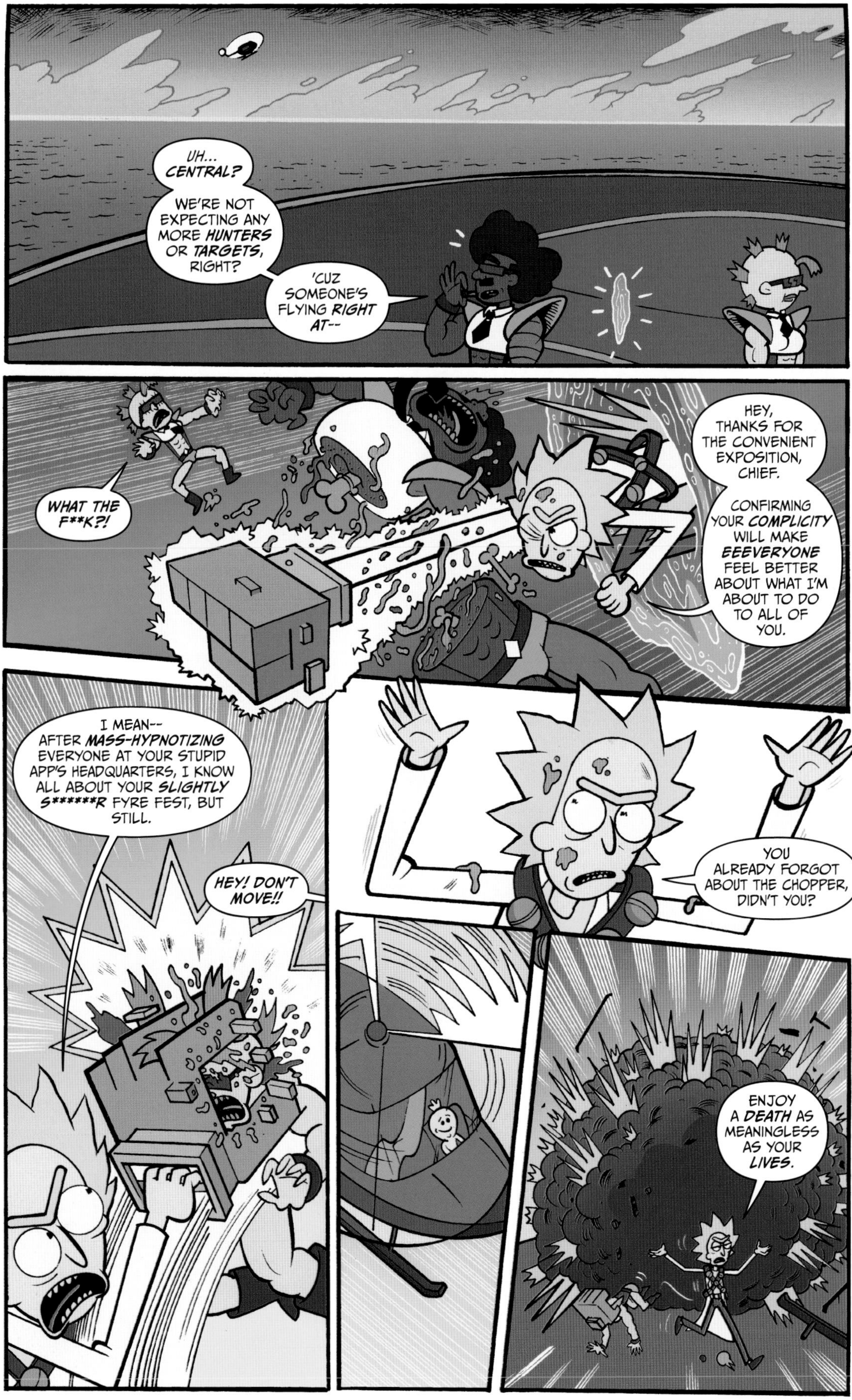
UH... CENTRAL?
WE'RE NOT EXPECTING ANY MORE HUNTERS OR TARGETS, RIGHT?
'CUZ SOMEONE'S FLYING RIGHT AT--
WHAT THE F**K?!
HEY, THANKS FOR THE CONVENIENT EXPOSITION, CHIEF.
CONFIRMING YOUR COMPLICITY WILL MAKE EEEVERYONE FEEL BETTER ABOUT WHAT I'M ABOUT TO DO TO ALL OF YOU.
I MEAN-- AFTER MASS-HYPNOTIZING EVERYONE AT YOUR STUPID APP'S HEADQUARTERS, I KNOW ALL ABOUT YOUR SLIGHTLY S******R FYRE FEST, BUT STILL.
HEY! DON'T MOVE!!
YOU ALREADY FORGOT ABOUT THE CHOPPER, DIDN'T YOU?
ENJOY A DEATH AS MEANINGLESS AS YOUR LIVES.

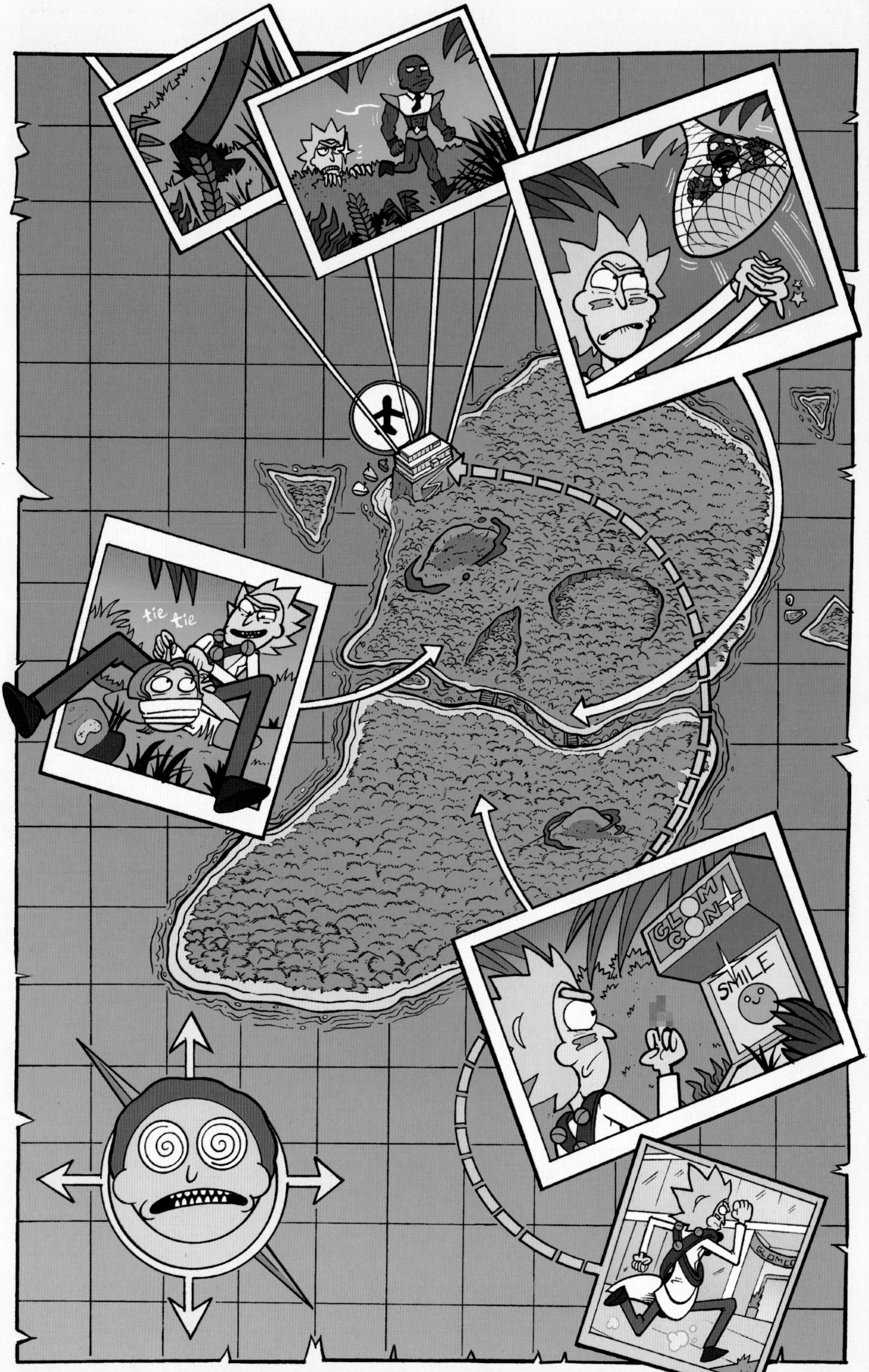
tie tie
SMILE

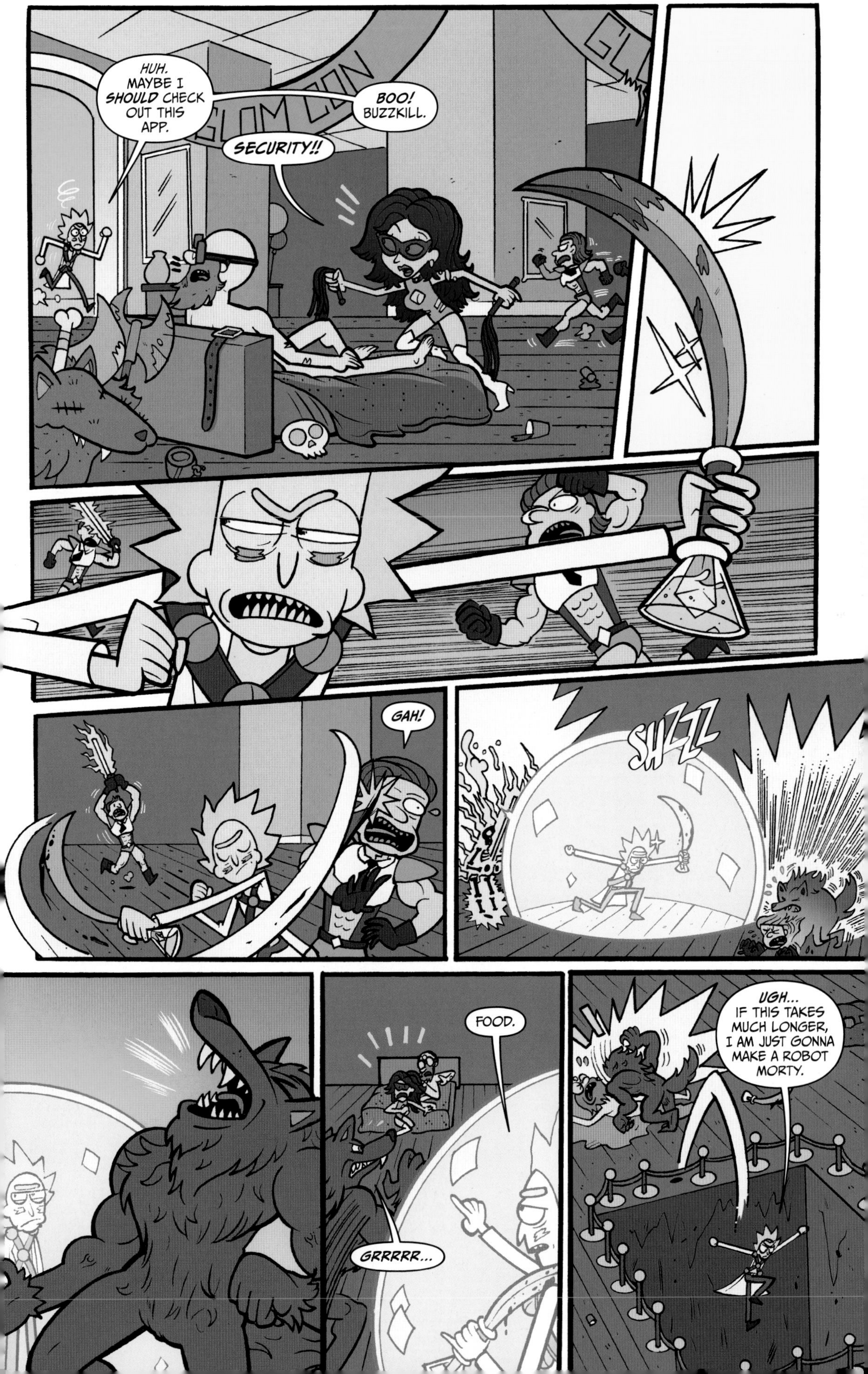
GLOM CON
HUH. MAYBE I SHOULD CHECK OUT THIS APP.
BOO! BUZZKILL.
SECURITY!!
GAH!
SHZZZ
FOOD.
GRRRRR...
UGH... IF THIS TAKES MUCH LONGER, I AM JUST GONNA MAKE A ROBOT MORTY.

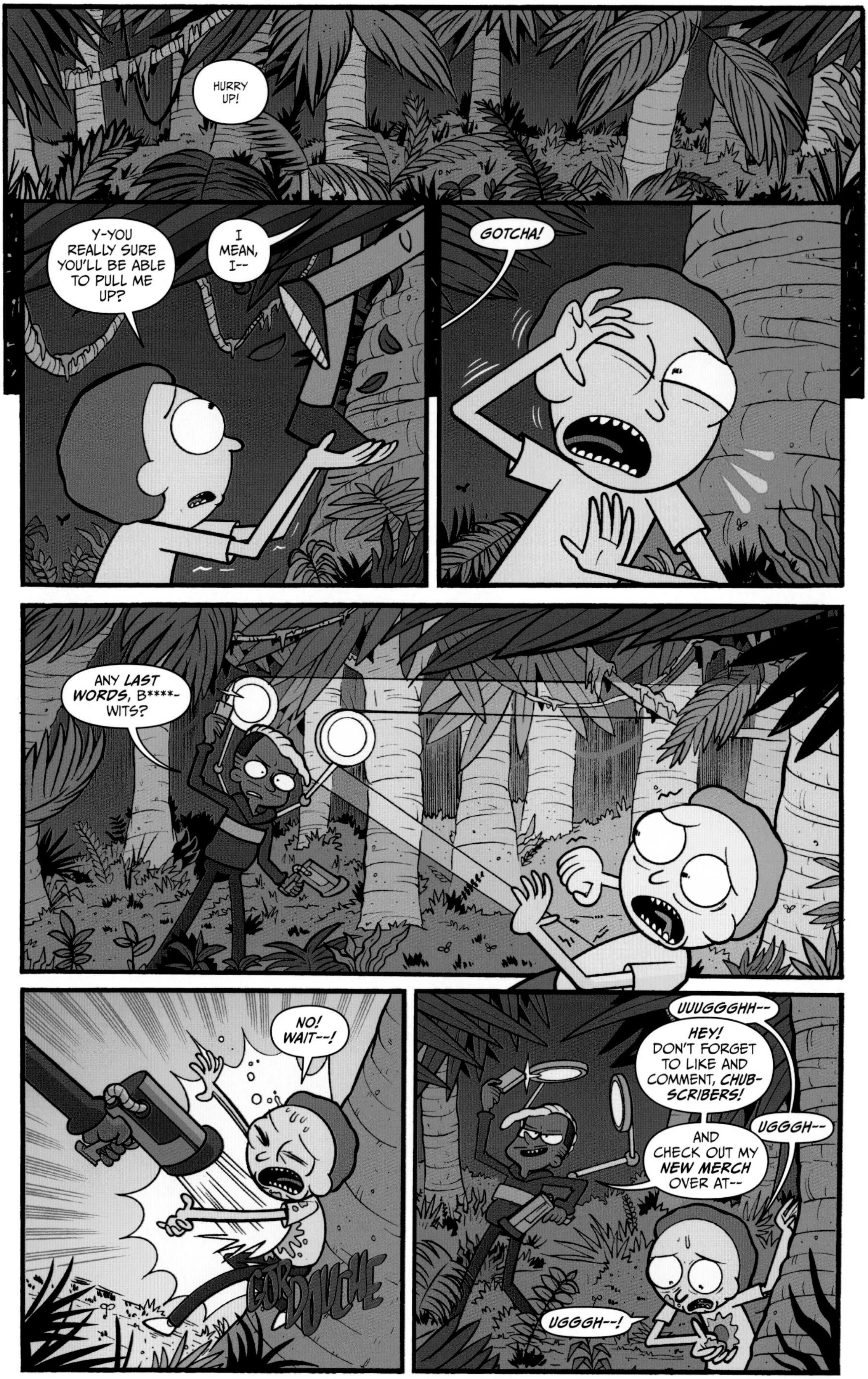
HURRY UP!
Y-YOU REALLY SURE YOU'LL BE ABLE TO PULL ME UP?
I MEAN, I--
GOTCHA!
ANY LAST WORDS, B****-WITS?
NO! WAIT--!
GORDOUCHE
UUUGGGHH--
HEY! DON'T FORGET TO LIKE AND COMMENT, CHUB-SCRIBERS!
UGGGH--
AND CHECK OUT MY NEW MERCH OVER AT--
UGGGH--!

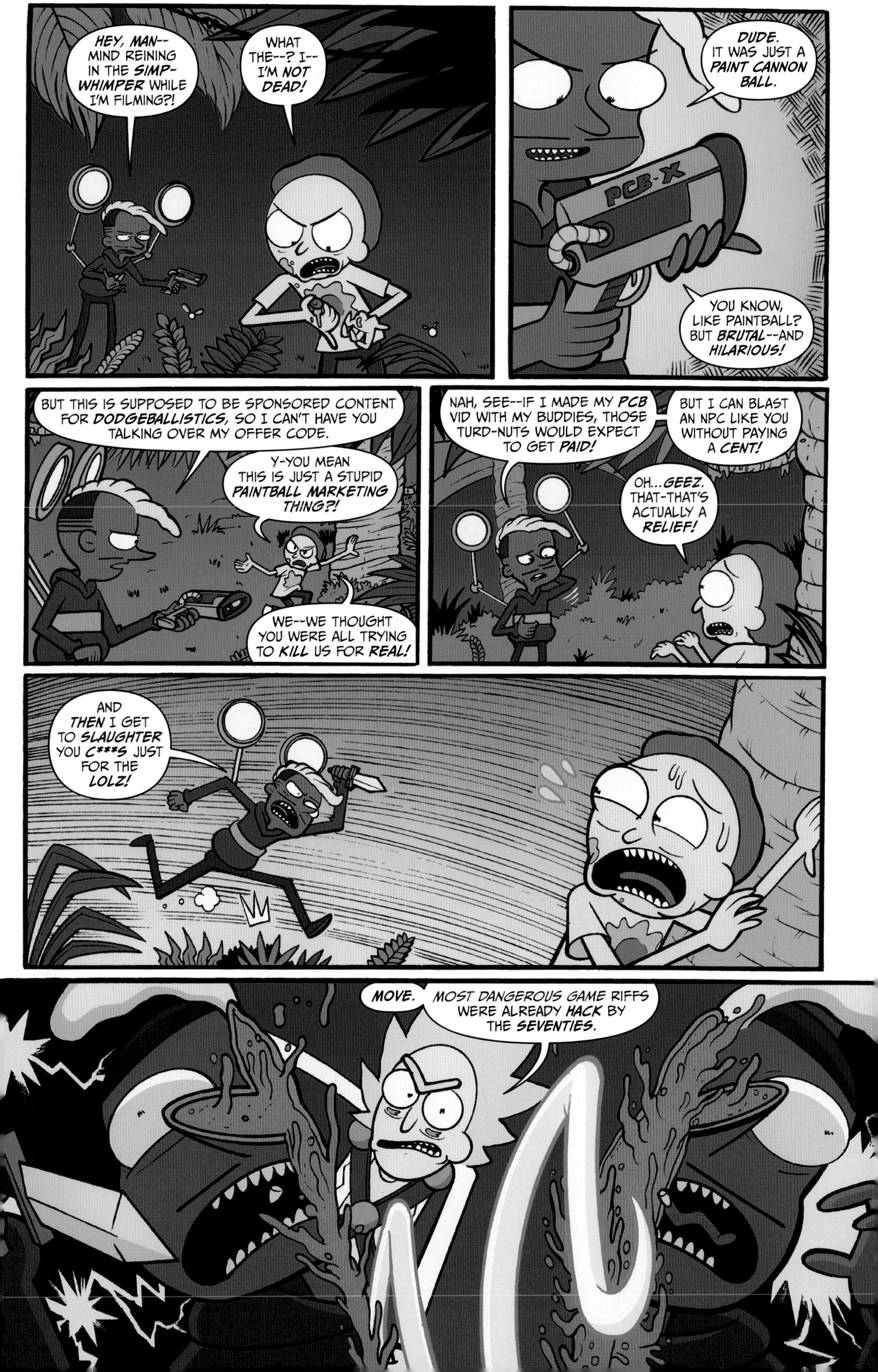
HEY, MAN--MIND REINING IN THE SIMP-WHIMPER WHILE I'M FILMING?!
WHAT THE--? I--I'M NOT DEAD!
DUDE. IT WAS JUST A PAINT CANNON BALL.
PCB-X
YOU KNOW, LIKE PAINTBALL? BUT BRUTAL--AND HILARIOUS!
BUT THIS IS SUPPOSED TO BE SPONSORED CONTENT FOR DODGEBALLISTICS, SO I CAN'T HAVE YOU TALKING OVER MY OFFER CODE.
Y-YOU MEAN THIS IS JUST A STUPID PAINTBALL MARKETING THING?!
WE--WE THOUGHT YOU WERE ALL TRYING TO KILL US FOR REAL!
NAH, SEE--IF I MADE MY PCB VID WITH MY BUDDIES, THOSE TURD-NUTS WOULD EXPECT TO GET PAID!
BUT I CAN BLAST AN NPC LIKE YOU WITHOUT PAYING A CENT!
OH...GEEZ. THAT-THAT'S ACTUALLY A RELIEF!
AND THEN I GET TO SLAUGHTER YOU C***S JUST FOR THE LOLZ!
MOVE.
MOST DANGEROUS GAME RIFFS WERE ALREADY HACK BY THE SEVENTIES.

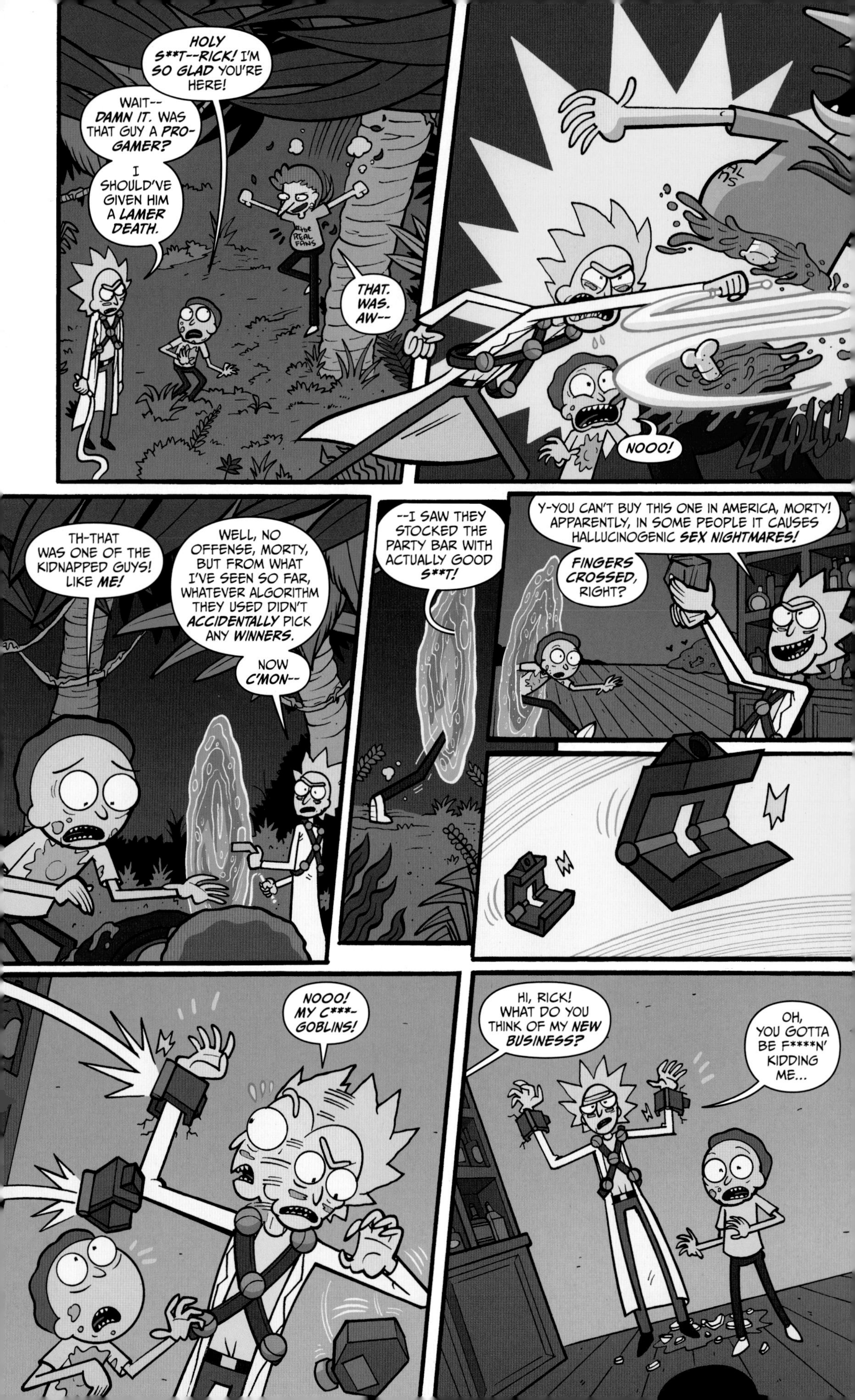
HOLY S**T--RICK! I'M SO GLAD YOU'RE HERE!
WAIT-- DAMN IT. WAS THAT GUY A PRO-GAMER?
I SHOULD'VE GIVEN HIM A LAMER DEATH.
THE REAL FANS
THAT. WAS. AW--
NOOO!
ZZZPLCH
TH-THAT WAS ONE OF THE KIDNAPPED GUYS! LIKE ME!
WELL, NO OFFENSE, MORTY, BUT FROM WHAT I'VE SEEN SO FAR, WHATEVER ALGORITHM THEY USED DIDN'T ACCIDENTALLY PICK ANY WINNERS.
NOW C'MON--
--I SAW THEY STOCKED THE PARTY BAR WITH ACTUALLY GOOD S**T!
Y-YOU CAN'T BUY THIS ONE IN AMERICA, MORTY! APPARENTLY, IN SOME PEOPLE IT CAUSES HALLUCINOGENIC SEX NIGHTMARES!
FINGERS CROSSED, RIGHT?
NOOO! MY C***-GOBLINS!
HI, RICK! WHAT DO YOU THINK OF MY NEW BUSINESS?
OH, YOU GOTTA BE F****N' KIDDING ME...

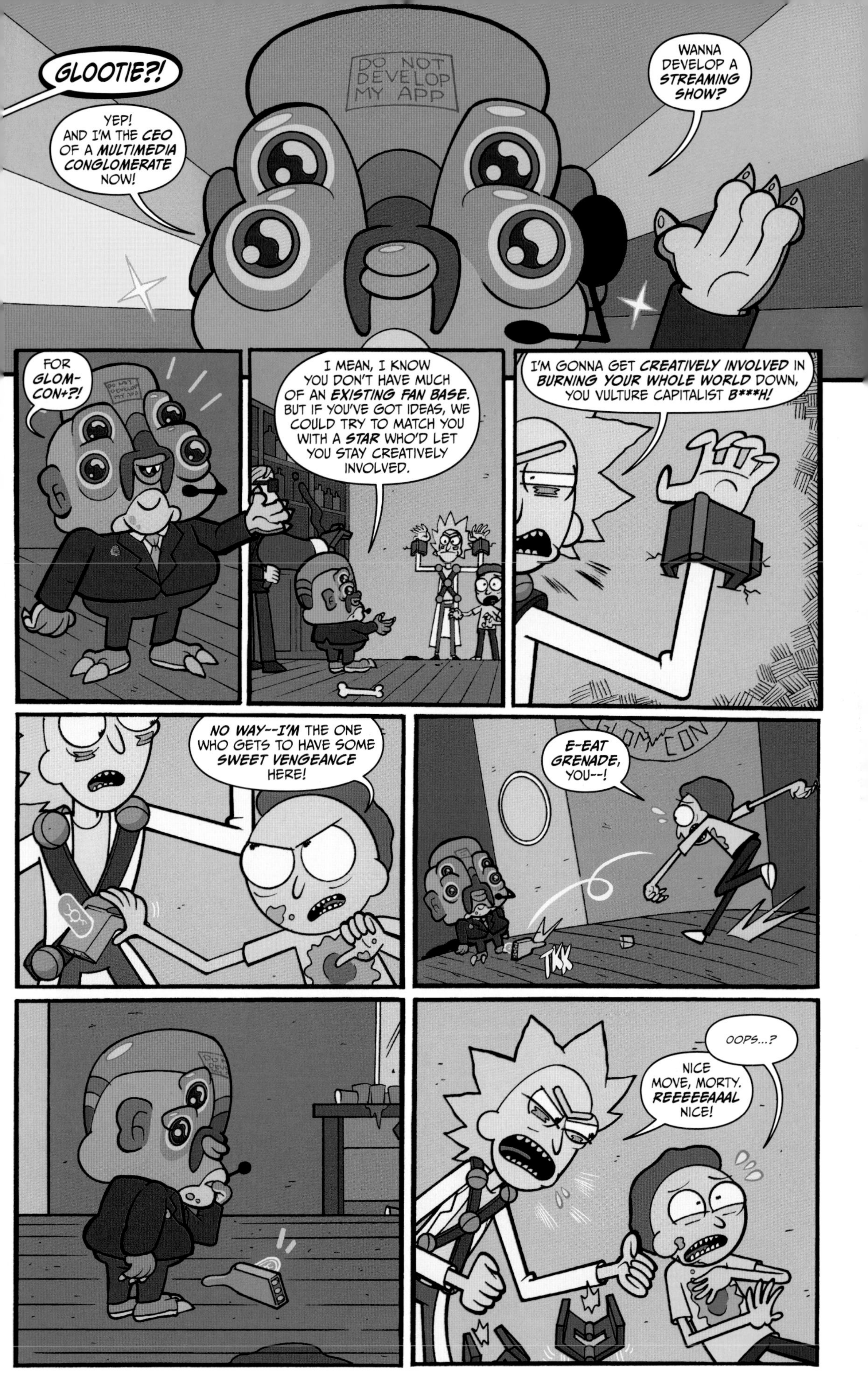

GLOOTIE?!
YEP! AND I'M THE CEO OF A MULTIMEDIA CONGLOMERATE NOW!
DO NOT DEVELOP MY APP
WANNA DEVELOP A STREAMING SHOW?
FOR GLOM-CON+?!
I MEAN, I KNOW YOU DON'T HAVE MUCH OF AN EXISTING FAN BASE. BUT IF YOU'VE GOT IDEAS, WE COULD TRY TO MATCH YOU WITH A STAR WHO'D LET YOU STAY CREATIVELY INVOLVED.
I'M GONNA GET CREATIVELY INVOLVED IN BURNING YOUR WHOLE WORLD DOWN, YOU VULTURE CAPITALIST B***H!
NO WAY--I'M THE ONE WHO GETS TO HAVE SOME SWEET VENGEANCE HERE!
E-EAT GRENADE, YOU--!
TKK
OOPS...?
NICE MOVE, MORTY. REEEEEAAAL NICE!

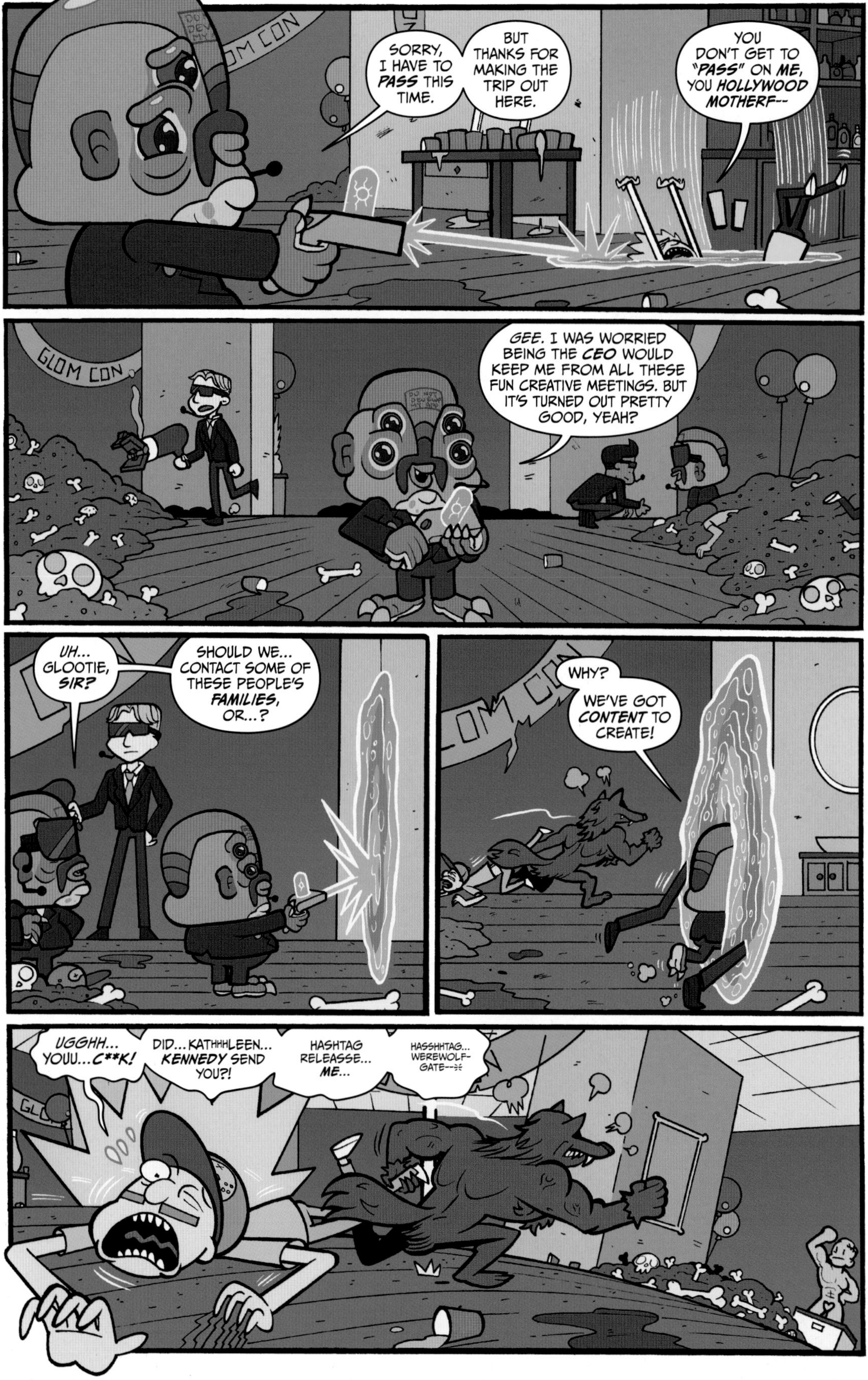
SORRY, I HAVE TO PASS THIS TIME.
BUT THANKS FOR MAKING THE TRIP OUT HERE.
YOU DON'T GET TO "PASS" ON ME, YOU HOLLYWOOD MOTHERF--
GLOM CON
GEE. I WAS WORRIED BEING THE CEO WOULD KEEP ME FROM ALL THESE FUN CREATIVE MEETINGS. BUT IT'S TURNED OUT PRETTY GOOD, YEAH?
UH... GLOOTIE, SIR?
SHOULD WE... CONTACT SOME OF THESE PEOPLE'S FAMILIES, OR...?
WHY?
WE'VE GOT CONTENT TO CREATE!
UGGHH... YOUU... C**K!
DID... KATHHHLEEN... KENNEDY SEND YOU?!
HASHTAG RELEASSE... ME...
HASSHHTAG... WEREWOLF-GATE--

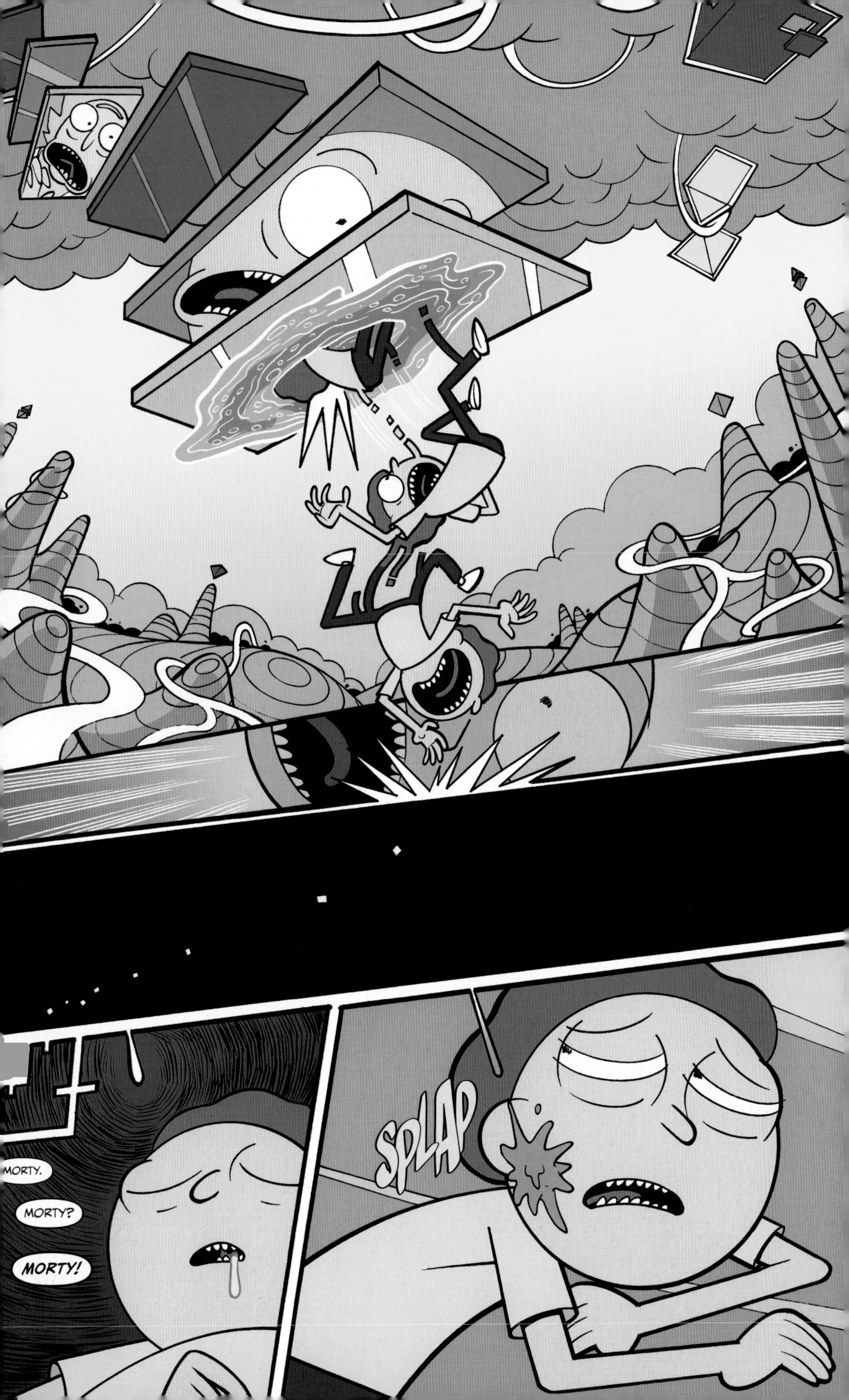

MORTY.
MORTY?
MORTY!
SPLAP

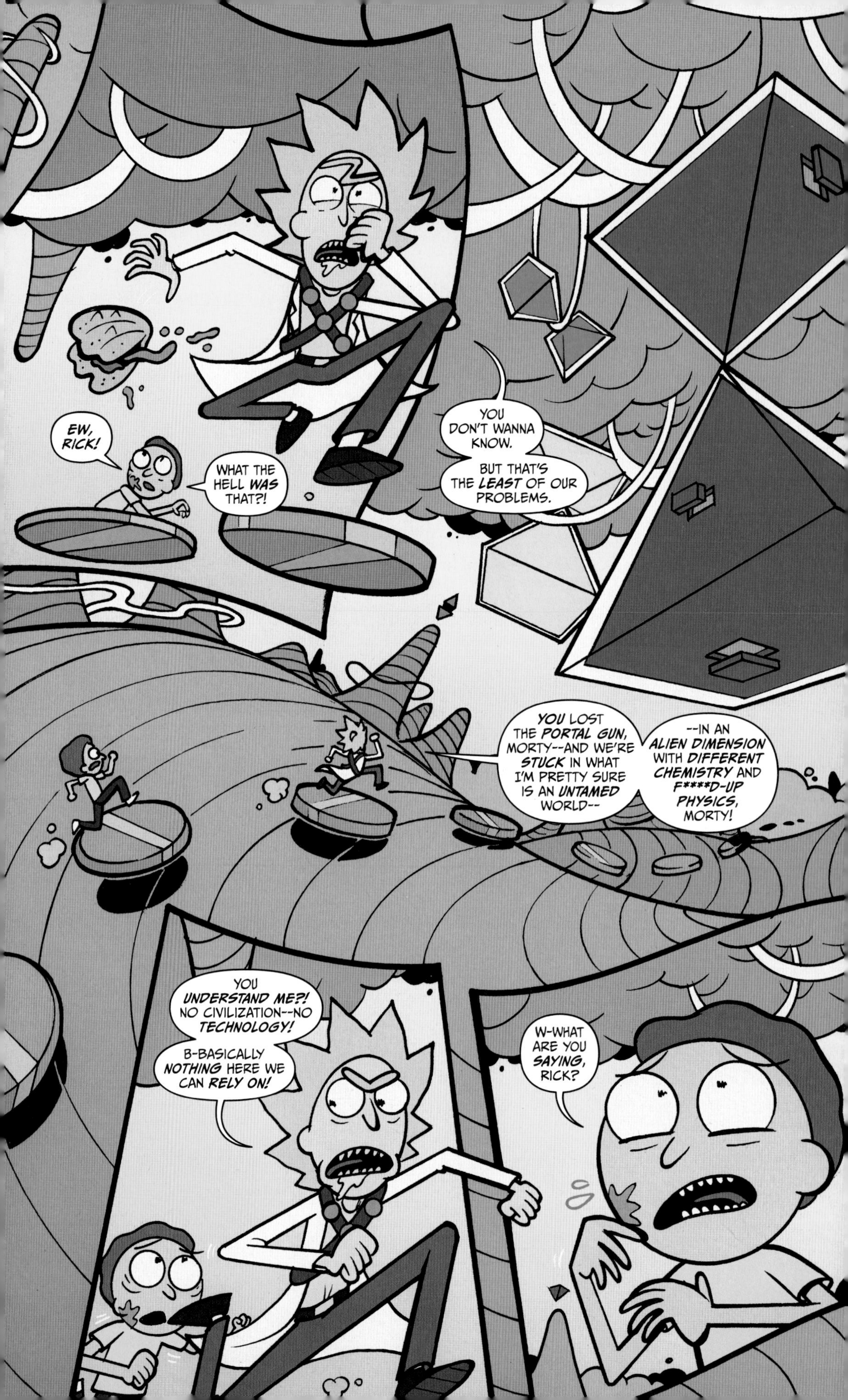

EW, RICK!
WHAT THE HELL WAS THAT?!
YOU DON'T WANNA KNOW.
BUT THAT'S THE LEAST OF OUR PROBLEMS.
YOU LOST THE PORTAL GUN, MORTY--AND WE'RE STUCK IN WHAT I'M PRETTY SURE IS AN UNTAMED WORLD--
--IN AN ALIEN DIMENSION WITH DIFFERENT CHEMISTRY AND F****D-UP PHYSICS, MORTY!
YOU UNDERSTAND ME?! NO CIVILIZATION--NO TECHNOLOGY!
B-BASICALLY NOTHING HERE WE CAN RELY ON!
W-WHAT ARE YOU SAYING, RICK?

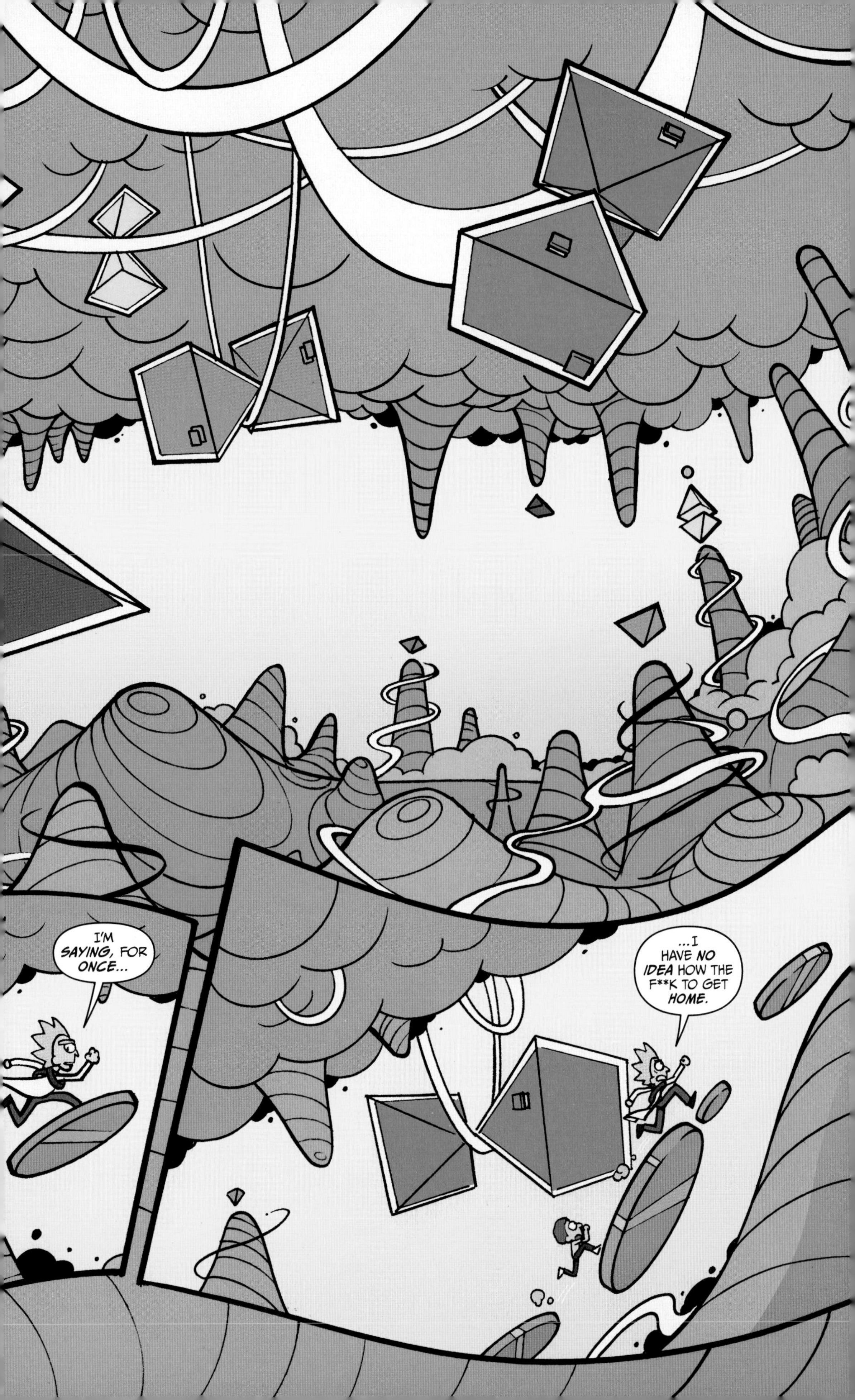
I'M SAYING, FOR ONCE...
...I HAVE NO IDEA HOW THE F**K TO GET HOME.

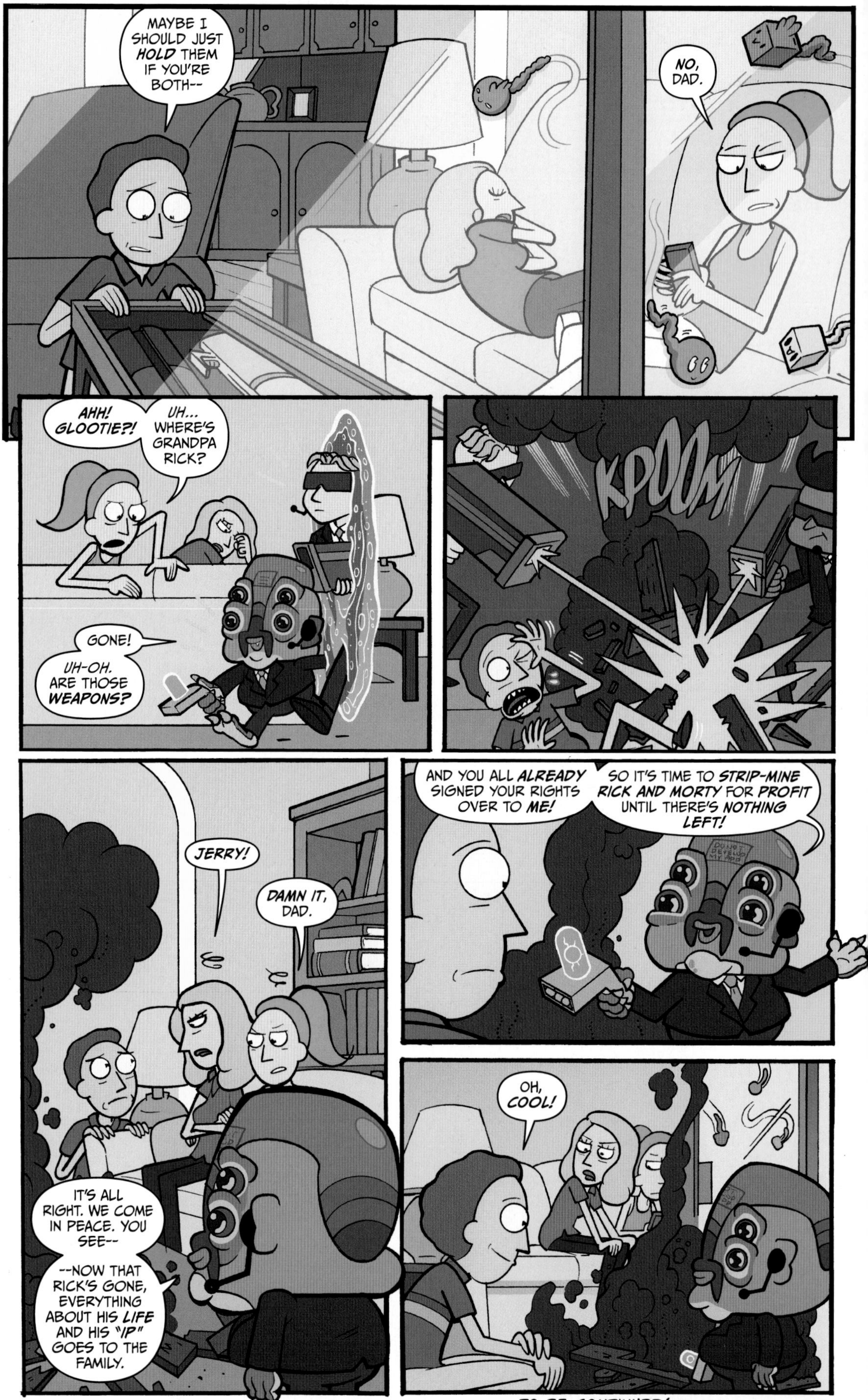
MAYBE I SHOULD JUST HOLD THEM IF YOU'RE BOTH--
NO, DAD.
AHH! GLOOTIE?!
UH... WHERE'S GRANDPA RICK?
GONE!
UH-OH. ARE THOSE WEAPONS?
KPOOM
JERRY!
DAMN IT, DAD.
IT'S ALL RIGHT. WE COME IN PEACE. YOU SEE--
--NOW THAT RICK'S GONE, EVERYTHING ABOUT HIS LIFE AND HIS "IP" GOES TO THE FAMILY.
AND YOU ALL ALREADY SIGNED YOUR RIGHTS OVER TO ME!
SO IT'S TIME TO STRIP-MINE RICK AND MORTY FOR PROFIT UNTIL THERE'S NOTHING LEFT!
OH, COOL!

TO BE CONTINUED! (SO GET YOUR $$$ READY!!)

CHAPTER 2

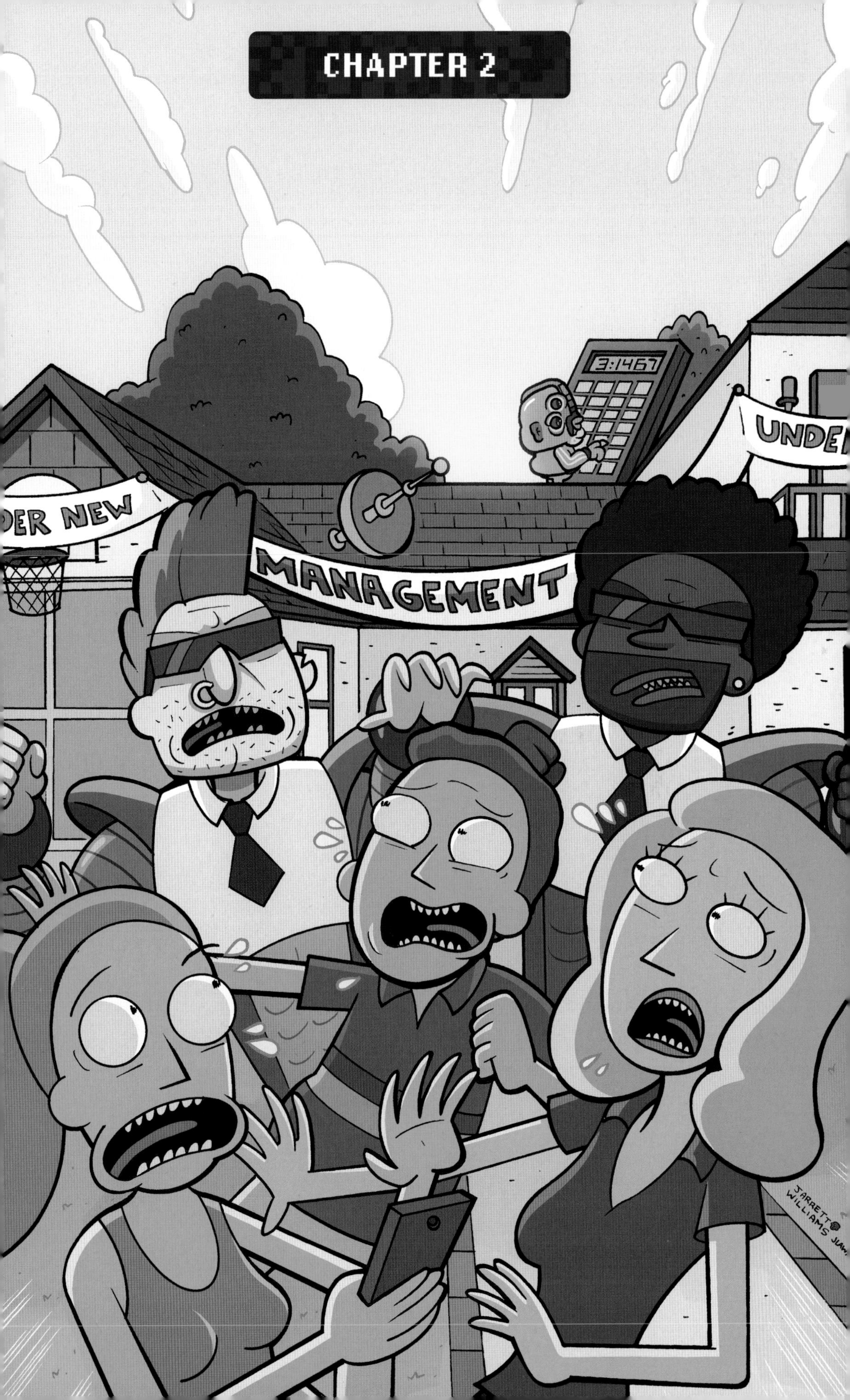

DER NEW
MANAGEMENT
UNDE
3:1467
JARRETT WILLIAMS

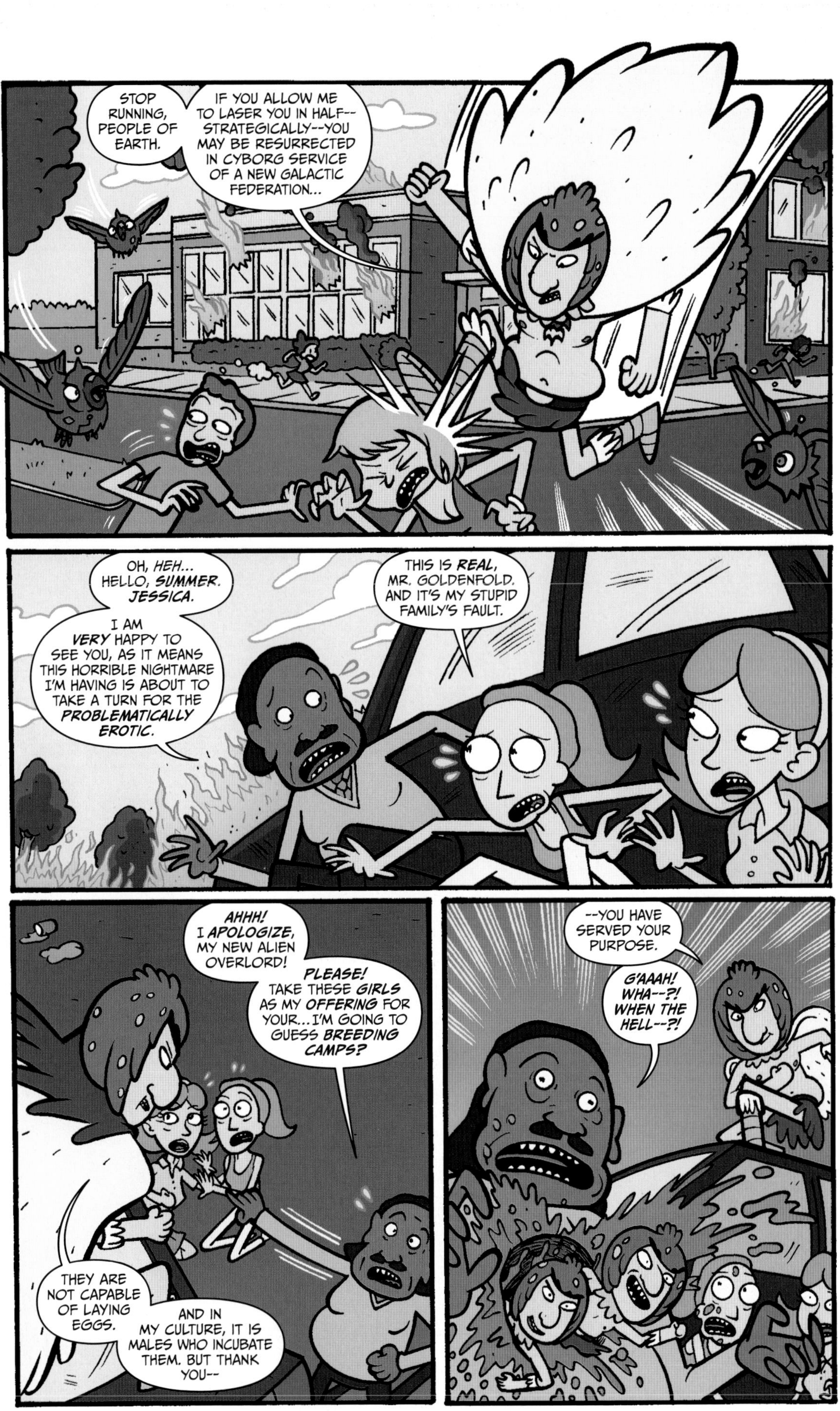
STOP RUNNING, PEOPLE OF EARTH.
IF YOU ALLOW ME TO LASER YOU IN HALF-- STRATEGICALLY--YOU MAY BE RESURRECTED IN CYBORG SERVICE OF A NEW GALACTIC FEDERATION...
OH, *HEH*... HELLO, **SUMMER**. **JESSICA.**
I AM **VERY** HAPPY TO SEE YOU, AS IT MEANS THIS HORRIBLE NIGHTMARE I'M HAVING IS ABOUT TO TAKE A TURN FOR THE **PROBLEMATICALLY EROTIC.**
THIS IS **REAL**, MR. GOLDENFOLD. AND IT'S MY STUPID FAMILY'S FAULT.
AHHH! I **APOLOGIZE**, MY NEW ALIEN OVERLORD!
PLEASE! TAKE THESE **GIRLS** AS MY **OFFERING** FOR YOUR...I'M GOING TO GUESS **BREEDING CAMPS?**
THEY ARE NOT CAPABLE OF LAYING EGGS.
AND IN MY CULTURE, IT IS MALES WHO INCUBATE THEM. BUT THANK YOU--
--YOU HAVE SERVED YOUR PURPOSE.
G'AAAH! WHA--?! WHEN THE HELL--?!

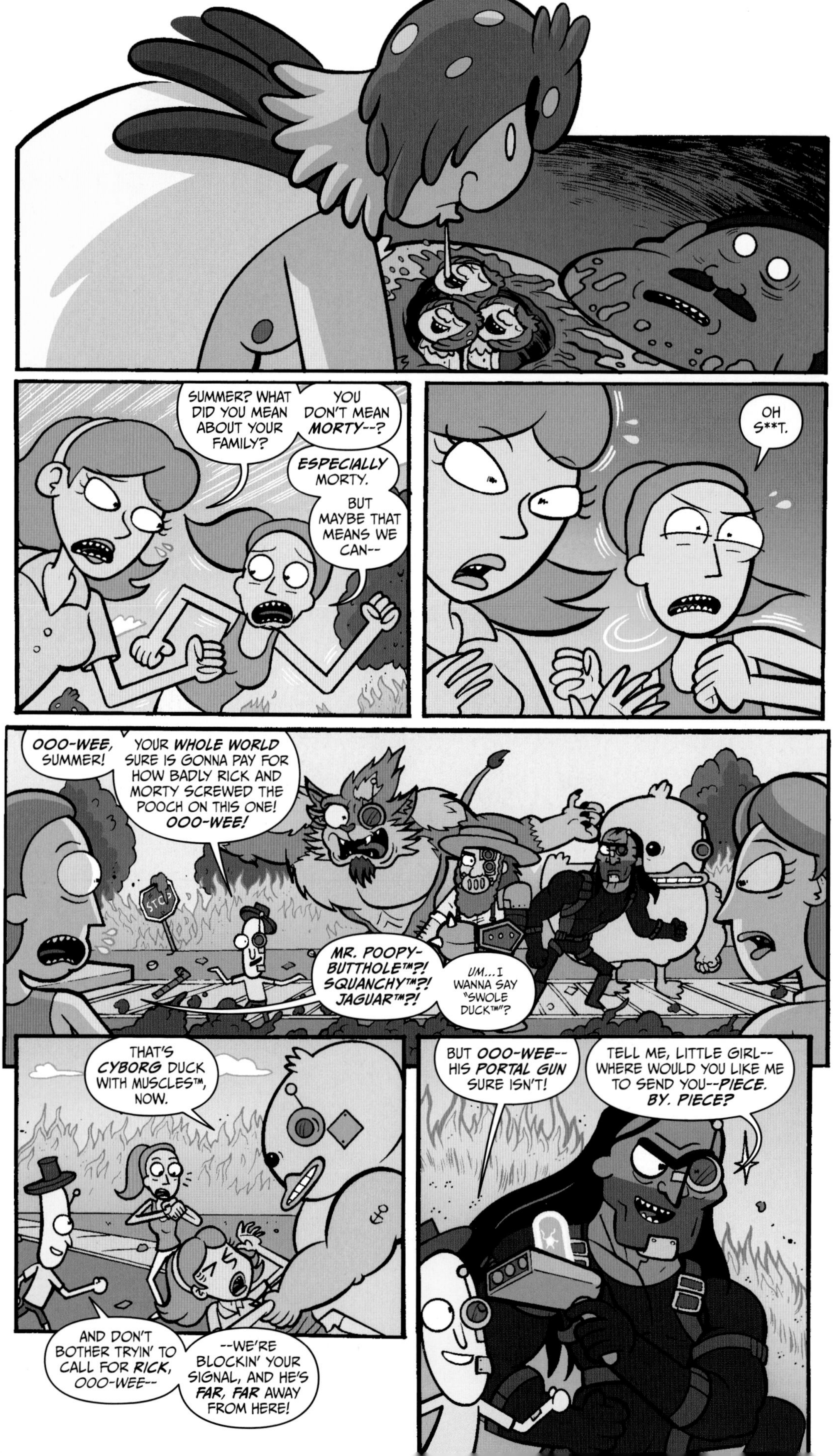
SUMMER? WHAT DID YOU MEAN ABOUT YOUR FAMILY?
YOU DON'T MEAN MORTY--?
ESPECIALLY MORTY.
BUT MAYBE THAT MEANS WE CAN--
OH S**T.
OOO-WEE, SUMMER!
YOUR WHOLE WORLD SURE IS GONNA PAY FOR HOW BADLY RICK AND MORTY SCREWED THE POOCH ON THIS ONE! OOO-WEE!
MR. POOPY-BUTTHOLE™?! SQUANCHY™?! JAGUAR™?!
UM...I WANNA SAY "SWOLE DUCK™"?
THAT'S CYBORG DUCK WITH MUSCLES™, NOW.
AND DON'T BOTHER TRYIN' TO CALL FOR RICK, OOO-WEE--
--WE'RE BLOCKIN' YOUR SIGNAL, AND HE'S FAR, FAR AWAY FROM HERE!
BUT OOO-WEE-- HIS PORTAL GUN SURE ISN'T!
TELL ME, LITTLE GIRL-- WHERE WOULD YOU LIKE ME TO SEND YOU--PIECE. BY. PIECE?

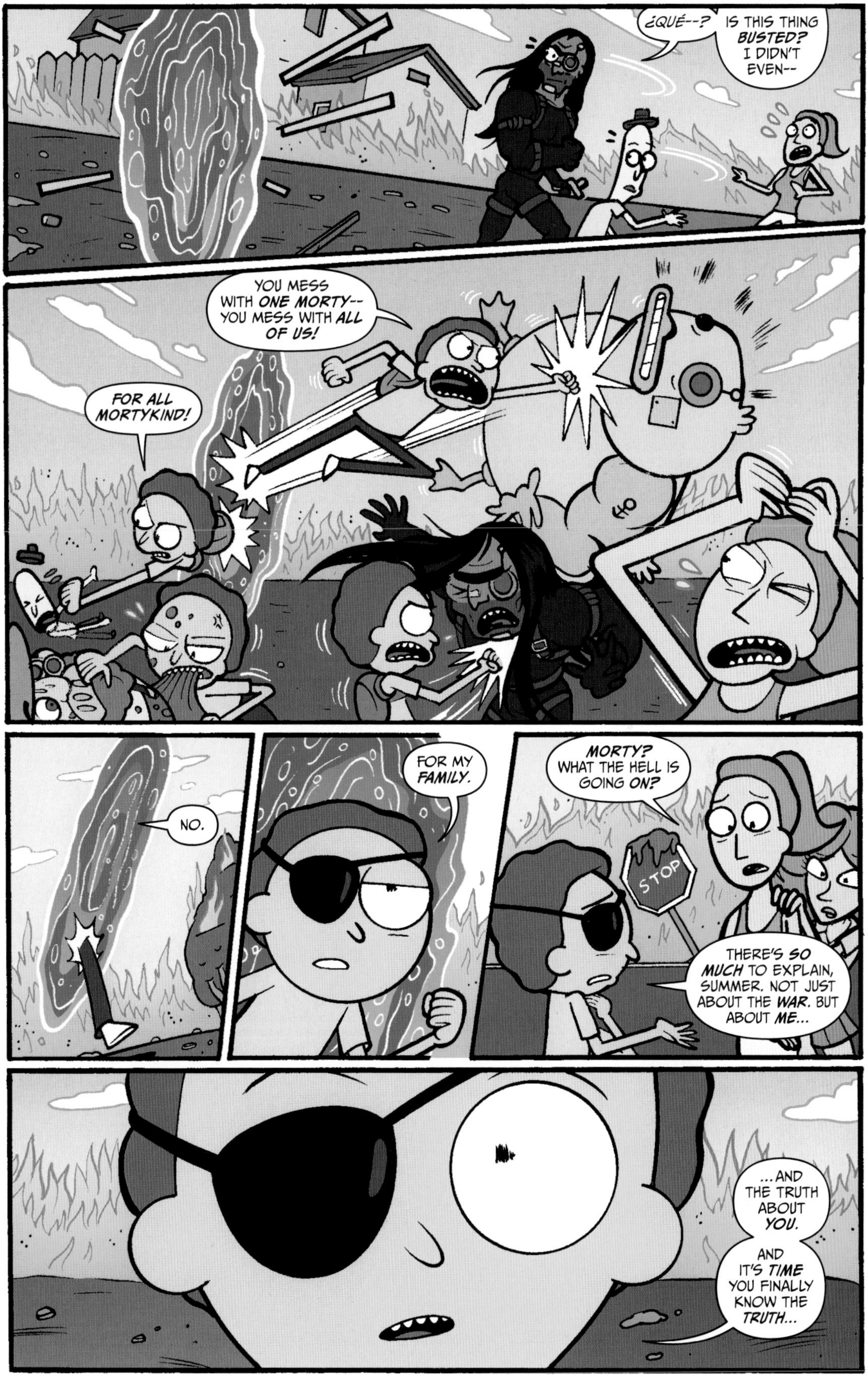
¿QUÉ--?
IS THIS THING BUSTED? I DIDN'T EVEN--
YOU MESS WITH ONE MORTY-- YOU MESS WITH ALL OF US!
FOR ALL MORTYKIND!
NO.
FOR MY FAMILY.
MORTY? WHAT THE HELL IS GOING ON?
STOP
THERE'S SO MUCH TO EXPLAIN, SUMMER. NOT JUST ABOUT THE WAR. BUT ABOUT ME...
...AND THE TRUTH ABOUT YOU.
AND IT'S TIME YOU FINALLY KNOW THE TRUTH...

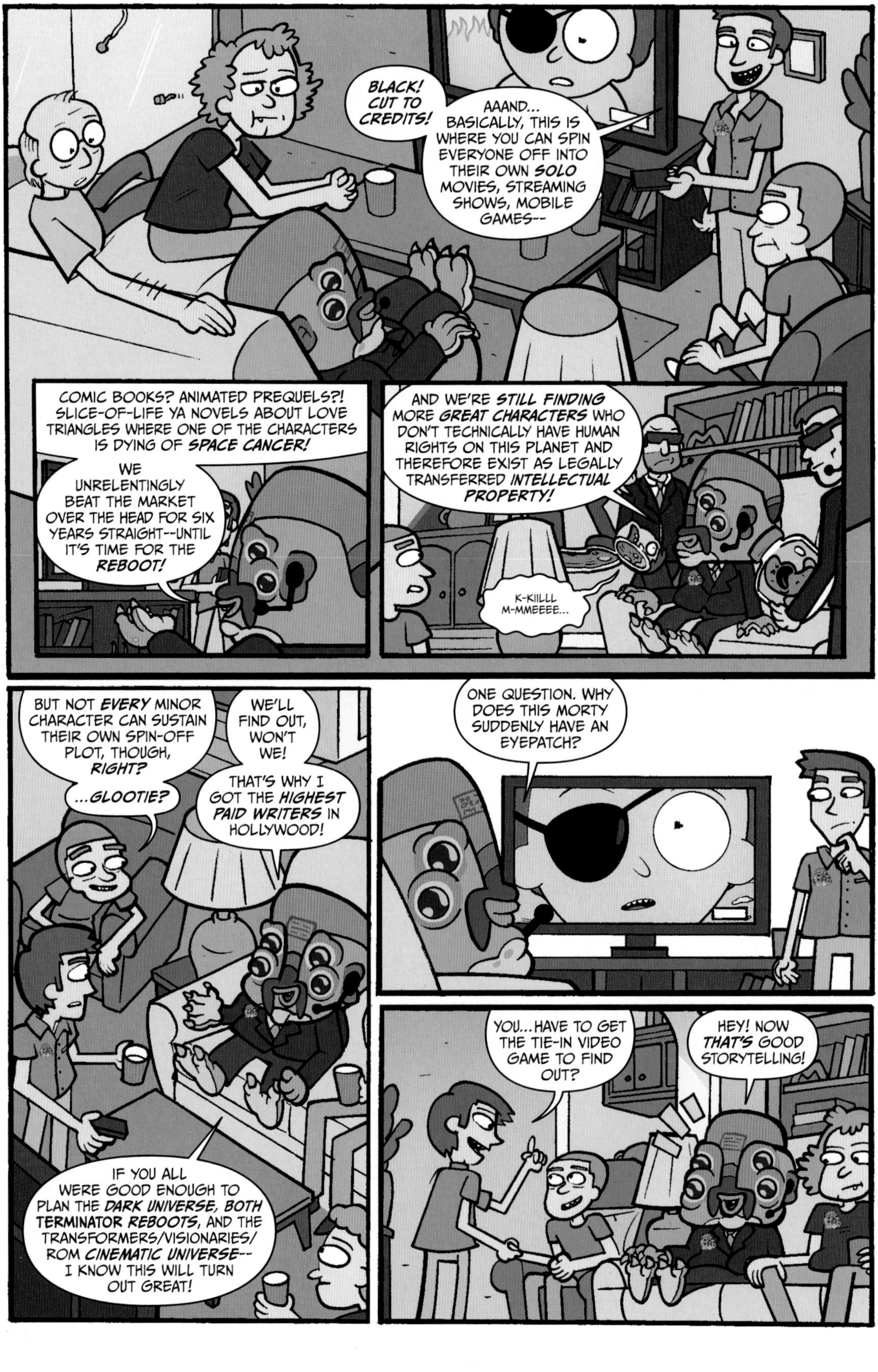
BLACK! CUT TO CREDITS!
AAAND... BASICALLY, THIS IS WHERE YOU CAN SPIN EVERYONE OFF INTO THEIR OWN SOLO MOVIES, STREAMING SHOWS, MOBILE GAMES--
COMIC BOOKS? ANIMATED PREQUELS?! SLICE-OF-LIFE YA NOVELS ABOUT LOVE TRIANGLES WHERE ONE OF THE CHARACTERS IS DYING OF SPACE CANCER!
WE UNRELENTINGLY BEAT THE MARKET OVER THE HEAD FOR SIX YEARS STRAIGHT--UNTIL IT'S TIME FOR THE REBOOT!
AND WE'RE STILL FINDING MORE GREAT CHARACTERS WHO DON'T TECHNICALLY HAVE HUMAN RIGHTS ON THIS PLANET AND THEREFORE EXIST AS LEGALLY TRANSFERRED INTELLECTUAL PROPERTY!
K-KIILLL M-MMEEEE...
BUT NOT EVERY MINOR CHARACTER CAN SUSTAIN THEIR OWN SPIN-OFF PLOT, THOUGH, RIGHT?
...GLOOTIE?
WE'LL FIND OUT, WON'T WE!
THAT'S WHY I GOT THE HIGHEST PAID WRITERS IN HOLLYWOOD!
IF YOU ALL WERE GOOD ENOUGH TO PLAN THE DARK UNIVERSE, BOTH TERMINATOR REBOOTS, AND THE TRANSFORMERS/VISIONARIES/ ROM CINEMATIC UNIVERSE-- I KNOW THIS WILL TURN OUT GREAT!
ONE QUESTION. WHY DOES THIS MORTY SUDDENLY HAVE AN EYEPATCH?
YOU...HAVE TO GET THE TIE-IN VIDEO GAME TO FIND OUT?
HEY! NOW THAT'S GOOD STORYTELLING!

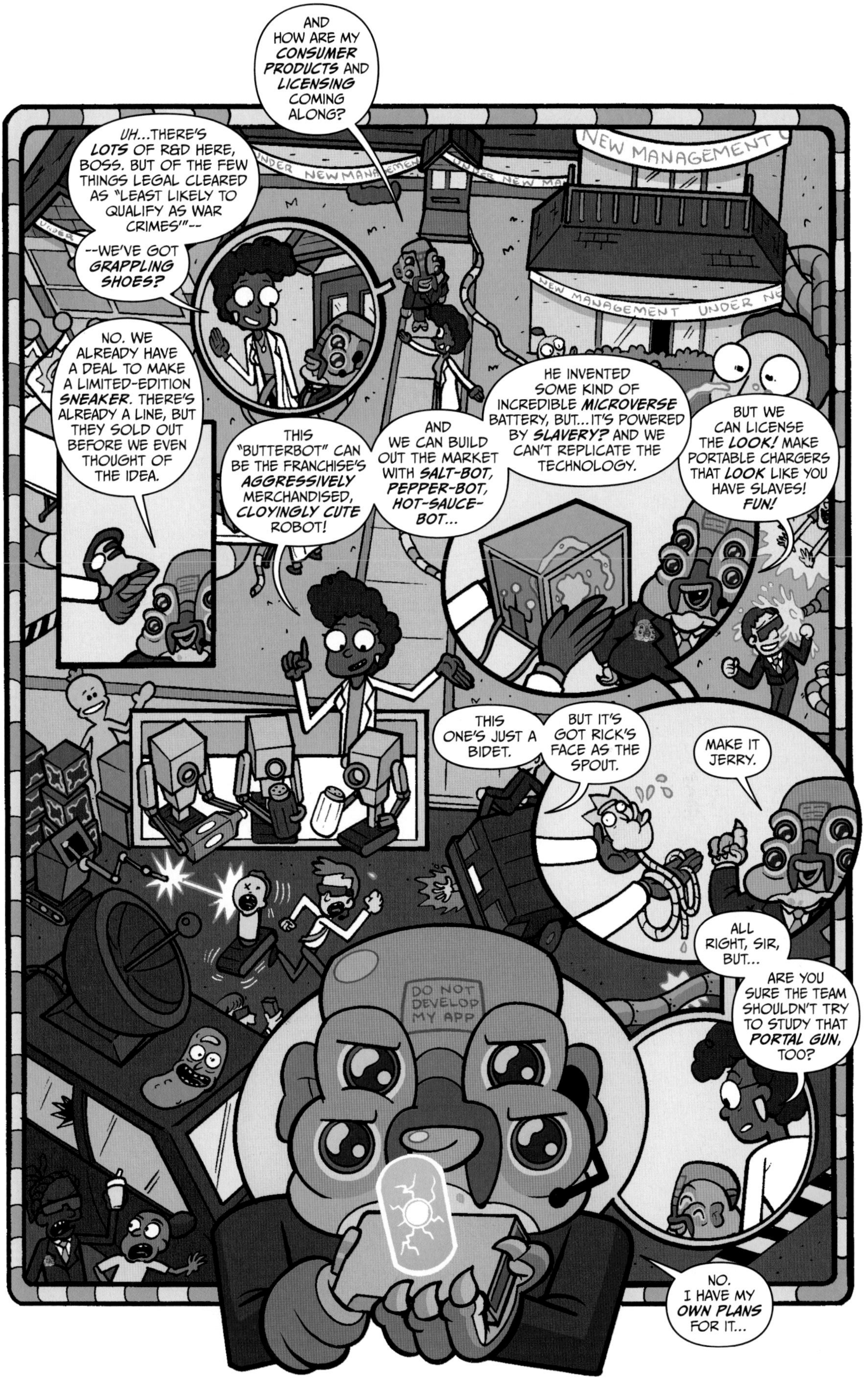
AND HOW ARE MY CONSUMER PRODUCTS AND LICENSING COMING ALONG?
UH...THERE'S LOTS OF R&D HERE, BOSS. BUT OF THE FEW THINGS LEGAL CLEARED AS "LEAST LIKELY TO QUALIFY AS WAR CRIMES'"--
--WE'VE GOT GRAPPLING SHOES?
NEW MANAGEMENT
UNDER NEW MANAGEMENT
UNDER NEW MA
NEW MANAGEMENT UNDER NE
NO. WE ALREADY HAVE A DEAL TO MAKE A LIMITED-EDITION SNEAKER. THERE'S ALREADY A LINE, BUT THEY SOLD OUT BEFORE WE EVEN THOUGHT OF THE IDEA.
THIS "BUTTERBOT" CAN BE THE FRANCHISE'S AGGRESSIVELY MERCHANDISED, CLOYINGLY CUTE ROBOT!
AND WE CAN BUILD OUT THE MARKET WITH SALT-BOT, PEPPER-BOT, HOT-SAUCE-BOT...
HE INVENTED SOME KIND OF INCREDIBLE MICROVERSE BATTERY, BUT...IT'S POWERED BY SLAVERY? AND WE CAN'T REPLICATE THE TECHNOLOGY.
BUT WE CAN LICENSE THE LOOK! MAKE PORTABLE CHARGERS THAT LOOK LIKE YOU HAVE SLAVES! FUN!
THIS ONE'S JUST A BIDET.
BUT IT'S GOT RICK'S FACE AS THE SPOUT.
MAKE IT JERRY.
ALL RIGHT, SIR, BUT...
ARE YOU SURE THE TEAM SHOULDN'T TRY TO STUDY THAT PORTAL GUN, TOO?
DO NOT DEVELOP MY APP
NO. I HAVE MY OWN PLANS FOR IT...

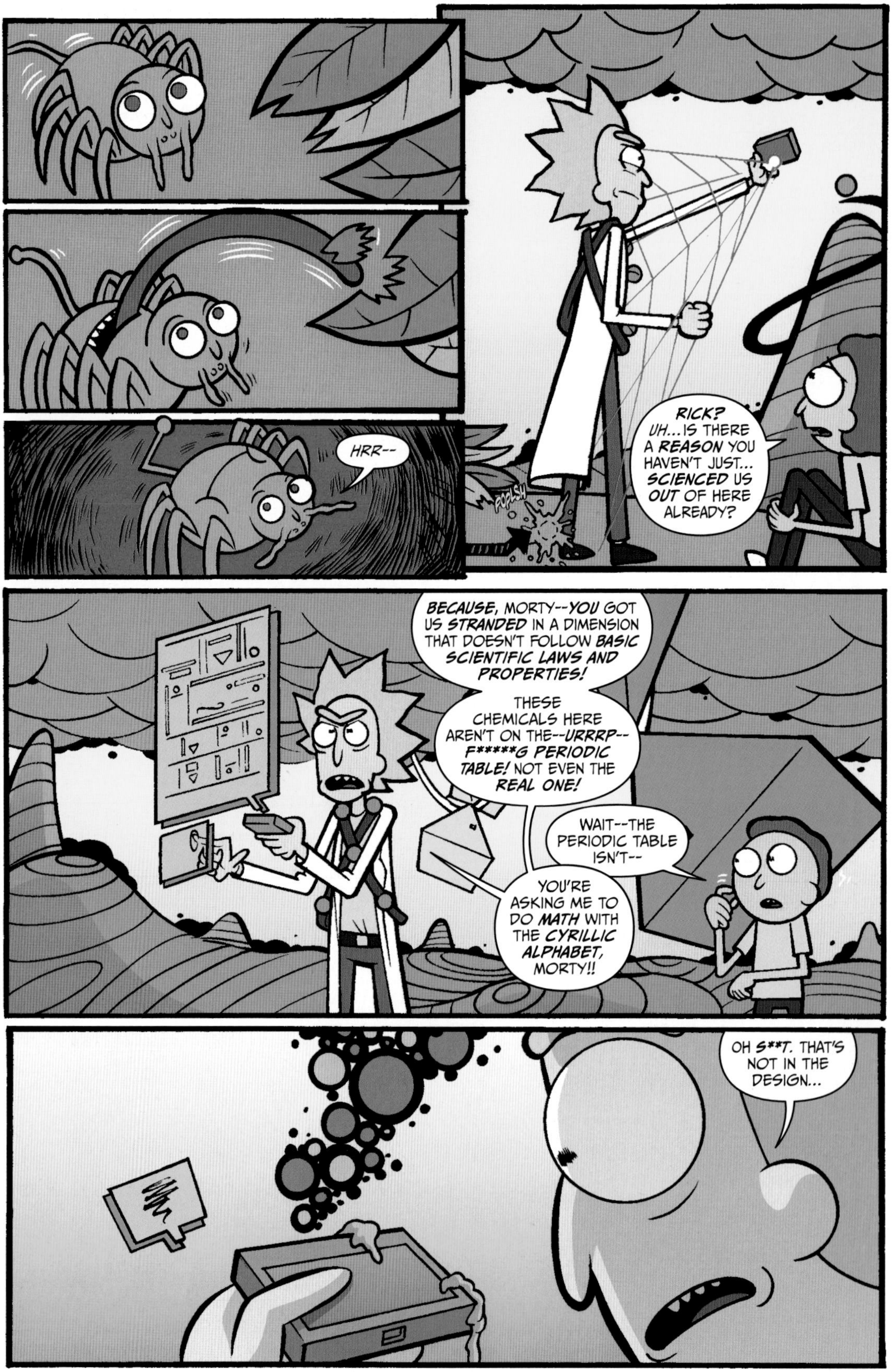
HRR--
RICK? UH...IS THERE A REASON YOU HAVEN'T JUST... SCIENCED US OUT OF HERE ALREADY?
POPLSH
BECAUSE, MORTY--YOU GOT US STRANDED IN A DIMENSION THAT DOESN'T FOLLOW BASIC SCIENTIFIC LAWS AND PROPERTIES!
THESE CHEMICALS HERE AREN'T ON THE--URRRP--F*****G PERIODIC TABLE! NOT EVEN THE REAL ONE!
WAIT--THE PERIODIC TABLE ISN'T--
YOU'RE ASKING ME TO DO MATH WITH THE CYRILLIC ALPHABET, MORTY!!
OH S**T. THAT'S NOT IN THE DESIGN...

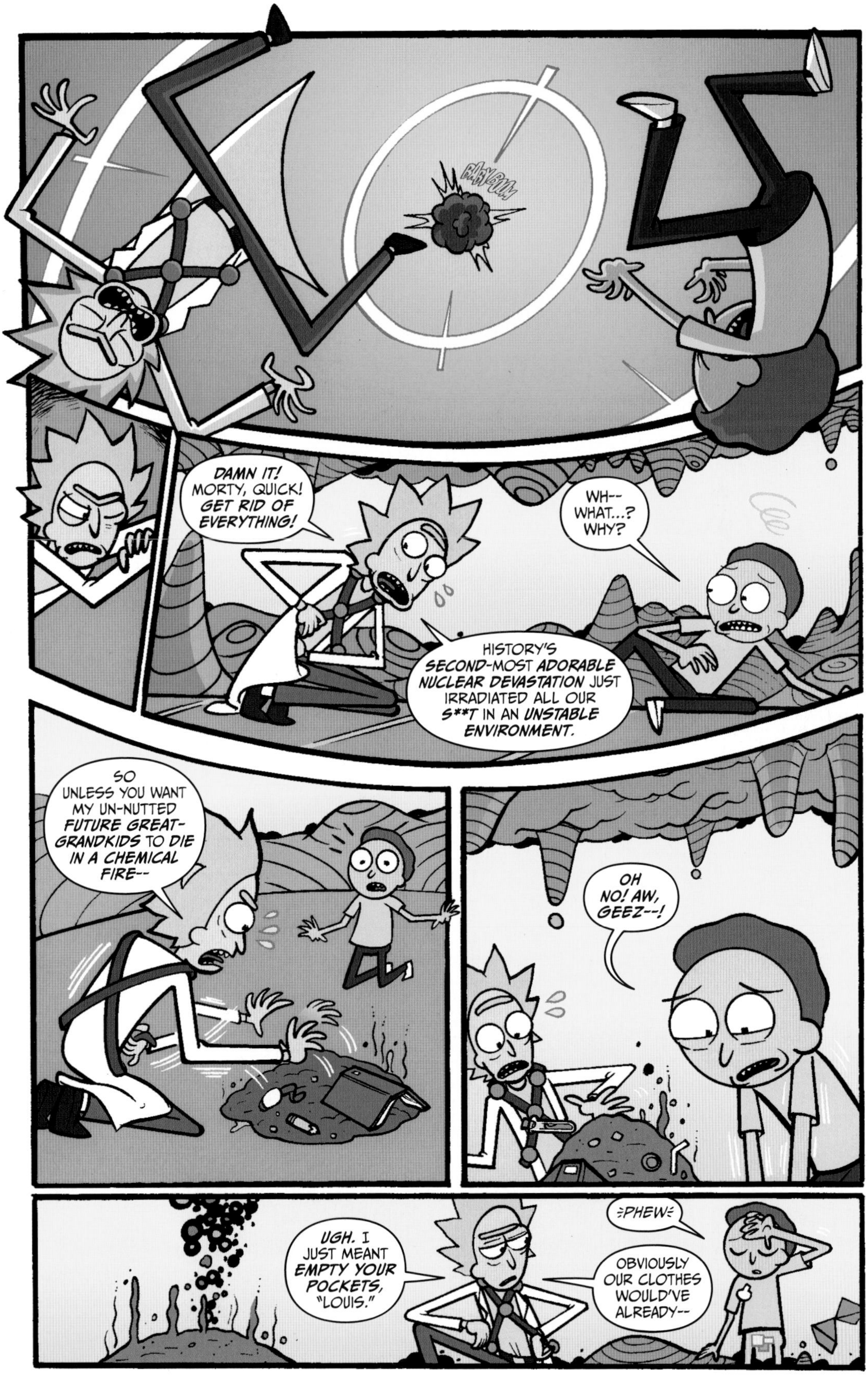
BABYBOOM
DAMN IT! MORTY, QUICK! GET RID OF EVERYTHING!
WH-- WHAT...? WHY?
HISTORY'S SECOND-MOST ADORABLE NUCLEAR DEVASTATION JUST IRRADIATED ALL OUR S**T IN AN UNSTABLE ENVIRONMENT.
SO UNLESS YOU WANT MY UN-NUTTED FUTURE GREAT-GRANDKIDS TO DIE IN A CHEMICAL FIRE--
OH NO! AW, GEEZ--!
UGH. I JUST MEANT EMPTY YOUR POCKETS, "LOUIS."
PHEW
OBVIOUSLY OUR CLOTHES WOULD'VE ALREADY--

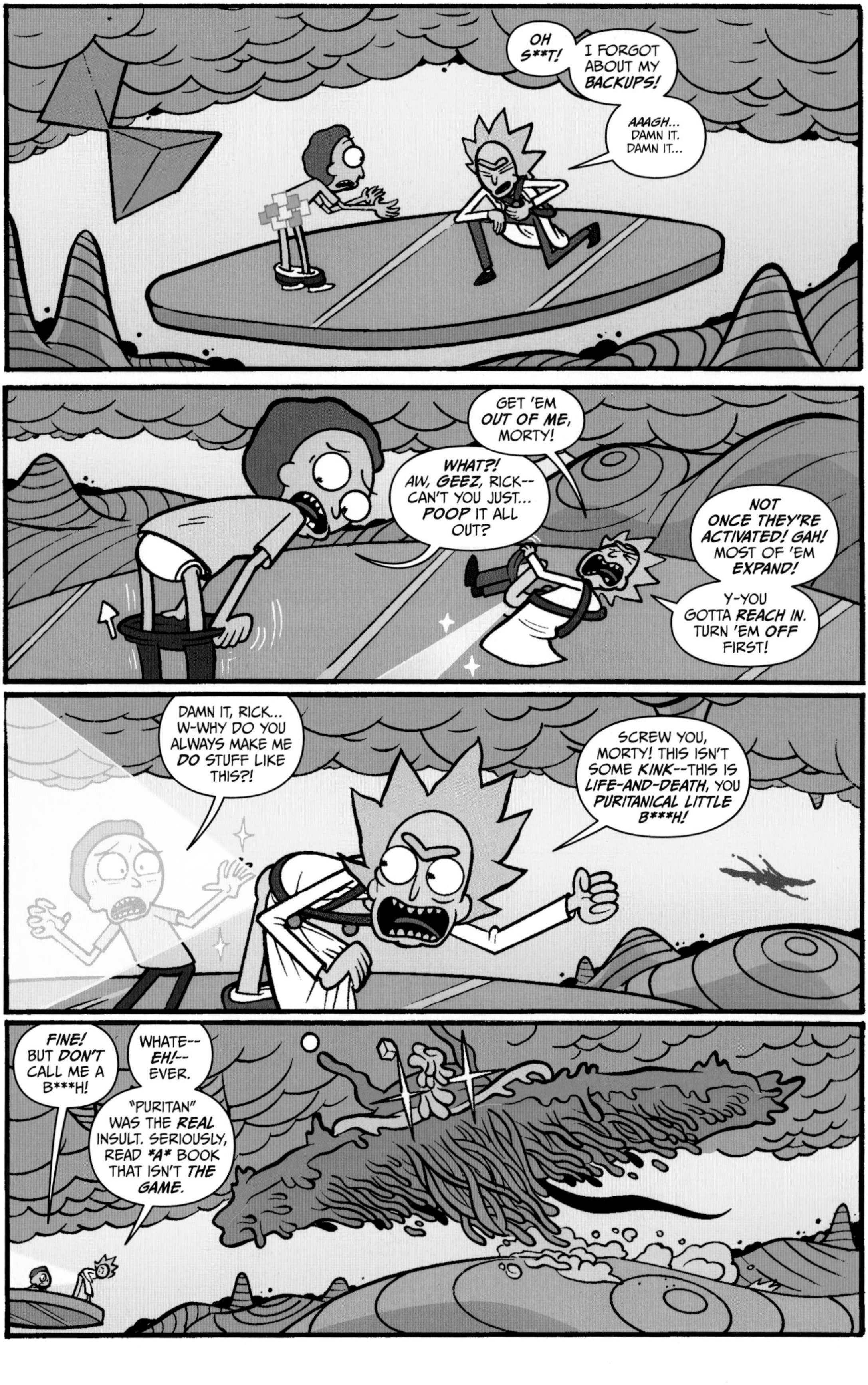
OH S**T!
I FORGOT ABOUT MY BACKUPS!
AAAGH... DAMN IT. DAMN IT...
GET 'EM OUT OF ME, MORTY!
WHAT?! AW, GEEZ, RICK-- CAN'T YOU JUST... POOP IT ALL OUT?
NOT ONCE THEY'RE ACTIVATED! GAH! MOST OF 'EM EXPAND!
Y-YOU GOTTA REACH IN. TURN 'EM OFF FIRST!
DAMN IT, RICK... W-WHY DO YOU ALWAYS MAKE ME DO STUFF LIKE THIS?!
SCREW YOU, MORTY! THIS ISN'T SOME KINK--THIS IS LIFE-AND-DEATH, YOU PURITANICAL LITTLE B***H!
FINE! BUT DON'T CALL ME A B***H!
WHATE-- EH!-- EVER.
"PURITAN" WAS THE REAL INSULT. SERIOUSLY, READ *A* BOOK THAT ISN'T THE GAME.

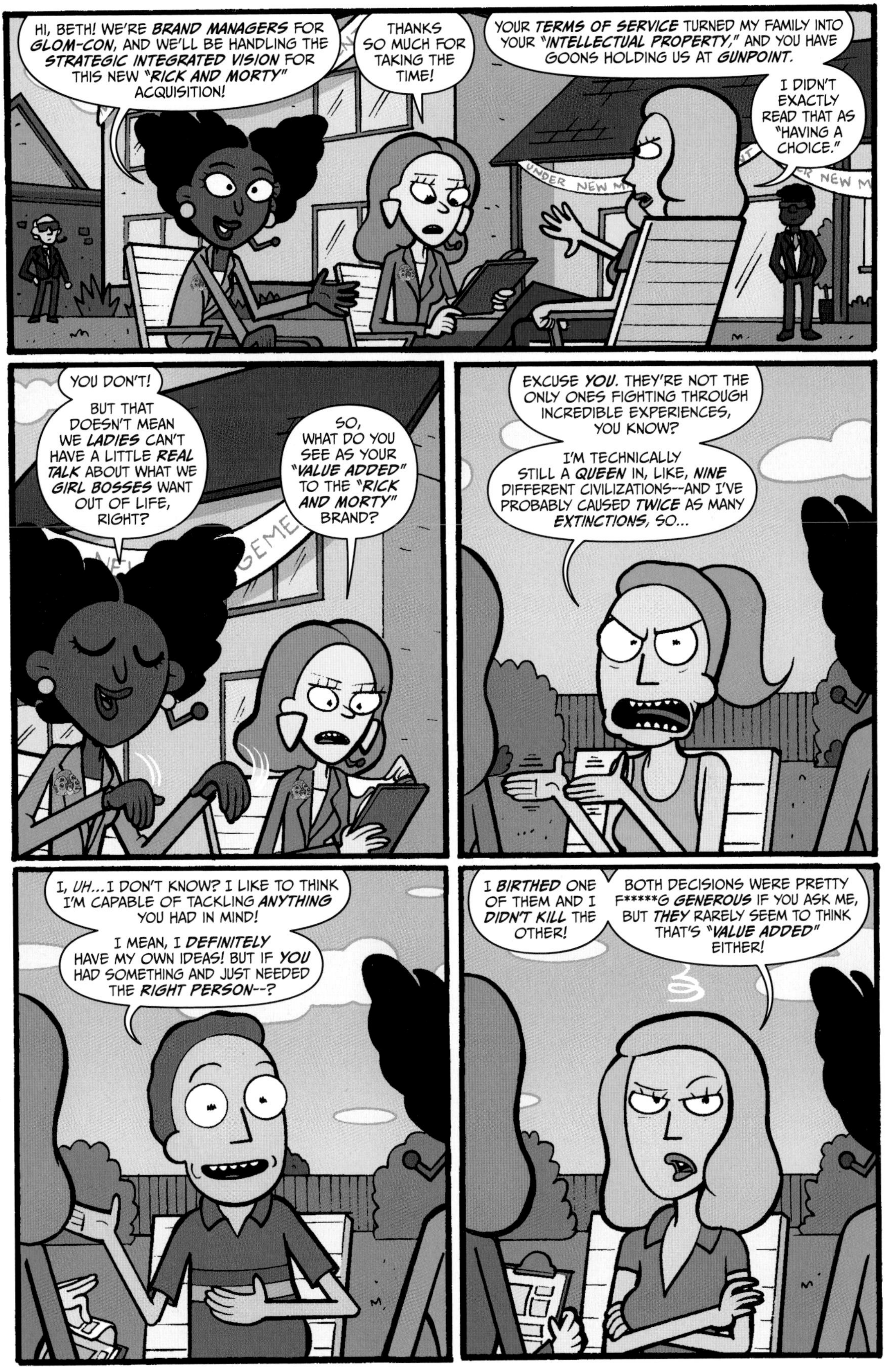
HI, BETH! WE'RE BRAND MANAGERS FOR GLOM-CON, AND WE'LL BE HANDLING THE STRATEGIC INTEGRATED VISION FOR THIS NEW "RICK AND MORTY" ACQUISITION!
THANKS SO MUCH FOR TAKING THE TIME!
YOUR TERMS OF SERVICE TURNED MY FAMILY INTO YOUR "INTELLECTUAL PROPERTY," AND YOU HAVE GOONS HOLDING US AT GUNPOINT.
I DIDN'T EXACTLY READ THAT AS "HAVING A CHOICE."
UNDER NEW M
YOU DON'T!
BUT THAT DOESN'T MEAN WE LADIES CAN'T HAVE A LITTLE REAL TALK ABOUT WHAT WE GIRL BOSSES WANT OUT OF LIFE, RIGHT?
SO, WHAT DO YOU SEE AS YOUR "VALUE ADDED" TO THE "RICK AND MORTY" BRAND?
EXCUSE YOU. THEY'RE NOT THE ONLY ONES FIGHTING THROUGH INCREDIBLE EXPERIENCES, YOU KNOW?
I'M TECHNICALLY STILL A QUEEN IN, LIKE, NINE DIFFERENT CIVILIZATIONS--AND I'VE PROBABLY CAUSED TWICE AS MANY EXTINCTIONS, SO...
I, UH...I DON'T KNOW? I LIKE TO THINK I'M CAPABLE OF TACKLING ANYTHING YOU HAD IN MIND!
I MEAN, I DEFINITELY HAVE MY OWN IDEAS! BUT IF YOU HAD SOMETHING AND JUST NEEDED THE RIGHT PERSON--?
I BIRTHED ONE OF THEM AND I DIDN'T KILL THE OTHER!
BOTH DECISIONS WERE PRETTY F*****G GENEROUS IF YOU ASK ME, BUT THEY RARELY SEEM TO THINK THAT'S "VALUE ADDED" EITHER!

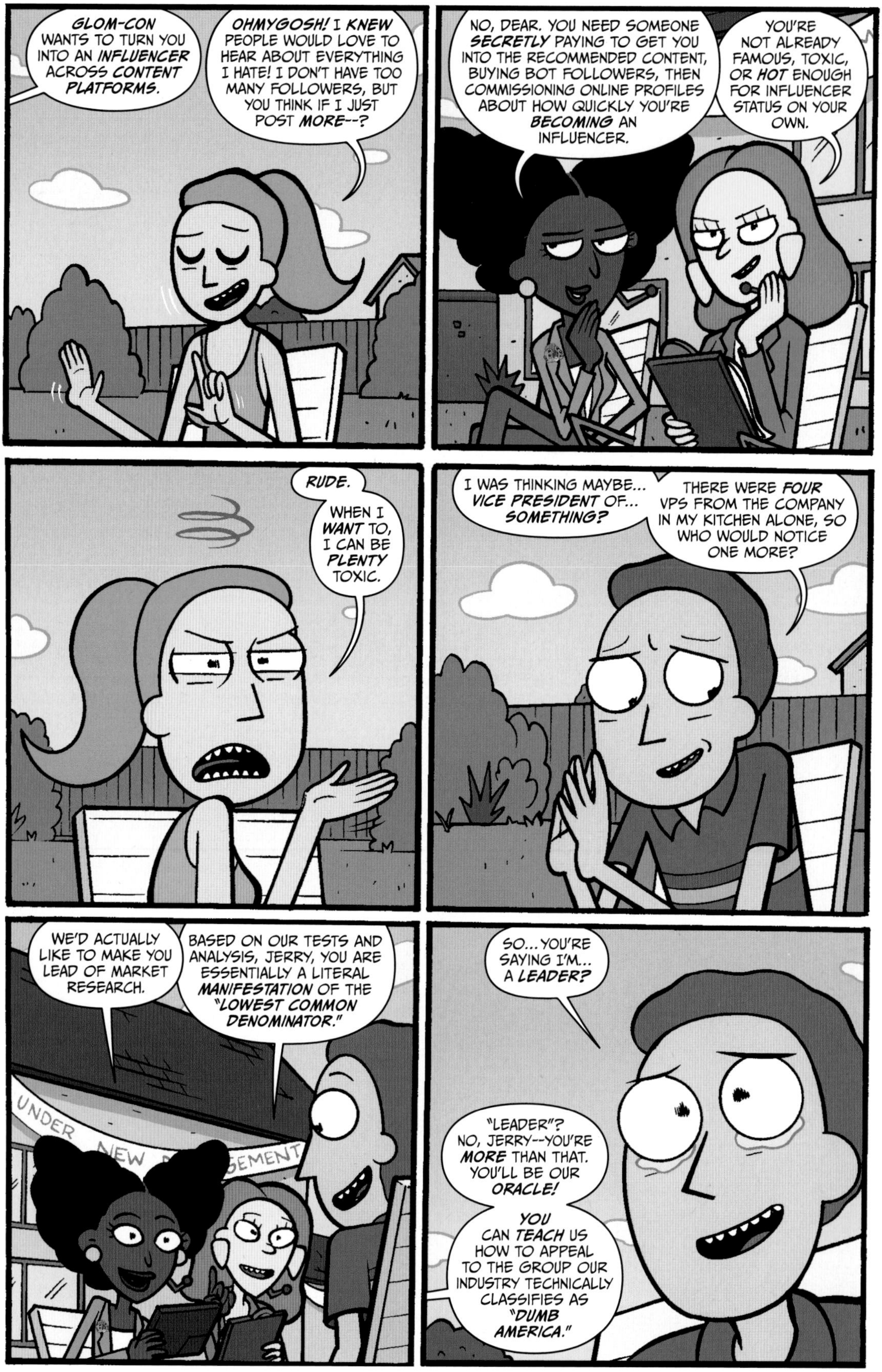
GLOM-CON WANTS TO TURN YOU INTO AN INFLUENCER ACROSS CONTENT PLATFORMS.
OHMYGOSH! I KNEW PEOPLE WOULD LOVE TO HEAR ABOUT EVERYTHING I HATE! I DON'T HAVE TOO MANY FOLLOWERS, BUT YOU THINK IF I JUST POST MORE--?
NO, DEAR. YOU NEED SOMEONE SECRETLY PAYING TO GET YOU INTO THE RECOMMENDED CONTENT, BUYING BOT FOLLOWERS, THEN COMMISSIONING ONLINE PROFILES ABOUT HOW QUICKLY YOU'RE BECOMING AN INFLUENCER.
YOU'RE NOT ALREADY FAMOUS, TOXIC, OR HOT ENOUGH FOR INFLUENCER STATUS ON YOUR OWN.
RUDE.
WHEN I WANT TO, I CAN BE PLENTY TOXIC.
I WAS THINKING MAYBE... VICE PRESIDENT OF... SOMETHING?
THERE WERE FOUR VPS FROM THE COMPANY IN MY KITCHEN ALONE, SO WHO WOULD NOTICE ONE MORE?
WE'D ACTUALLY LIKE TO MAKE YOU LEAD OF MARKET RESEARCH.
BASED ON OUR TESTS AND ANALYSIS, JERRY, YOU ARE ESSENTIALLY A LITERAL MANIFESTATION OF THE "LOWEST COMMON DENOMINATOR."
SO... YOU'RE SAYING I'M... A LEADER?
"LEADER"? NO, JERRY--YOU'RE MORE THAN THAT. YOU'LL BE OUR ORACLE!
YOU CAN TEACH US HOW TO APPEAL TO THE GROUP OUR INDUSTRY TECHNICALLY CLASSIFIES AS "DUMB AMERICA."

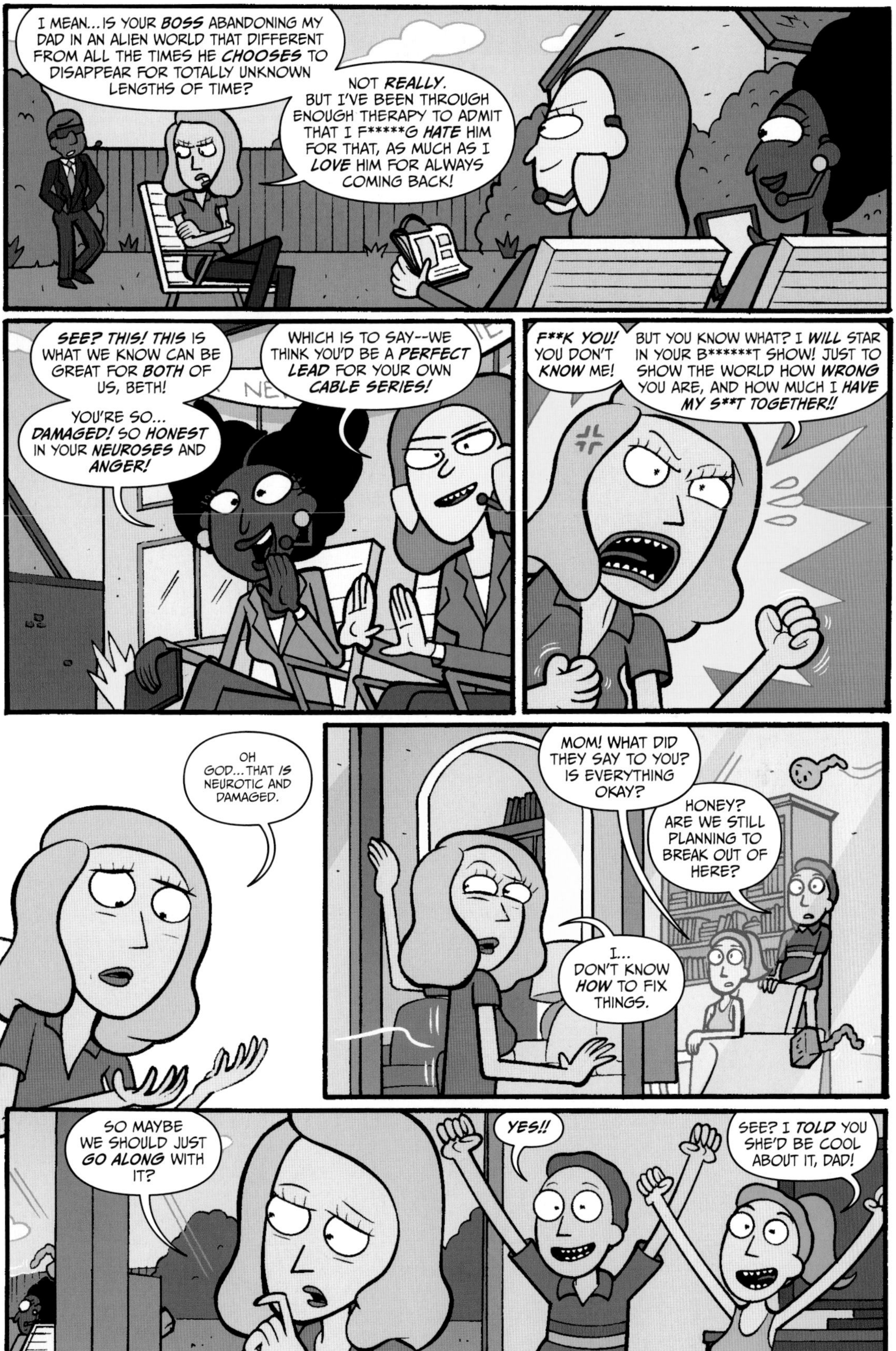
I MEAN... IS YOUR BOSS ABANDONING MY DAD IN AN ALIEN WORLD THAT DIFFERENT FROM ALL THE TIMES HE CHOOSES TO DISAPPEAR FOR TOTALLY UNKNOWN LENGTHS OF TIME?
NOT REALLY. BUT I'VE BEEN THROUGH ENOUGH THERAPY TO ADMIT THAT I F*****G HATE HIM FOR THAT, AS MUCH AS I LOVE HIM FOR ALWAYS COMING BACK!
SEE? THIS! THIS IS WHAT WE KNOW CAN BE GREAT FOR BOTH OF US, BETH!
YOU'RE SO... DAMAGED! SO HONEST IN YOUR NEUROSES AND ANGER!
WHICH IS TO SAY--WE THINK YOU'D BE A PERFECT LEAD FOR YOUR OWN CABLE SERIES!
F**K YOU! YOU DON'T KNOW ME!
BUT YOU KNOW WHAT? I WILL STAR IN YOUR B******T SHOW! JUST TO SHOW THE WORLD HOW WRONG YOU ARE, AND HOW MUCH I HAVE MY S**T TOGETHER!!
OH GOD... THAT IS NEUROTIC AND DAMAGED.
MOM! WHAT DID THEY SAY TO YOU? IS EVERYTHING OKAY?
HONEY? ARE WE STILL PLANNING TO BREAK OUT OF HERE?
I... DON'T KNOW HOW TO FIX THINGS.
SO MAYBE WE SHOULD JUST GO ALONG WITH IT?
YES!!
SEE? I TOLD YOU SHE'D BE COOL ABOUT IT, DAD!

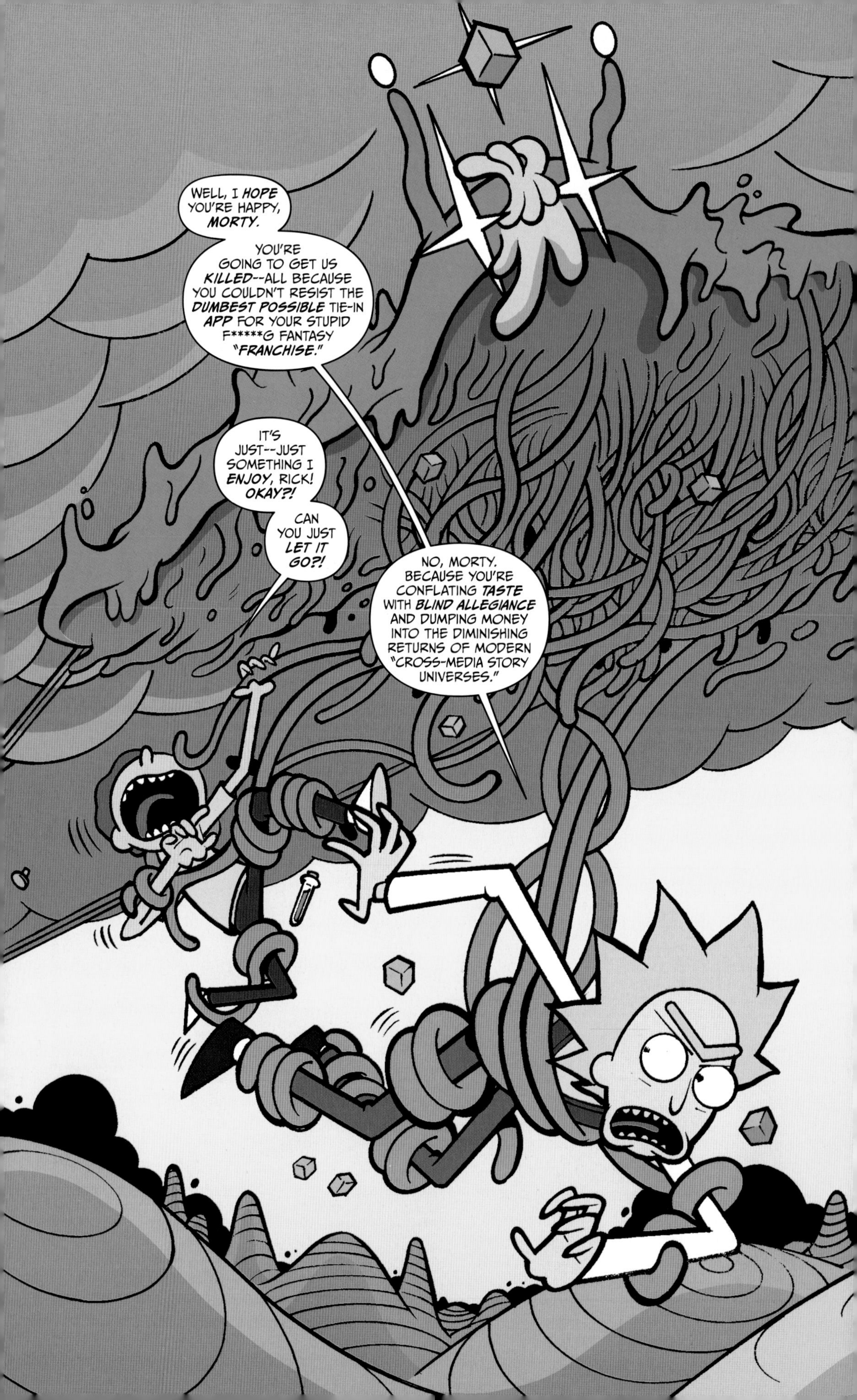
WELL, I HOPE YOU'RE HAPPY, MORTY.
YOU'RE GOING TO GET US KILLED--ALL BECAUSE YOU COULDN'T RESIST THE DUMBEST POSSIBLE TIE-IN APP FOR YOUR STUPID F*****G FANTASY "FRANCHISE."
IT'S JUST--JUST SOMETHING I ENJOY, RICK! OKAY?!
CAN YOU JUST LET IT GO?!
NO, MORTY. BECAUSE YOU'RE CONFLATING TASTE WITH BLIND ALLEGIANCE AND DUMPING MONEY INTO THE DIMINISHING RETURNS OF MODERN "CROSS-MEDIA STORY UNIVERSES."

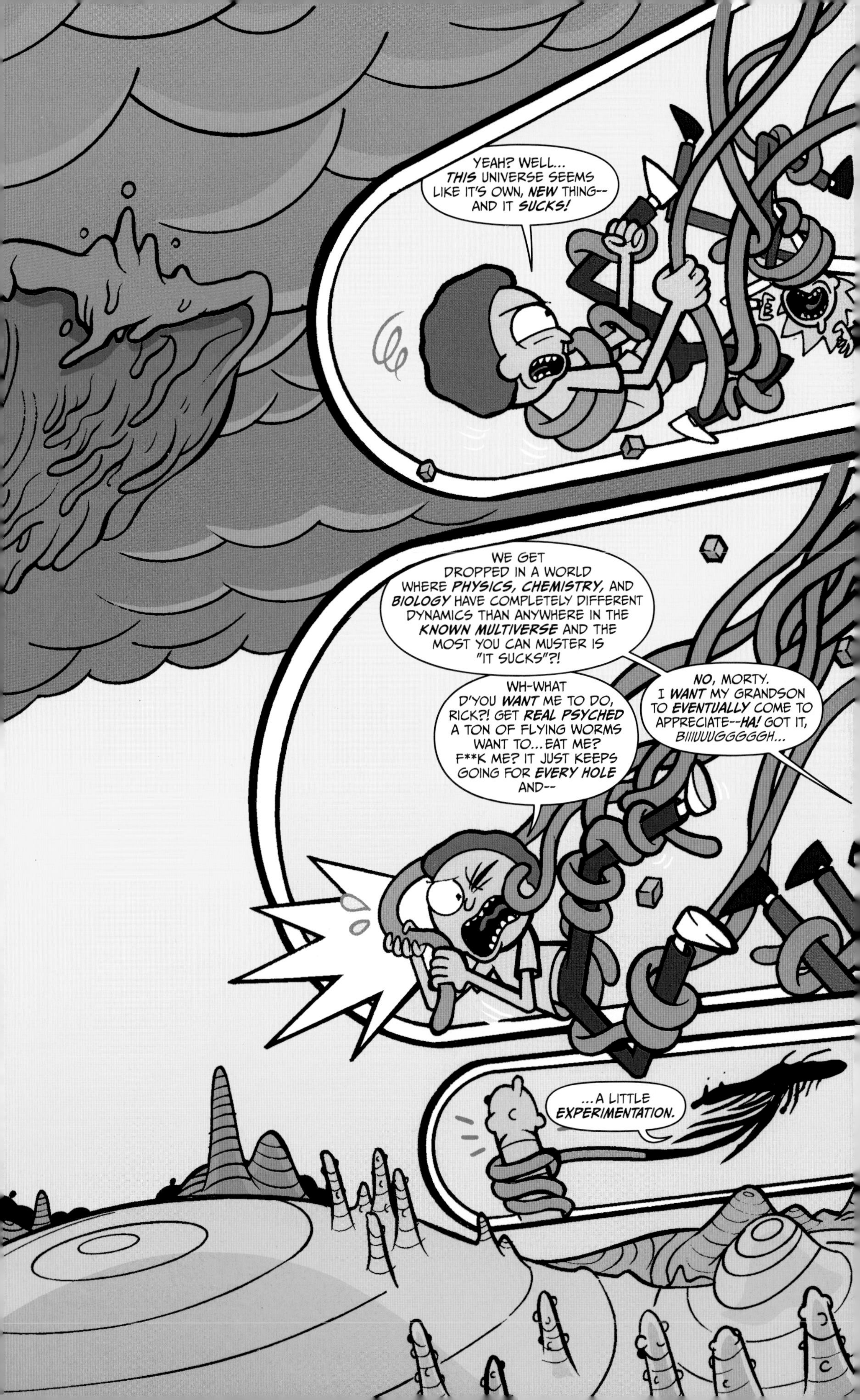
YEAH? WELL... THIS UNIVERSE SEEMS LIKE IT'S OWN, NEW THING-- AND IT SUCKS!
WE GET DROPPED IN A WORLD WHERE PHYSICS, CHEMISTRY, AND BIOLOGY HAVE COMPLETELY DIFFERENT DYNAMICS THAN ANYWHERE IN THE KNOWN MULTIVERSE AND THE MOST YOU CAN MUSTER IS "IT SUCKS"?!
WH-WHAT D'YOU WANT ME TO DO, RICK?! GET REAL PSYCHED A TON OF FLYING WORMS WANT TO... EAT ME? F**K ME? IT JUST KEEPS GOING FOR EVERY HOLE AND--
NO, MORTY. I WANT MY GRANDSON TO EVENTUALLY COME TO APPRECIATE--HA! GOT IT, BIIIUUUGGGGH...
...A LITTLE EXPERIMENTATION.

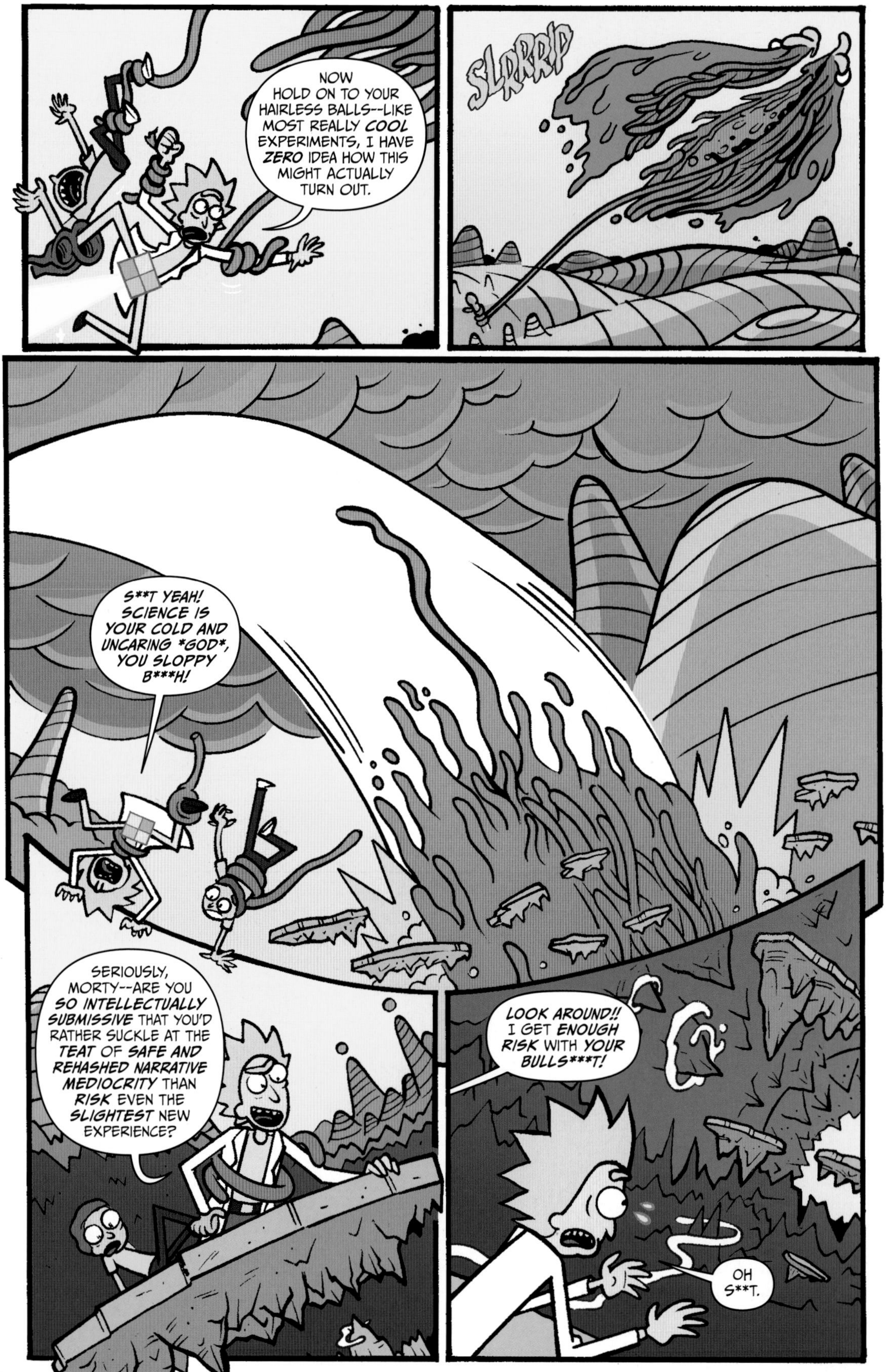
NOW HOLD ON TO YOUR HAIRLESS BALLS--LIKE MOST REALLY COOL EXPERIMENTS, I HAVE ZERO IDEA HOW THIS MIGHT ACTUALLY TURN OUT.
SLRRRIP
S**T YEAH! SCIENCE IS YOUR COLD AND UNCARING *GOD*, YOU SLOPPY B***H!
SERIOUSLY, MORTY--ARE YOU SO INTELLECTUALLY SUBMISSIVE THAT YOU'D RATHER SUCKLE AT THE TEAT OF SAFE AND REHASHED NARRATIVE MEDIOCRITY THAN RISK EVEN THE SLIGHTEST NEW EXPERIENCE?
LOOK AROUND!! I GET ENOUGH RISK WITH YOUR BULLS***T!
OH S**T.

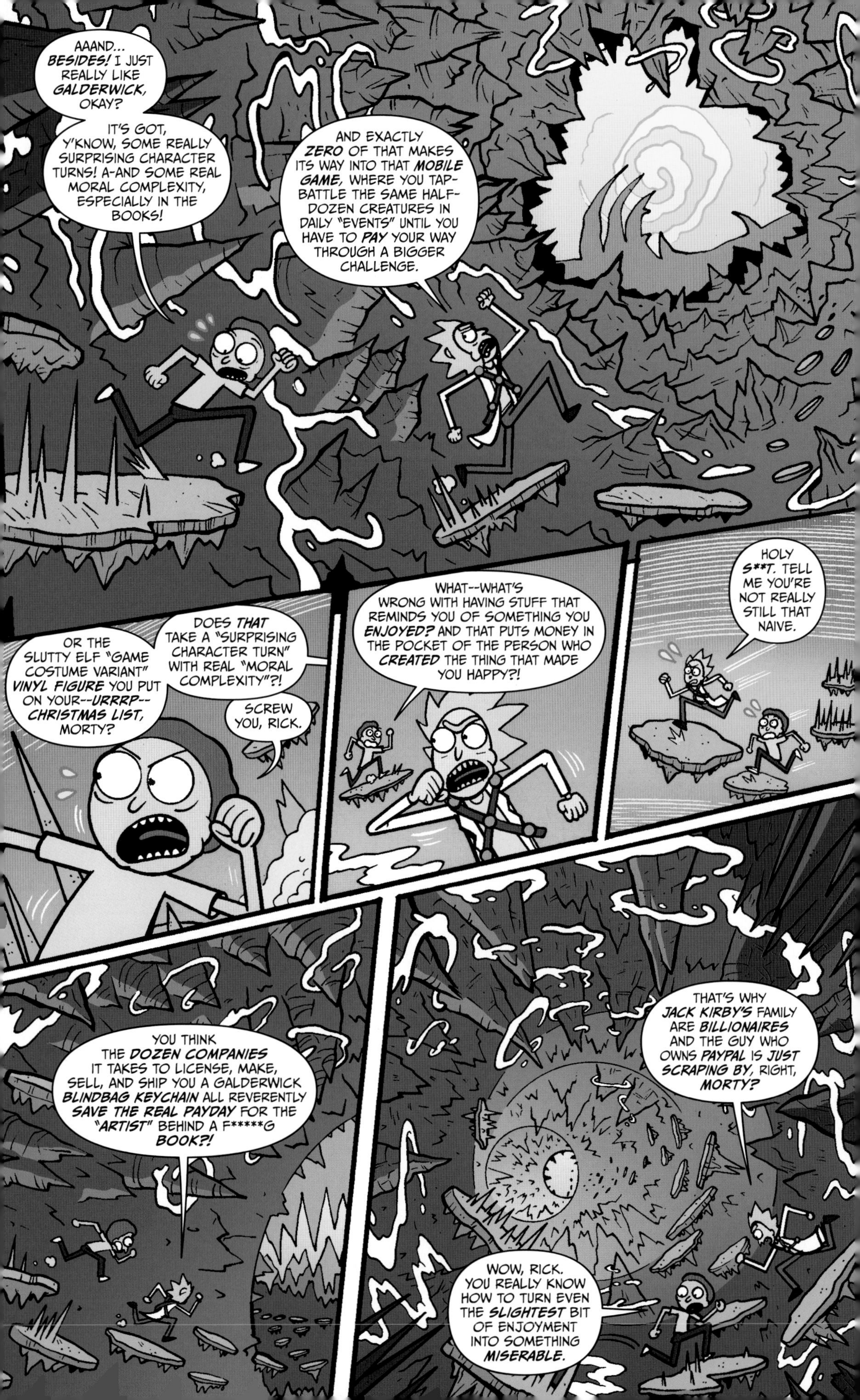
AAAND... BESIDES! I JUST REALLY LIKE GALDERWICK, OKAY?
IT'S GOT, Y'KNOW, SOME REALLY SURPRISING CHARACTER TURNS! A-AND SOME REAL MORAL COMPLEXITY, ESPECIALLY IN THE BOOKS!
AND EXACTLY ZERO OF THAT MAKES ITS WAY INTO THAT MOBILE GAME, WHERE YOU TAP-BATTLE THE SAME HALF-DOZEN CREATURES IN DAILY "EVENTS" UNTIL YOU HAVE TO PAY YOUR WAY THROUGH A BIGGER CHALLENGE.
OR THE SLUTTY ELF "GAME COSTUME VARIANT" VINYL FIGURE YOU PUT ON YOUR--URRRP--CHRISTMAS LIST, MORTY?
DOES THAT TAKE A "SURPRISING CHARACTER TURN" WITH REAL "MORAL COMPLEXITY"?!
SCREW YOU, RICK.
WHAT--WHAT'S WRONG WITH HAVING STUFF THAT REMINDS YOU OF SOMETHING YOU ENJOYED? AND THAT PUTS MONEY IN THE POCKET OF THE PERSON WHO CREATED THE THING THAT MADE YOU HAPPY?!
HOLY S**T. TELL ME YOU'RE NOT REALLY STILL THAT NAIVE.
YOU THINK THE DOZEN COMPANIES IT TAKES TO LICENSE, MAKE, SELL, AND SHIP YOU A GALDERWICK BLINDBAG KEYCHAIN ALL REVERENTLY SAVE THE REAL PAYDAY FOR THE "ARTIST" BEHIND A F*****G BOOK?!
THAT'S WHY JACK KIRBY'S FAMILY ARE BILLIONAIRES AND THE GUY WHO OWNS PAYPAL IS JUST SCRAPING BY, RIGHT, MORTY?
WOW, RICK. YOU REALLY KNOW HOW TO TURN EVEN THE SLIGHTEST BIT OF ENJOYMENT INTO SOMETHING MISERABLE.

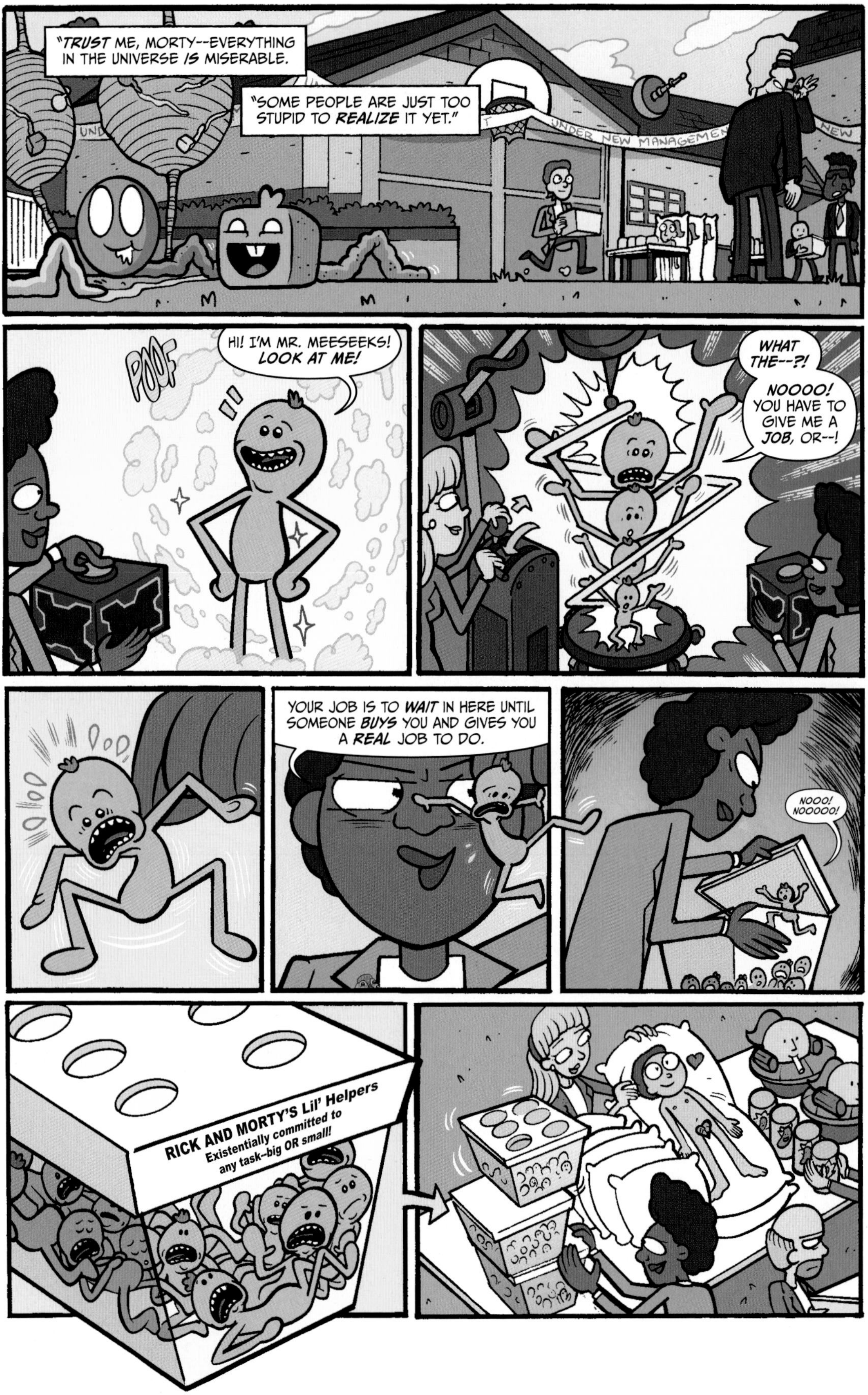
"TRUST ME, MORTY--EVERYTHING IN THE UNIVERSE IS MISERABLE.
"SOME PEOPLE ARE JUST TOO STUPID TO REALIZE IT YET."
UNDER NEW MANAGEMENT
POOF
HI! I'M MR. MEESEEKS! LOOK AT ME!
WHAT THE--?!
NOOOO! YOU HAVE TO GIVE ME A JOB, OR--!
YOUR JOB IS TO WAIT IN HERE UNTIL SOMEONE BUYS YOU AND GIVES YOU A REAL JOB TO DO.
NOOO! NOOOOO!
RICK AND MORTY'S Lil' Helpers
Existentially committed to any task--big OR small!

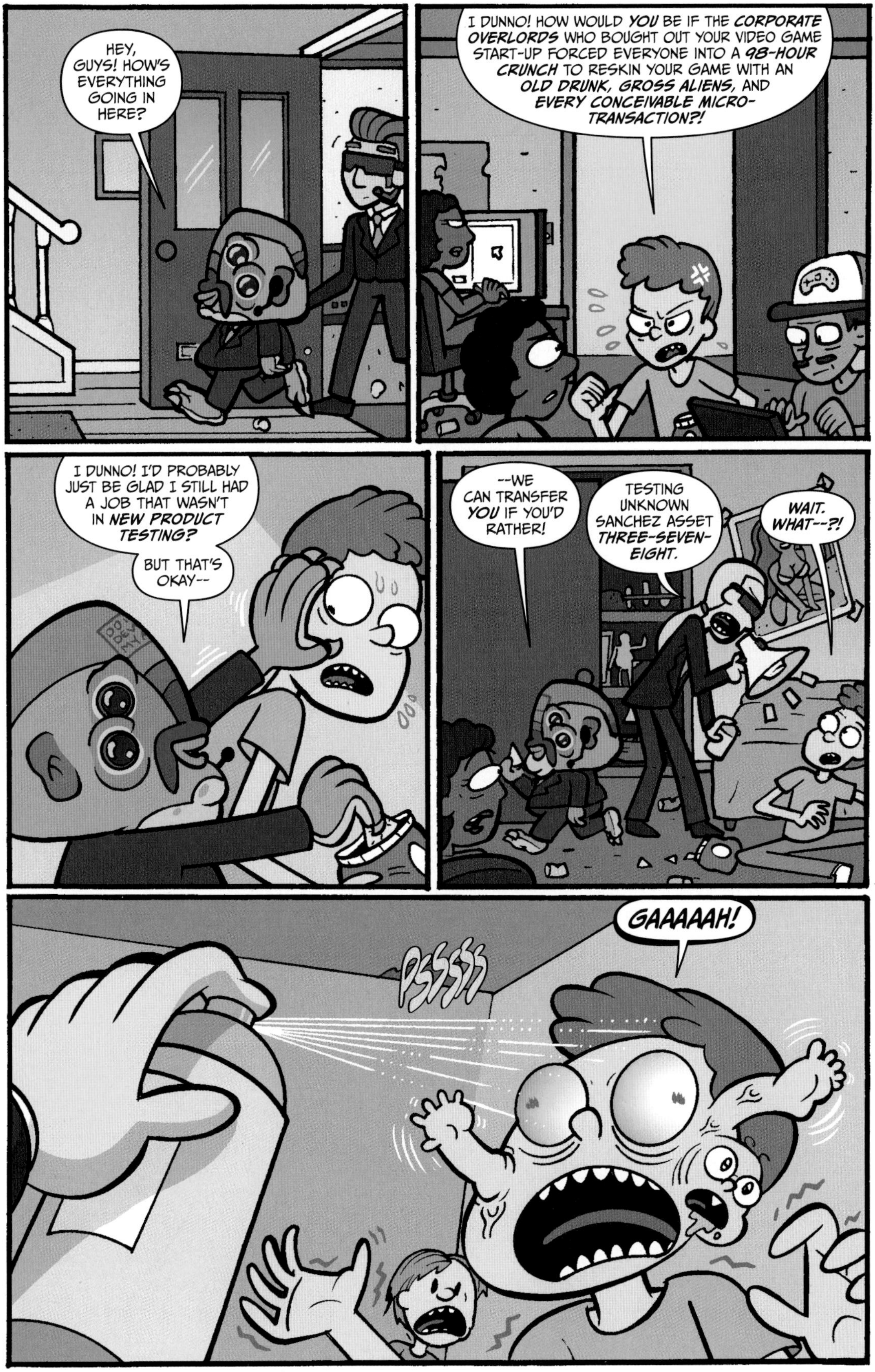
HEY, GUYS! HOW'S EVERYTHING GOING IN HERE?
I DUNNO! HOW WOULD YOU BE IF THE CORPORATE OVERLORDS WHO BOUGHT OUT YOUR VIDEO GAME START-UP FORCED EVERYONE INTO A 98-HOUR CRUNCH TO RESKIN YOUR GAME WITH AN OLD DRUNK, GROSS ALIENS, AND EVERY CONCEIVABLE MICRO-TRANSACTION?!
I DUNNO! I'D PROBABLY JUST BE GLAD I STILL HAD A JOB THAT WASN'T IN NEW PRODUCT TESTING?
BUT THAT'S OKAY--
--WE CAN TRANSFER YOU IF YOU'D RATHER!
TESTING UNKNOWN SANCHEZ ASSET THREE-SEVEN-EIGHT.
WAIT. WHAT--?!
PSSSSS
GAAAAAH!

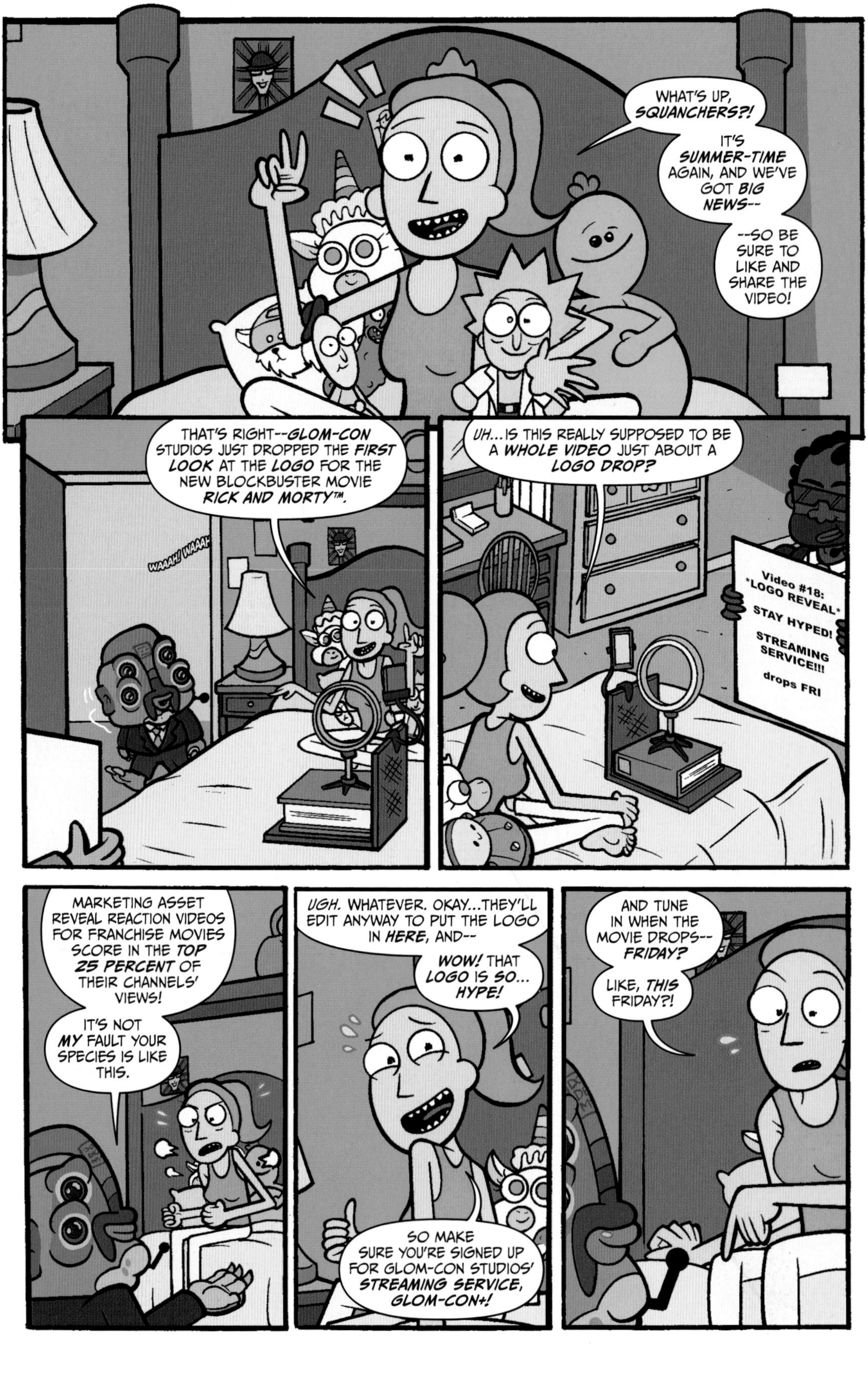
WHAT'S UP, SQUANCHERS?!
IT'S SUMMER-TIME AGAIN, AND WE'VE GOT BIG NEWS--
--SO BE SURE TO LIKE AND SHARE THE VIDEO!
THAT'S RIGHT--GLOM-CON STUDIOS JUST DROPPED THE FIRST LOOK AT THE LOGO FOR THE NEW BLOCKBUSTER MOVIE RICK AND MORTY™.
WAAAH! WAAAH
UH...IS THIS REALLY SUPPOSED TO BE A WHOLE VIDEO JUST ABOUT A LOGO DROP?
Video #18: *LOGO REVEAL* STAY HYPED! STREAMING SERVICE!!! drops FRI
MARKETING ASSET REVEAL REACTION VIDEOS FOR FRANCHISE MOVIES SCORE IN THE TOP 25 PERCENT OF THEIR CHANNELS' VIEWS!
IT'S NOT MY FAULT YOUR SPECIES IS LIKE THIS.
UGH. WHATEVER. OKAY...THEY'LL EDIT ANYWAY TO PUT THE LOGO IN HERE, AND--
WOW! THAT LOGO IS SO... HYPE!
SO MAKE SURE YOU'RE SIGNED UP FOR GLOM-CON STUDIOS' STREAMING SERVICE, GLOM-CON+!
AND TUNE IN WHEN THE MOVIE DROPS-- FRIDAY?
LIKE, THIS FRIDAY?!

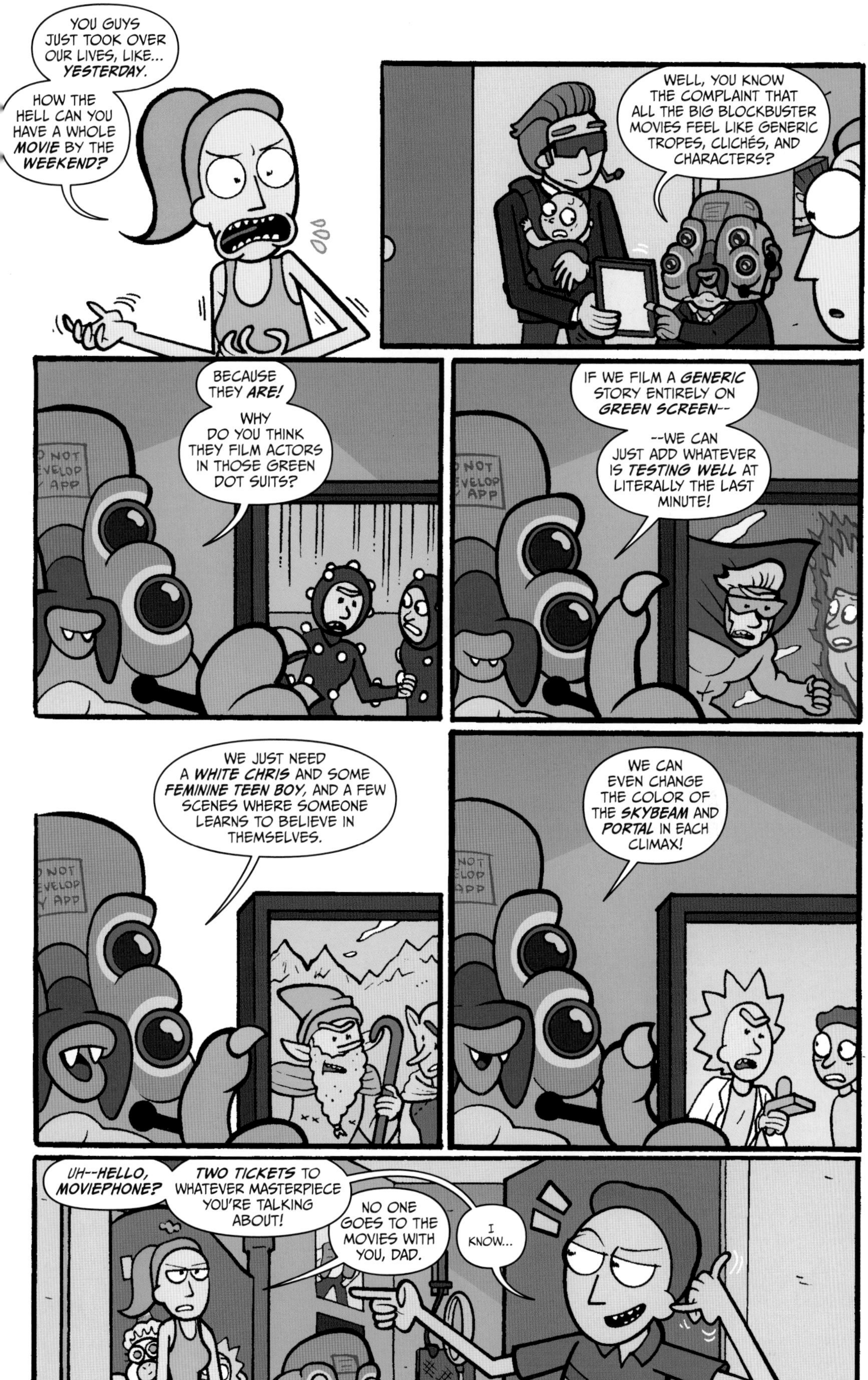
YOU GUYS JUST TOOK OVER OUR LIVES, LIKE... YESTERDAY.
HOW THE HELL CAN YOU HAVE A WHOLE MOVIE BY THE WEEKEND?
WELL, YOU KNOW THE COMPLAINT THAT ALL THE BIG BLOCKBUSTER MOVIES FEEL LIKE GENERIC TROPES, CLICHÉS, AND CHARACTERS?
BECAUSE THEY ARE!
WHY DO YOU THINK THEY FILM ACTORS IN THOSE GREEN DOT SUITS?
IF WE FILM A GENERIC STORY ENTIRELY ON GREEN SCREEN--
--WE CAN JUST ADD WHATEVER IS TESTING WELL AT LITERALLY THE LAST MINUTE!
WE JUST NEED A WHITE CHRIS AND SOME FEMININE TEEN BOY, AND A FEW SCENES WHERE SOMEONE LEARNS TO BELIEVE IN THEMSELVES.
WE CAN EVEN CHANGE THE COLOR OF THE SKYBEAM AND PORTAL IN EACH CLIMAX!
UH--HELLO, MOVIEPHONE?
TWO TICKETS TO WHATEVER MASTERPIECE YOU'RE TALKING ABOUT!
NO ONE GOES TO THE MOVIES WITH YOU, DAD.
I KNOW...

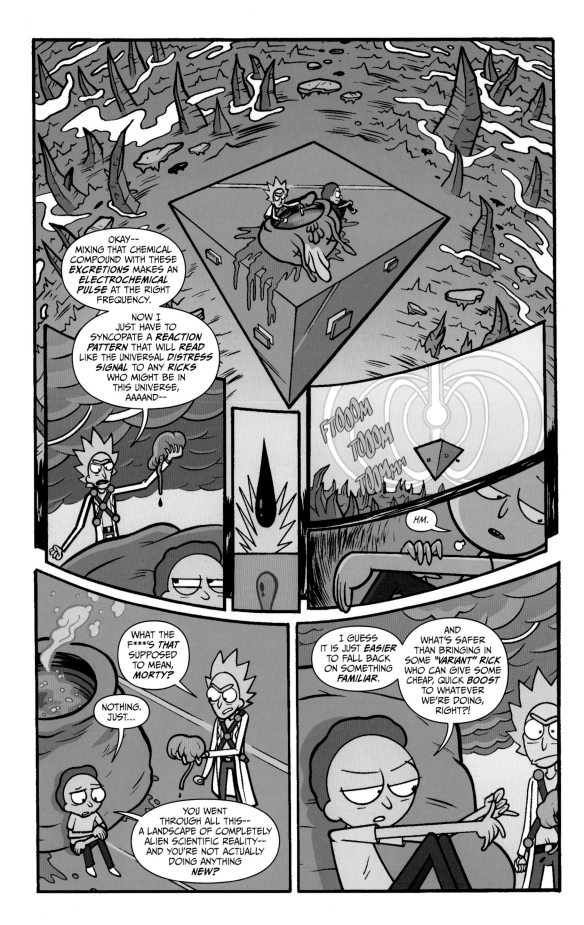

OKAY-- MIXING THAT CHEMICAL COMPOUND WITH THESE *EXCRETIONS* MAKES AN *ELECTROCHEMICAL PULSE* AT THE RIGHT FREQUENCY.

NOW I JUST HAVE TO SYNCOPATE A *REACTION PATTERN* THAT WILL *READ* LIKE THE UNIVERSAL *DISTRESS SIGNAL* TO ANY *RICKS* WHO MIGHT BE IN THIS UNIVERSE, AAAAND--

FTOOOOM TOOOM TOOOMmm

HM.

WHAT THE F***'S *THAT* SUPPOSED TO MEAN, *MORTY?*

NOTHING. JUST...

YOU WENT THROUGH ALL THIS-- A LANDSCAPE OF COMPLETELY ALIEN SCIENTIFIC REALITY-- AND YOU'RE NOT ACTUALLY DOING ANYTHING *NEW?*

I GUESS IT IS JUST *EASIER* TO FALL BACK ON SOMETHING *FAMILIAR.*

AND WHAT'S SAFER THAN BRINGING IN SOME *"VARIANT"* RICK WHO CAN GIVE SOME CHEAP, QUICK *BOOST* TO WHATEVER WE'RE DOING, RIGHT?!

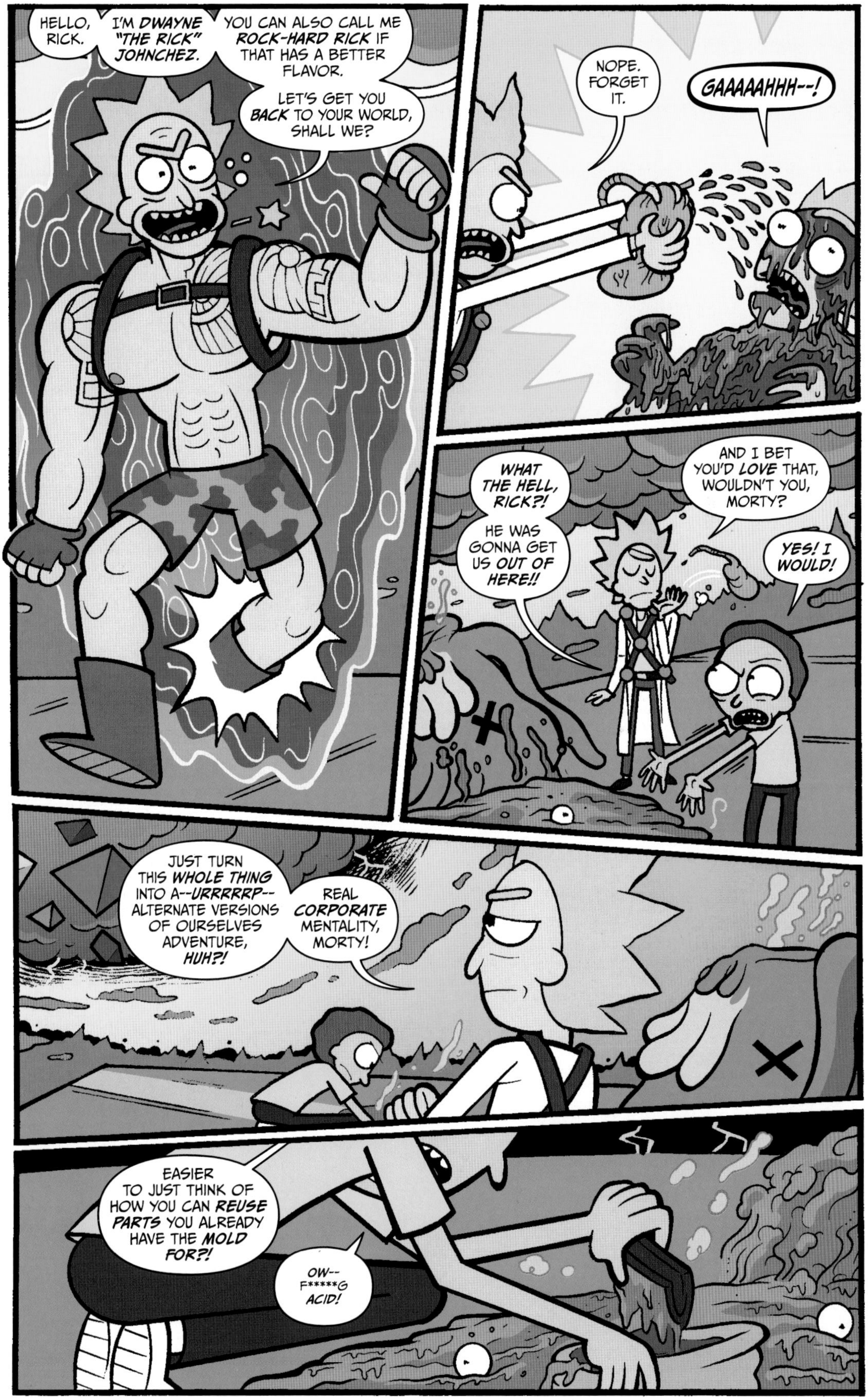
HELLO, RICK.
I'M DWAYNE "THE RICK" JOHNCHEZ.
YOU CAN ALSO CALL ME ROCK-HARD RICK IF THAT HAS A BETTER FLAVOR.
LET'S GET YOU BACK TO YOUR WORLD, SHALL WE?
NOPE. FORGET IT.
GAAAAAHHH--!
WHAT THE HELL, RICK?!
HE WAS GONNA GET US OUT OF HERE!!
AND I BET YOU'D LOVE THAT, WOULDN'T YOU, MORTY?
YES! I WOULD!
JUST TURN THIS WHOLE THING INTO A--URRRRRP--ALTERNATE VERSIONS OF OURSELVES ADVENTURE, HUH?!
REAL CORPORATE MENTALITY, MORTY!
EASIER TO JUST THINK OF HOW YOU CAN REUSE PARTS YOU ALREADY HAVE THE MOLD FOR?!
OW-- F*****G ACID!

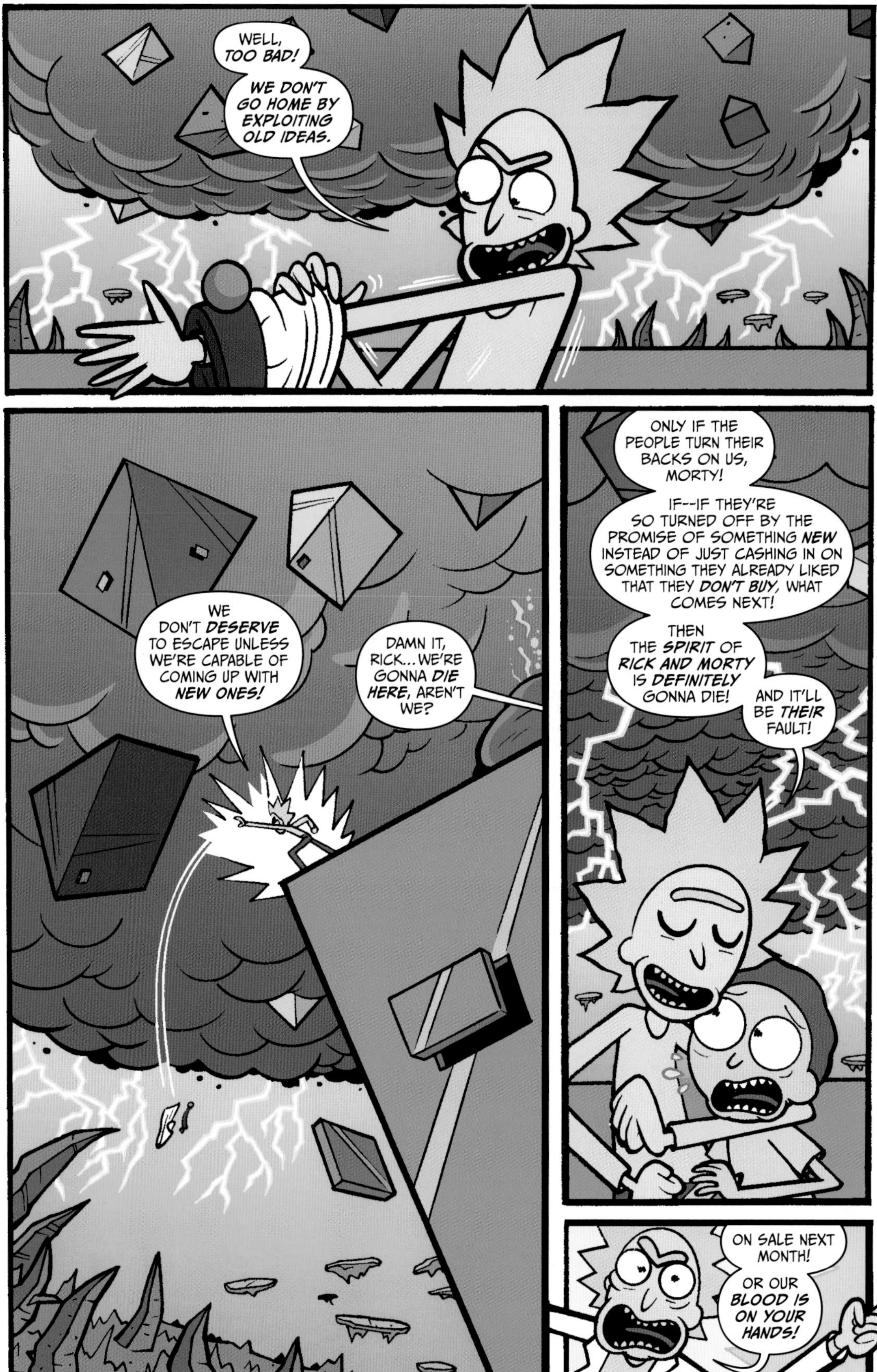
WELL, TOO BAD!
WE DON'T GO HOME BY EXPLOITING OLD IDEAS.
WE DON'T DESERVE TO ESCAPE UNLESS WE'RE CAPABLE OF COMING UP WITH NEW ONES!
DAMN IT, RICK...WE'RE GONNA DIE HERE, AREN'T WE?
ONLY IF THE PEOPLE TURN THEIR BACKS ON US, MORTY!
IF--IF THEY'RE SO TURNED OFF BY THE PROMISE OF SOMETHING NEW INSTEAD OF JUST CASHING IN ON SOMETHING THEY ALREADY LIKED THAT THEY DON'T BUY, WHAT COMES NEXT!
THEN THE SPIRIT OF RICK AND MORTY IS DEFINITELY GONNA DIE!
AND IT'LL BE THEIR FAULT!
ON SALE NEXT MONTH!
OR OUR BLOOD IS ON YOUR HANDS!

NEXT ISSUE: RICK AND MORTY: THE MOVIE!!
*(CALL YOUR COMIC SHOP **RIGHT NOW** TO MAKE SURE THEY HAVE EXTRA BECAUSE THAT'S HOW F*****G GOOD THIS IS. **TELL THEM. DO IT.** CHAMPIONING THIS UNDERAPPRECIATED GEM IS **YOUR JOB** AS A FAN, AND THE WAY TO PROVE YOUR CULTURAL CLOUT WITHIN YOUR SOCIAL CIRCLE OF NERDS!)*

CHAPTER 3

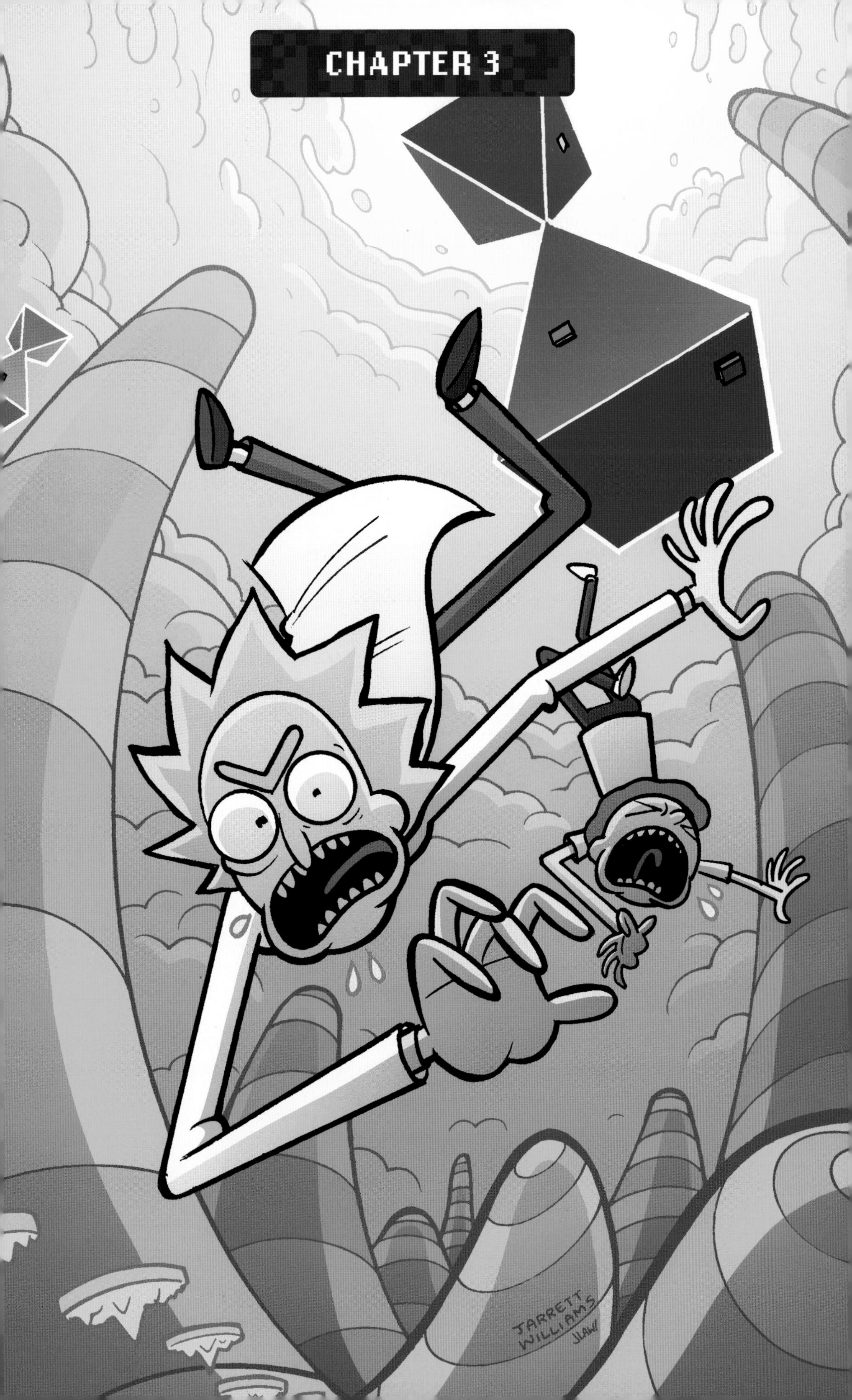
JARRETT WILLIAMS
JLAW

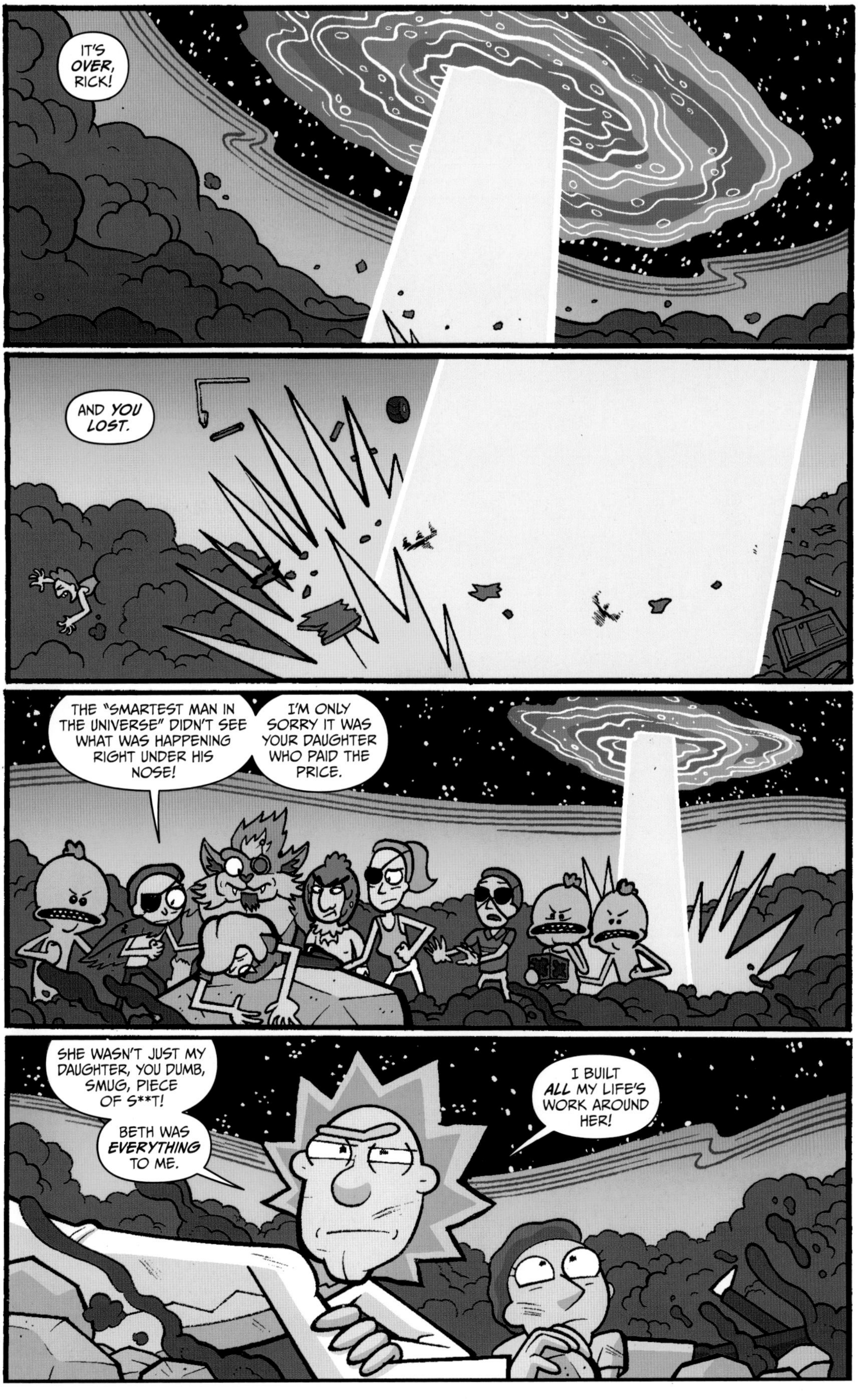
IT'S OVER, RICK!
AND YOU LOST.
THE "SMARTEST MAN IN THE UNIVERSE" DIDN'T SEE WHAT WAS HAPPENING RIGHT UNDER HIS NOSE!
I'M ONLY SORRY IT WAS YOUR DAUGHTER WHO PAID THE PRICE.
SHE WASN'T JUST MY DAUGHTER, YOU DUMB, SMUG, PIECE OF S**T!
BETH WAS EVERYTHING TO ME.
I BUILT ALL MY LIFE'S WORK AROUND HER!

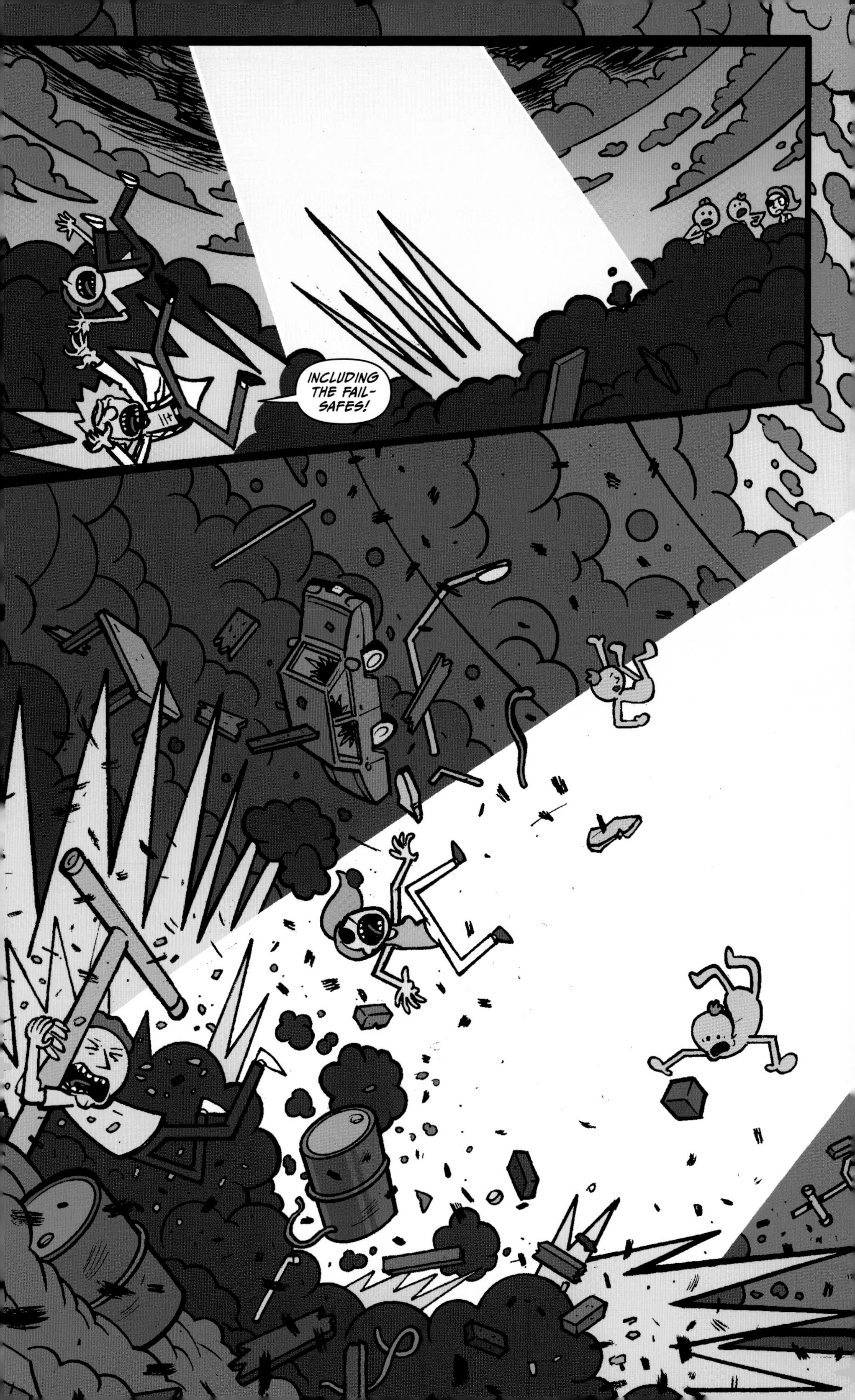
INCLUDING THE FAIL-SAFES!

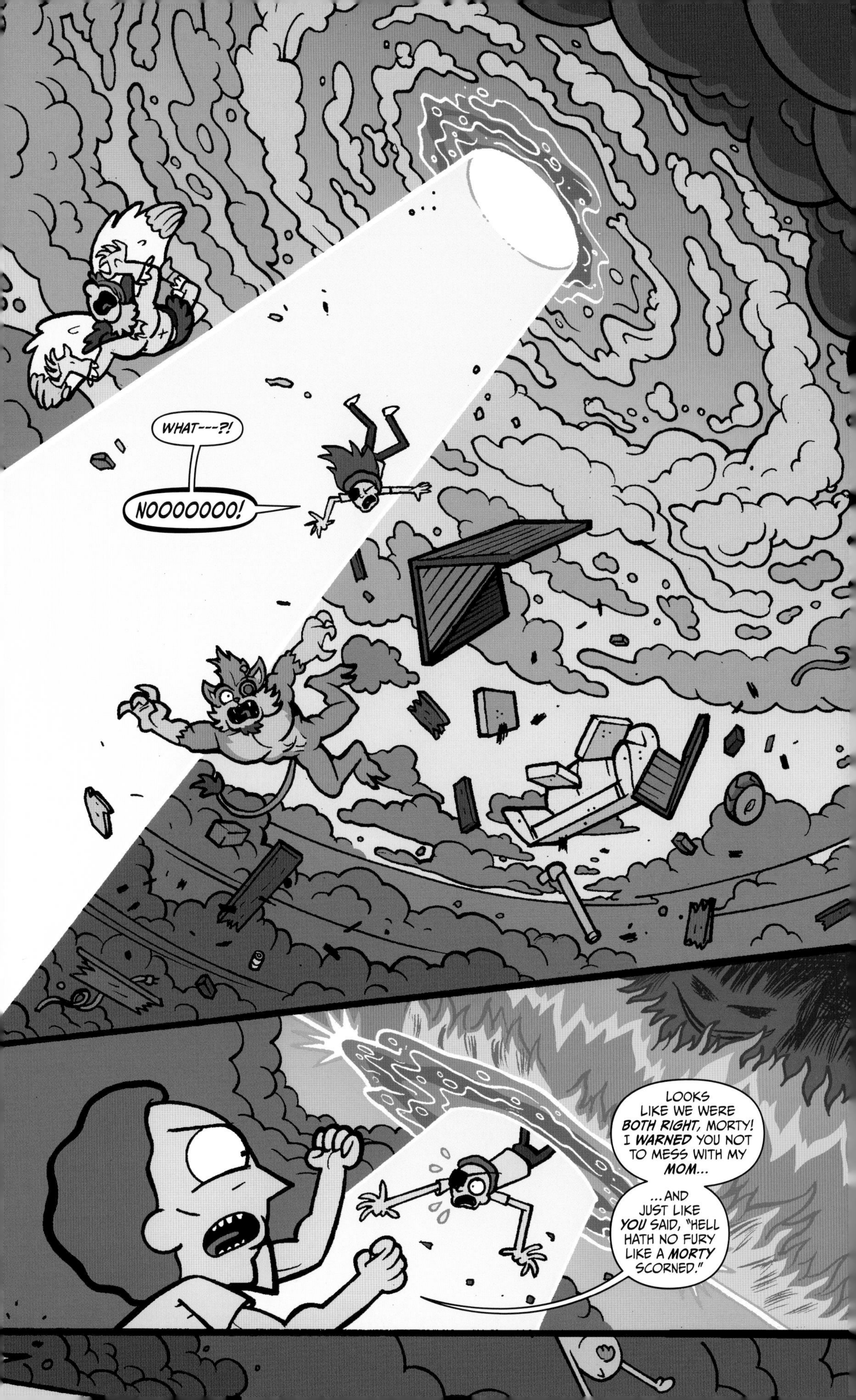
WHAT---?!
NOOOOOOO!
LOOKS LIKE WE WERE BOTH RIGHT, MORTY! I WARNED YOU NOT TO MESS WITH MY MOM...
...AND JUST LIKE YOU SAID, "HELL HATH NO FURY LIKE A MORTY SCORNED."

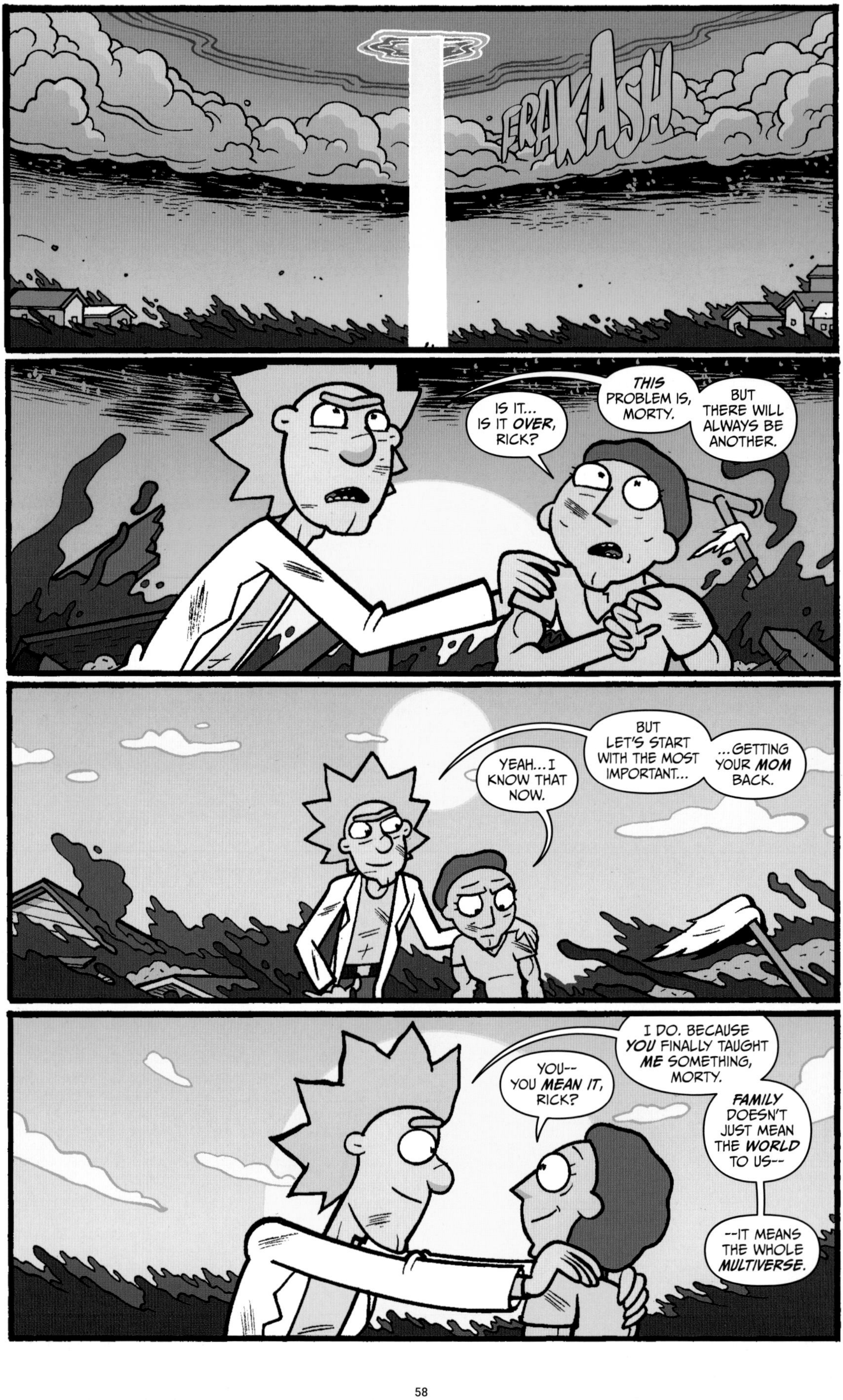
FRAKASH
IS IT... IS IT *OVER*, RICK?
THIS PROBLEM IS, MORTY.
BUT THERE WILL ALWAYS BE ANOTHER.
YEAH... I KNOW THAT NOW.
BUT LET'S START WITH THE MOST IMPORTANT...
...GETTING YOUR *MOM* BACK.
YOU-- YOU *MEAN IT*, RICK?
I DO. BECAUSE *YOU* FINALLY TAUGHT *ME* SOMETHING, MORTY.
FAMILY DOESN'T JUST MEAN THE *WORLD* TO US--
--IT MEANS THE WHOLE *MULTIVERSE*.

GLOM-CON's

Rick and Morty

Directed by

GLOM-CON's

GUY WHITEMAN

Written by

GUY WHITEMAN & WHITNEY MANSON

and

CHAD OTHERBOY & B.A. RICHSON

and

CAUCASION PALEFELLOW & THE CIA'S ARTISTIC PSY-OPS UNIT

MART
NO HOPE
FINE...
...I'LL DO IT MYSELF.
WATCH NEXT!
RICK AND MORTY 2 Teaser Trailer
RICK AND MORTY: ORIGINS: anime
TALKING RICK w/Chris Harbwick for some f*****g reason
MEESEEKS HOME-WISH RENOVATION

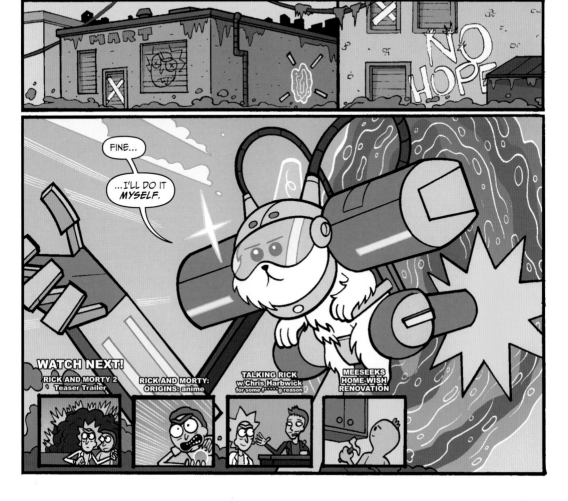

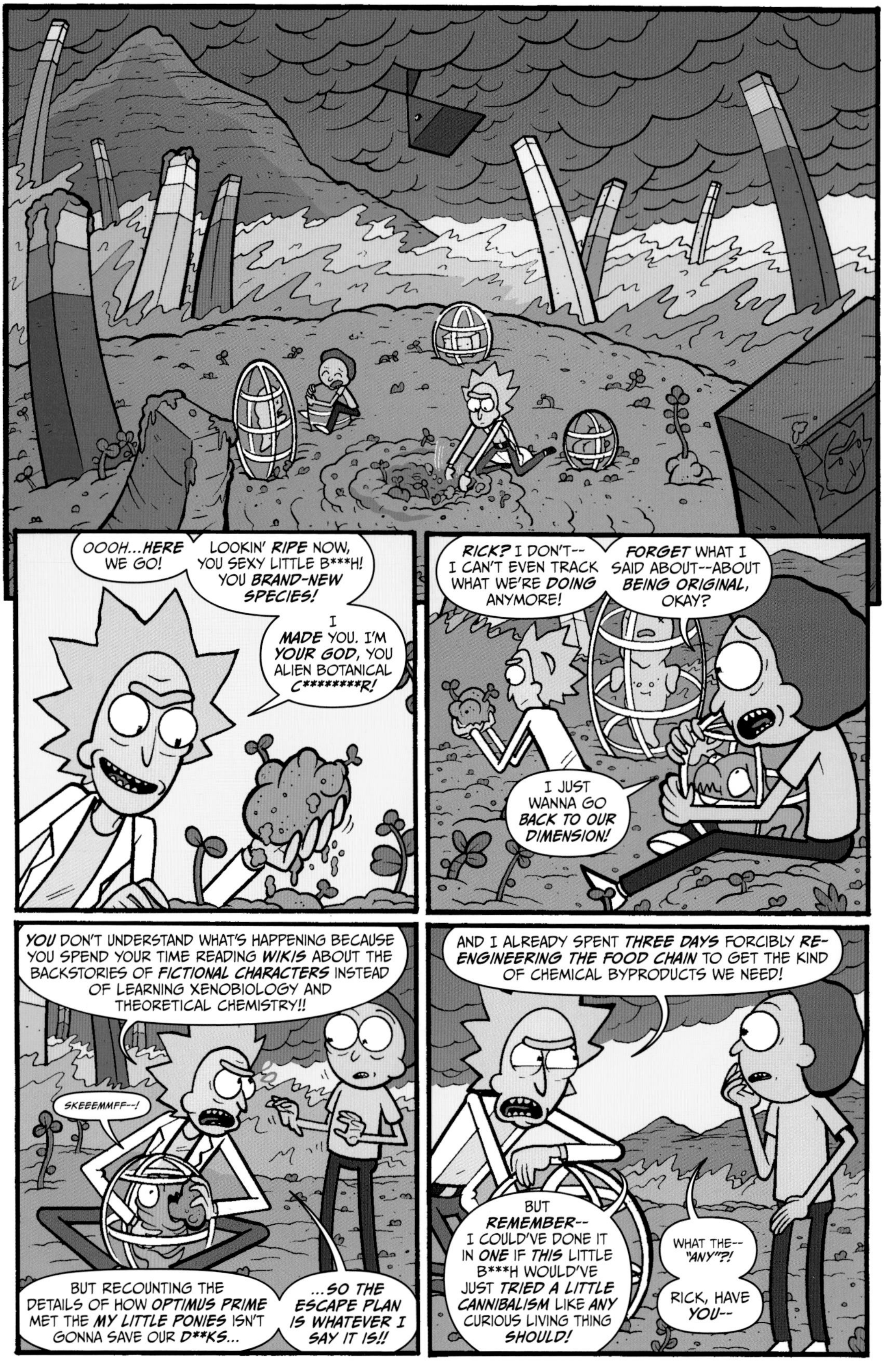

OOOH...HERE WE GO!
LOOKIN' RIPE NOW, YOU SEXY LITTLE B***H! YOU BRAND-NEW SPECIES!
I MADE YOU. I'M YOUR GOD, YOU ALIEN BOTANICAL C*********R!
RICK? I DON'T-- I CAN'T EVEN TRACK WHAT WE'RE DOING ANYMORE!
FORGET WHAT I SAID ABOUT--ABOUT BEING ORIGINAL, OKAY?
I JUST WANNA GO BACK TO OUR DIMENSION!
YOU DON'T UNDERSTAND WHAT'S HAPPENING BECAUSE YOU SPEND YOUR TIME READING WIKIS ABOUT THE BACKSTORIES OF FICTIONAL CHARACTERS INSTEAD OF LEARNING XENOBIOLOGY AND THEORETICAL CHEMISTRY!!
SKEEEMMFF--!
BUT RECOUNTING THE DETAILS OF HOW OPTIMUS PRIME MET THE MY LITTLE PONIES ISN'T GONNA SAVE OUR D**KS...
...SO THE ESCAPE PLAN IS WHATEVER I SAY IT IS!!
AND I ALREADY SPENT THREE DAYS FORCIBLY RE-ENGINEERING THE FOOD CHAIN TO GET THE KIND OF CHEMICAL BYPRODUCTS WE NEED!
BUT REMEMBER-- I COULD'VE DONE IT IN ONE IF THIS LITTLE B***H WOULD'VE JUST TRIED A LITTLE CANNIBALISM LIKE ANY CURIOUS LIVING THING SHOULD!
WHAT THE-- "ANY"?!
RICK, HAVE YOU--

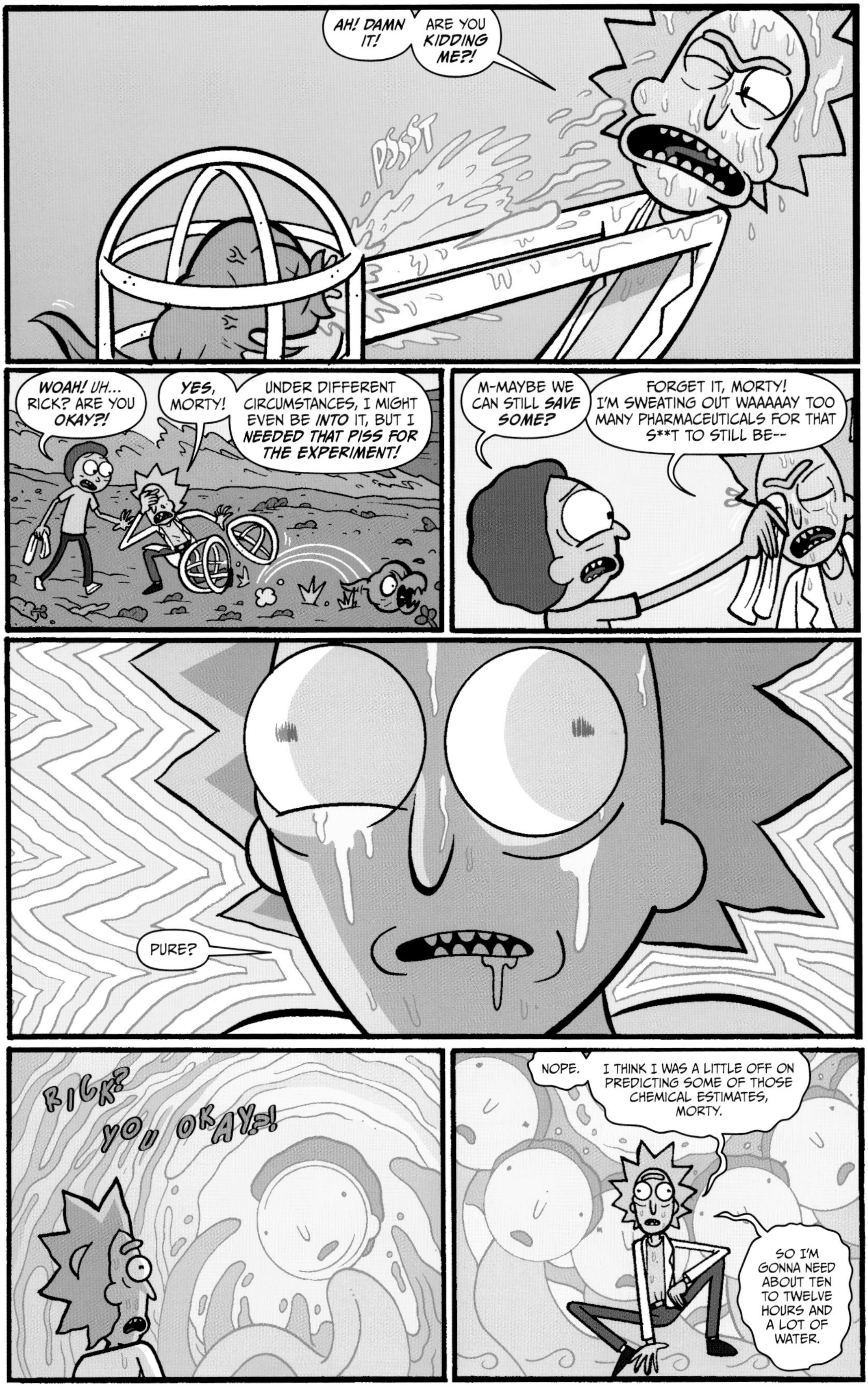

PSSST
AH! DAMN IT!
ARE YOU KIDDING ME?!
WOAH! UH... RICK? ARE YOU OKAY?!
YES, MORTY!
UNDER DIFFERENT CIRCUMSTANCES, I MIGHT EVEN BE INTO IT, BUT I NEEDED THAT PISS FOR THE EXPERIMENT!
M-MAYBE WE CAN STILL SAVE SOME?
FORGET IT, MORTY! I'M SWEATING OUT WAAAAAY TOO MANY PHARMACEUTICALS FOR THAT S**T TO STILL BE--
PURE?
RICK? YOU OKAY?!
NOPE.
I THINK I WAS A LITTLE OFF ON PREDICTING SOME OF THOSE CHEMICAL ESTIMATES, MORTY.
SO I'M GONNA NEED ABOUT TEN TO TWELVE HOURS AND A LOT OF WATER.

ORDER *YOUR* FAVORITE ITEM STRAIGHT FROM THE WORLD OF RICK AND MORTY

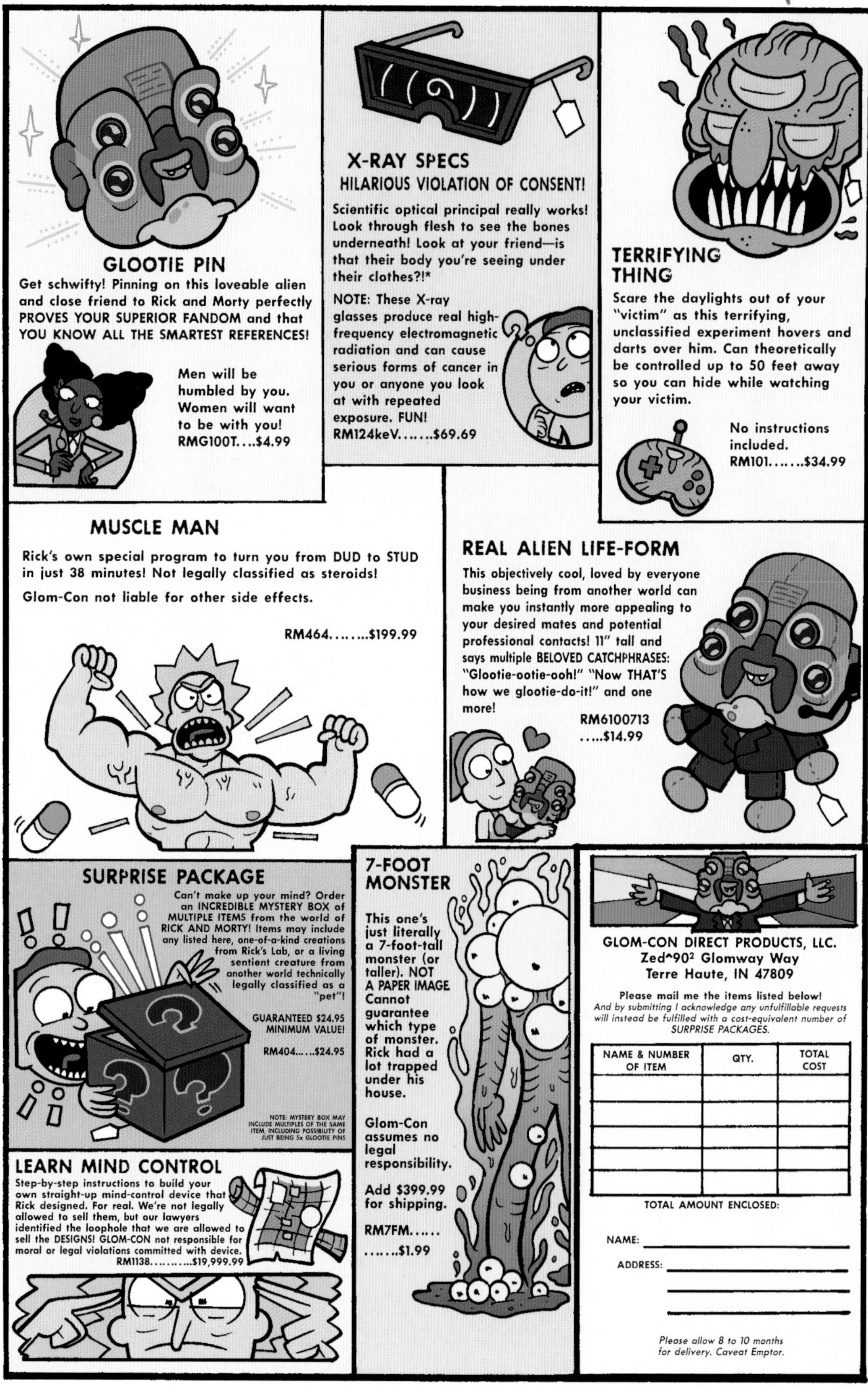
GLOOTIE PIN
Get schwifty! Pinning on this loveable alien and close friend to Rick and Morty perfectly PROVES YOUR SUPERIOR FANDOM and that YOU KNOW ALL THE SMARTEST REFERENCES!
Men will be humbled by you. Women will want to be with you!
RMG100T....$4.99
X-RAY SPECS
HILARIOUS VIOLATION OF CONSENT!
Scientific optical principal really works! Look through flesh to see the bones underneath! Look at your friend—is that their body you're seeing under their clothes?!*
NOTE: These X-ray glasses produce real high-frequency electromagnetic radiation and can cause serious forms of cancer in you or anyone you look at with repeated exposure. FUN!
RM124keV.......$69.69
TERRIFYING THING
Scare the daylights out of your "victim" as this terrifying, unclassified experiment hovers and darts over him. Can theoretically be controlled up to 50 feet away so you can hide while watching your victim.
No instructions included.
RM101.......$34.99
MUSCLE MAN
Rick's own special program to turn you from DUD to STUD in just 38 minutes! Not legally classified as steroids!
Glom-Con not liable for other side effects.
RM464........$199.99
REAL ALIEN LIFE-FORM
This objectively cool, loved by everyone business being from another world can make you instantly more appealing to your desired mates and potential professional contacts! 11" tall and says multiple BELOVED CATCHPHRASES: "Glootie-ootie-ooh!" "Now THAT'S how we glootie-do-it!" and one more!
RM6100713
.....$14.99
SURPRISE PACKAGE
Can't make up your mind? Order an INCREDIBLE MYSTERY BOX of MULTIPLE ITEMS from the world of RICK AND MORTY! Items may include any listed here, one-of-a-kind creations from Rick's Lab, or a living sentient creature from another world technically legally classified as a "pet"!
GUARANTEED $24.95 MINIMUM VALUE!
RM404......$24.95
NOTE: MYSTERY BOX MAY INCLUDE MULTIPLES OF THE SAME ITEM, INCLUDING POSSIBILITY OF JUST BEING 5x GLOOTIE PINS
LEARN MIND CONTROL
Step-by-step instructions to build your own straight-up mind-control device that Rick designed. For real. We're not legally allowed to sell them, but our lawyers identified the loophole that we are allowed to sell the DESIGNS! GLOM-CON not responsible for moral or legal violations committed with device.
RM1138...........$19,999.99
7-FOOT MONSTER
This one's just literally a 7-foot-tall monster (or taller). NOT A PAPER IMAGE Cannot guarantee which type of monster. Rick had a lot trapped under his house.
Glom-Con assumes no legal responsibility.
Add $399.99 for shipping.
RM7FM......
.......$1.99
GLOM-CON DIRECT PRODUCTS, LLC.
Zed^90² Glomway Way
Terre Haute, IN 47809
Please mail me the items listed below!
And by submitting I acknowledge any unfulfillable requests will instead be fulfilled with a cost-equivalent number of SURPRISE PACKAGES.
NAME & NUMBER OF ITEM
QTY.
TOTAL COST
TOTAL AMOUNT ENCLOSED:
NAME:
ADDRESS:
Please allow 8 to 10 months for delivery. Caveat Emptor.

*No. That's not how X-rays work.

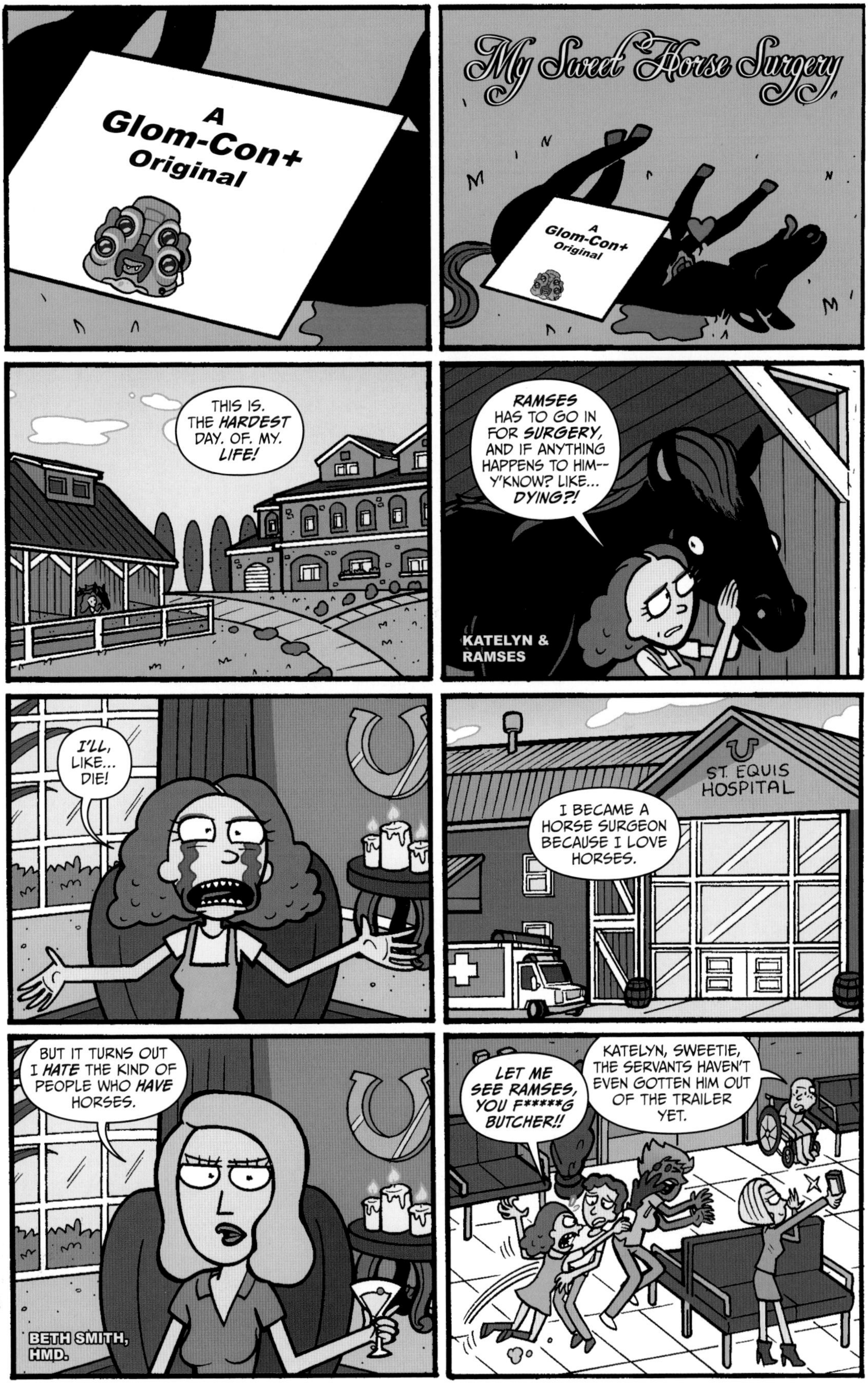
A Glom-Con+ Original
My Sweet Horse Surgery
A Glom-Con+ Original
THIS IS. THE HARDEST DAY. OF. MY. LIFE!
RAMSES HAS TO GO IN FOR SURGERY, AND IF ANYTHING HAPPENS TO HIM-- Y'KNOW? LIKE... DYING?!
KATELYN & RAMSES
I'LL, LIKE... DIE!
ST. EQUIS HOSPITAL
I BECAME A HORSE SURGEON BECAUSE I LOVE HORSES.
BUT IT TURNS OUT I HATE THE KIND OF PEOPLE WHO HAVE HORSES.
BETH SMITH, HMD.
LET ME SEE RAMSES, YOU F*****G BUTCHER!!
KATELYN, SWEETIE, THE SERVANTS HAVEN'T EVEN GOTTEN HIM OUT OF THE TRAILER YET.

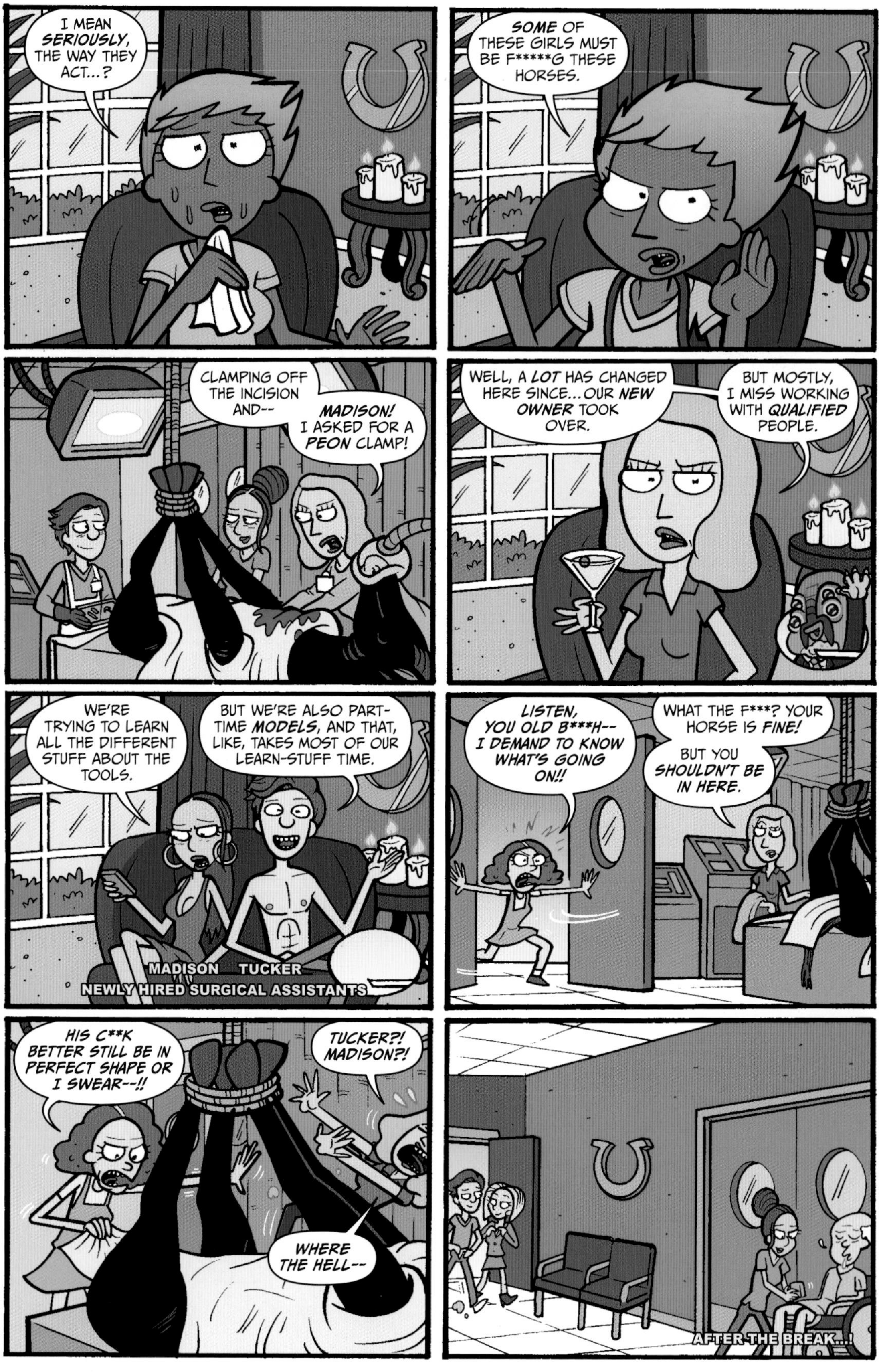
I MEAN SERIOUSLY, THE WAY THEY ACT...?
SOME OF THESE GIRLS MUST BE F*****G THESE HORSES.
CLAMPING OFF THE INCISION AND--
MADISON! I ASKED FOR A PEON CLAMP!
WELL, A LOT HAS CHANGED HERE SINCE...OUR NEW OWNER TOOK OVER.
BUT MOSTLY, I MISS WORKING WITH QUALIFIED PEOPLE.
WE'RE TRYING TO LEARN ALL THE DIFFERENT STUFF ABOUT THE TOOLS.
BUT WE'RE ALSO PART-TIME MODELS, AND THAT, LIKE, TAKES MOST OF OUR LEARN-STUFF TIME.
MADISON TUCKER
NEWLY HIRED SURGICAL ASSISTANTS
LISTEN, YOU OLD B***H-- I DEMAND TO KNOW WHAT'S GOING ON!!
WHAT THE F***? YOUR HORSE IS FINE!
BUT YOU SHOULDN'T BE IN HERE.
HIS C**K BETTER STILL BE IN PERFECT SHAPE OR I SWEAR--!!
TUCKER?! MADISON?!
WHERE THE HELL--
AFTER THE BREAK...!

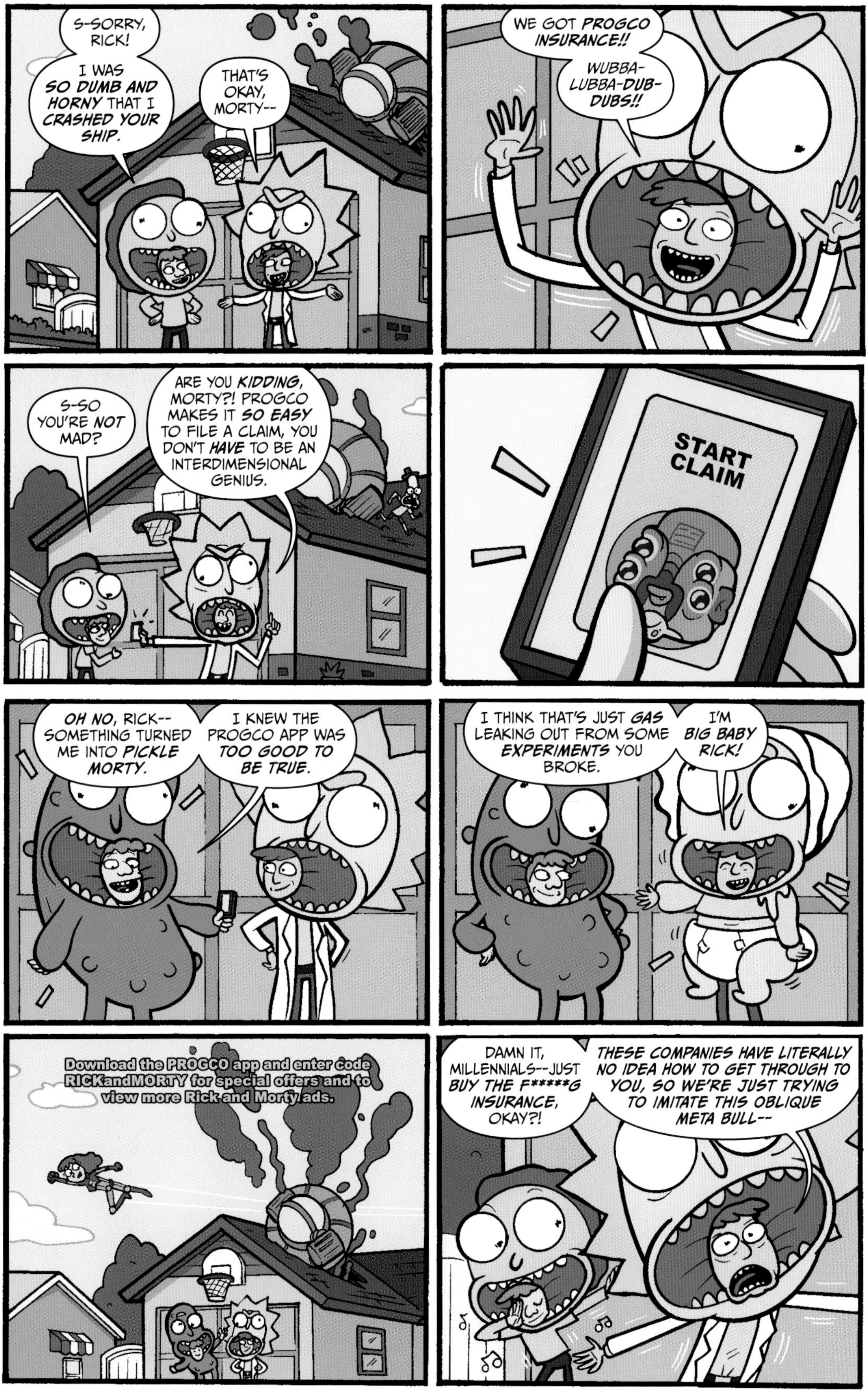
S-SORRY, RICK!
I WAS SO DUMB AND HORNY THAT I CRASHED YOUR SHIP.
THAT'S OKAY, MORTY--
WE GOT PROGCO INSURANCE!!
WUBBA-LUBBA-DUB-DUBS!!
S-SO YOU'RE NOT MAD?
ARE YOU KIDDING, MORTY?! PROGCO MAKES IT SO EASY TO FILE A CLAIM, YOU DON'T HAVE TO BE AN INTERDIMENSIONAL GENIUS.
START CLAIM
OH NO, RICK-- SOMETHING TURNED ME INTO PICKLE MORTY.
I KNEW THE PROGCO APP WAS TOO GOOD TO BE TRUE.
I THINK THAT'S JUST GAS LEAKING OUT FROM SOME EXPERIMENTS YOU BROKE.
I'M BIG BABY RICK!
Download the PROGCO app and enter code RICKandMORTY for special offers and to view more Rick and Morty ads.
DAMN IT, MILLENNIALS--JUST BUY THE F*****G INSURANCE, OKAY?!
THESE COMPANIES HAVE LITERALLY NO IDEA HOW TO GET THROUGH TO YOU, SO WE'RE JUST TRYING TO IMITATE THIS OBLIQUE META BULL--

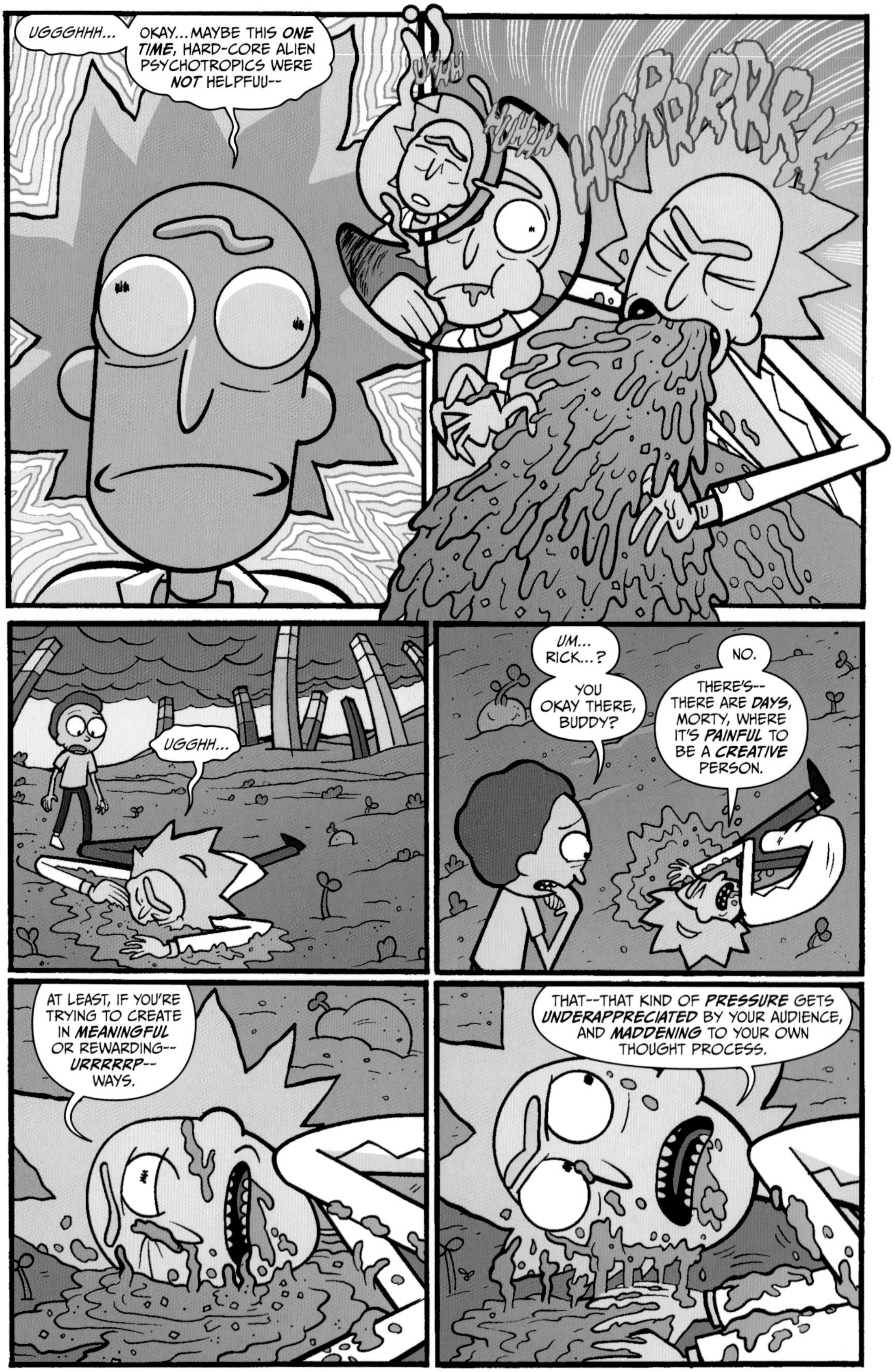
UGGGHHH...
OKAY...MAYBE THIS ONE TIME, HARD-CORE ALIEN PSYCHOTROPICS WERE NOT HELPFUU--
UMMM
WOMMM
HORRRRRK
UGGHH...
UM... RICK...?
YOU OKAY THERE, BUDDY?
NO.
THERE'S-- THERE ARE DAYS, MORTY, WHERE IT'S PAINFUL TO BE A CREATIVE PERSON.
AT LEAST, IF YOU'RE TRYING TO CREATE IN MEANINGFUL OR REWARDING-- URRRRRP-- WAYS.
THAT--THAT KIND OF PRESSURE GETS UNDERAPPRECIATED BY YOUR AUDIENCE, AND MADDENING TO YOUR OWN THOUGHT PROCESS.

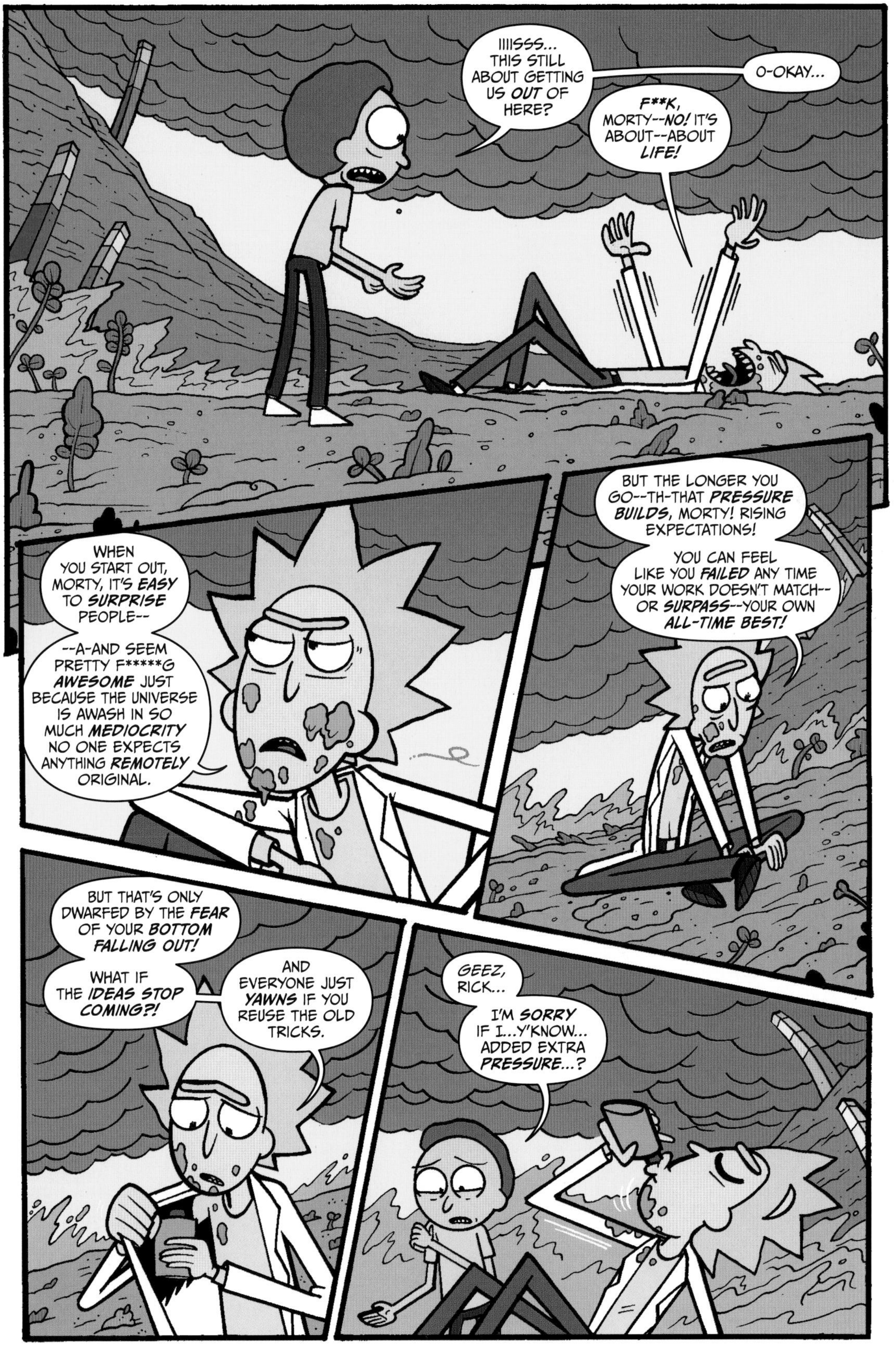
IIIISSS... THIS STILL ABOUT GETTING US OUT OF HERE?
F**K, MORTY--NO! IT'S ABOUT--ABOUT LIFE!
O-OKAY...
WHEN YOU START OUT, MORTY, IT'S EASY TO SURPRISE PEOPLE--
--A-AND SEEM PRETTY F*****G AWESOME JUST BECAUSE THE UNIVERSE IS AWASH IN SO MUCH MEDIOCRITY NO ONE EXPECTS ANYTHING REMOTELY ORIGINAL.
BUT THE LONGER YOU GO--TH-THAT PRESSURE BUILDS, MORTY! RISING EXPECTATIONS!
YOU CAN FEEL LIKE YOU FAILED ANY TIME YOUR WORK DOESN'T MATCH--OR SURPASS--YOUR OWN ALL-TIME BEST!
BUT THAT'S ONLY DWARFED BY THE FEAR OF YOUR BOTTOM FALLING OUT!
WHAT IF THE IDEAS STOP COMING?!
AND EVERYONE JUST YAWNS IF YOU REUSE THE OLD TRICKS.
GEEZ, RICK...
I'M SORRY IF I...Y'KNOW... ADDED EXTRA PRESSURE...?

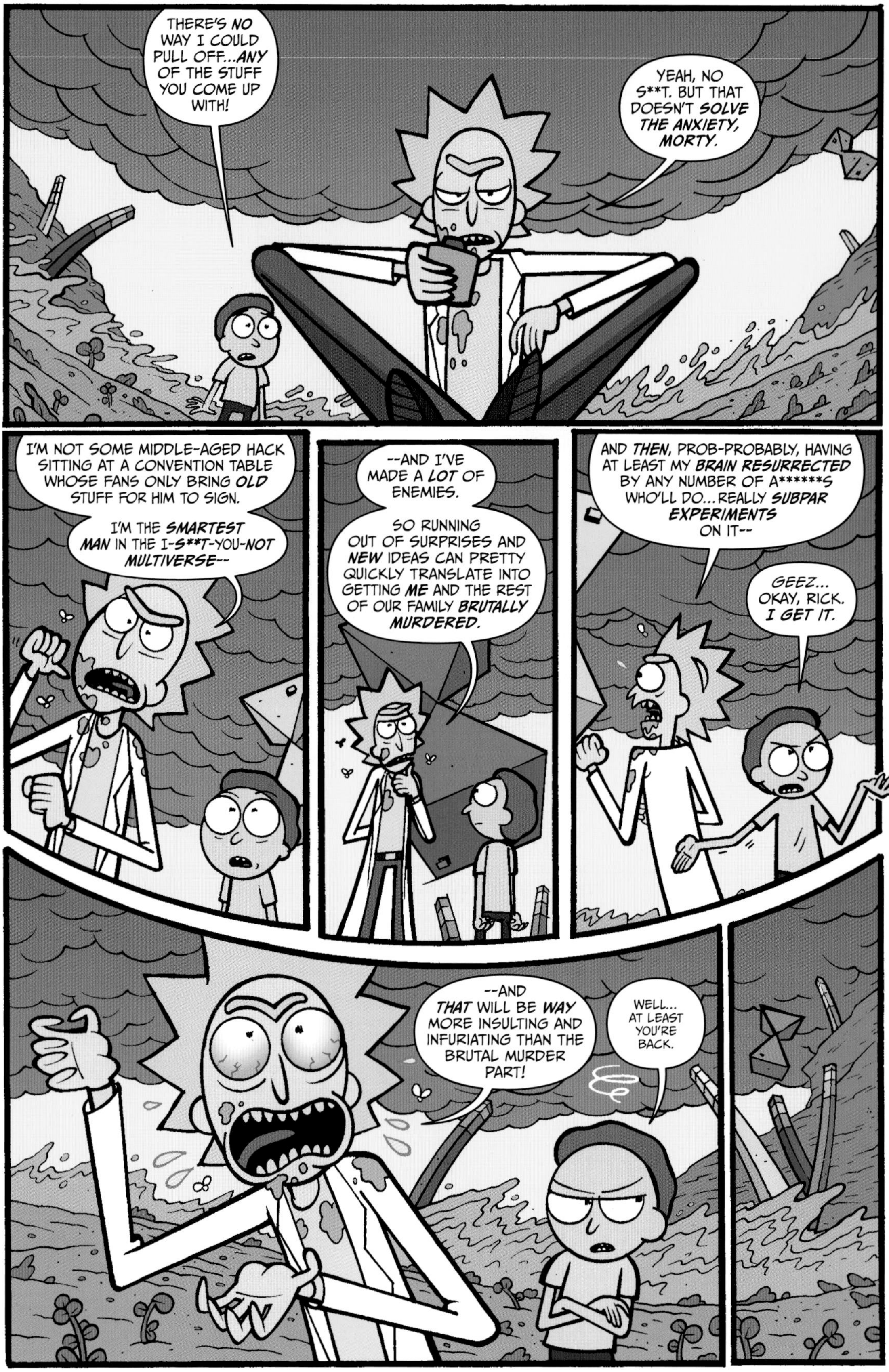
THERE'S NO WAY I COULD PULL OFF...ANY OF THE STUFF YOU COME UP WITH!
YEAH, NO S**T. BUT THAT DOESN'T SOLVE THE ANXIETY, MORTY.
I'M NOT SOME MIDDLE-AGED HACK SITTING AT A CONVENTION TABLE WHOSE FANS ONLY BRING OLD STUFF FOR HIM TO SIGN.
I'M THE SMARTEST MAN IN THE I-S**T-YOU-NOT MULTIVERSE--
--AND I'VE MADE A LOT OF ENEMIES.
SO RUNNING OUT OF SURPRISES AND NEW IDEAS CAN PRETTY QUICKLY TRANSLATE INTO GETTING ME AND THE REST OF OUR FAMILY BRUTALLY MURDERED.
AND THEN, PROB-PROBABLY, HAVING AT LEAST MY BRAIN RESURRECTED BY ANY NUMBER OF A******S WHO'LL DO...REALLY SUBPAR EXPERIMENTS ON IT--
GEEZ... OKAY, RICK. I GET IT.
--AND THAT WILL BE WAY MORE INSULTING AND INFURIATING THAN THE BRUTAL MURDER PART!
WELL... AT LEAST YOU'RE BACK.

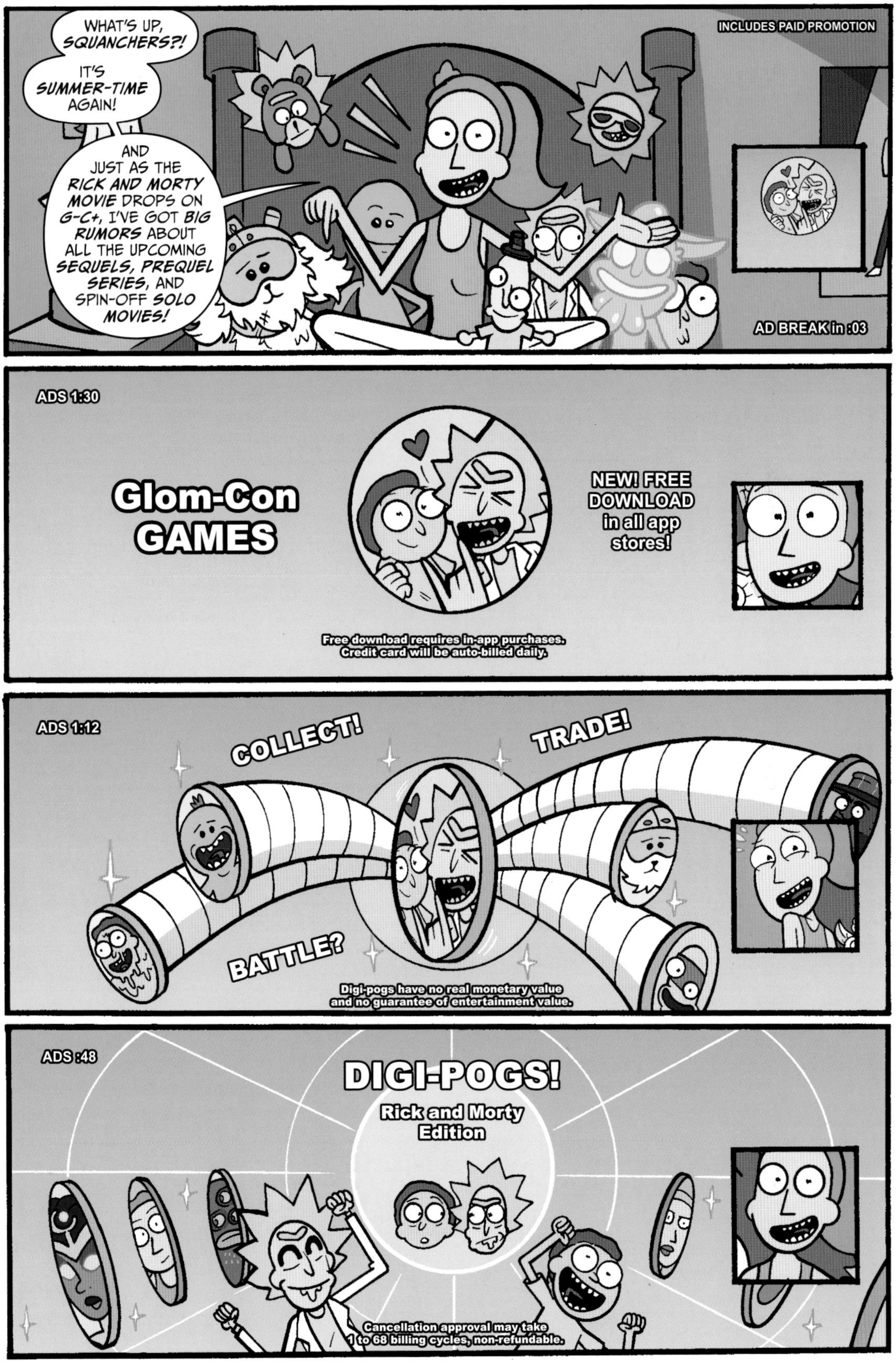
INCLUDES PAID PROMOTION
WHAT'S UP, SQUANCHERS?!
IT'S SUMMER-TIME AGAIN!
AND JUST AS THE RICK AND MORTY MOVIE DROPS ON G-C+, I'VE GOT BIG RUMORS ABOUT ALL THE UPCOMING SEQUELS, PREQUEL SERIES, AND SPIN-OFF SOLO MOVIES!
AD BREAK in :03
ADS 1:30
Glom-Con GAMES
NEW! FREE DOWNLOAD in all app stores!
Free download requires in-app purchases. Credit card will be auto-billed daily.
ADS 1:12
COLLECT!
TRADE!
BATTLE?
Digi-pogs have no real monetary value and no guarantee of entertainment value.
ADS :48
DIGI-POGS!
Rick and Morty Edition
Cancellation approval may take 1 to 68 billing cycles, non-refundable.

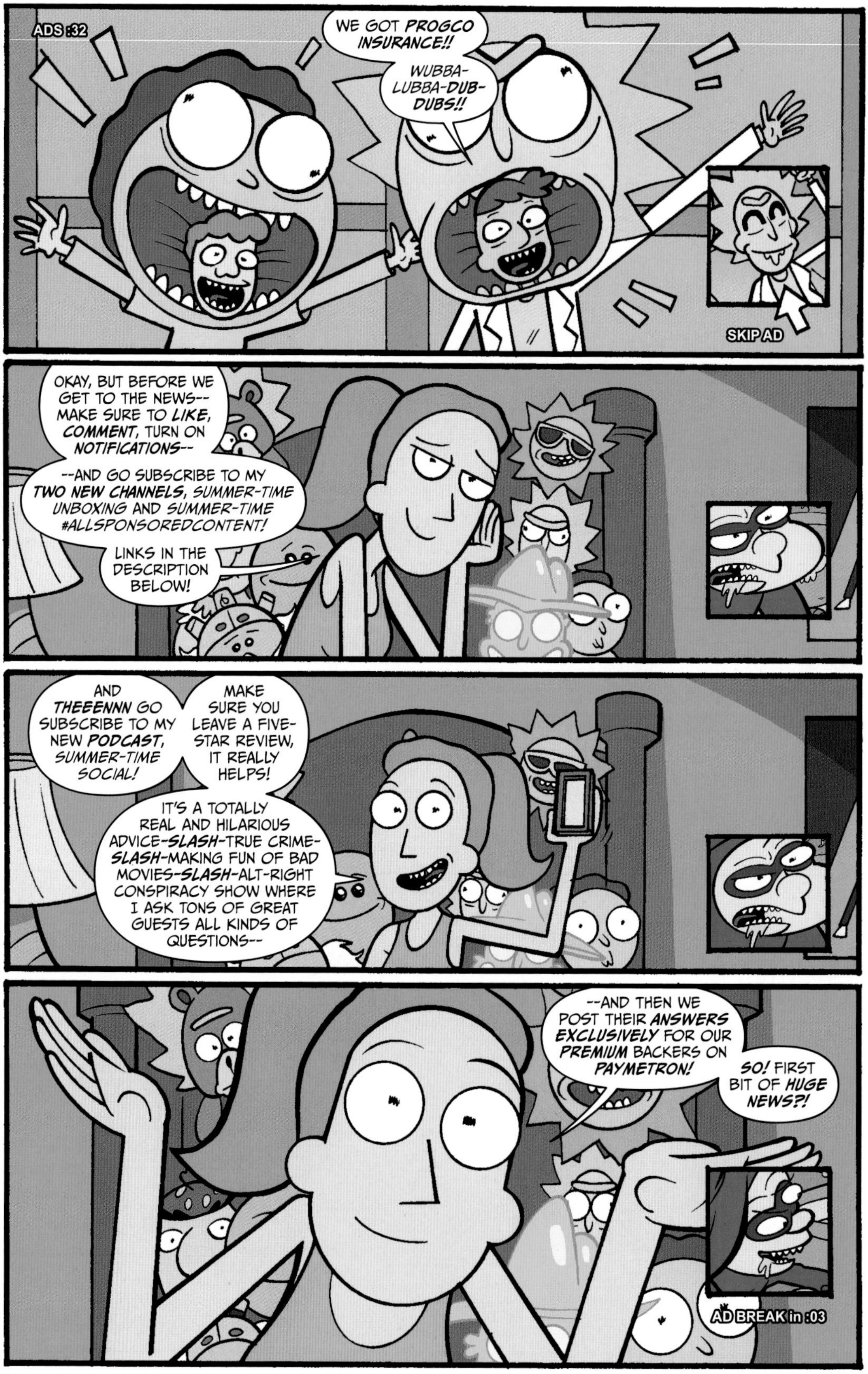
ADS :32
WE GOT PROGCO INSURANCE!!
WUBBA-LUBBA-DUB-DUBS!!
SKIP AD
OKAY, BUT BEFORE WE GET TO THE NEWS-- MAKE SURE TO LIKE, COMMENT, TURN ON NOTIFICATIONS--
--AND GO SUBSCRIBE TO MY TWO NEW CHANNELS, SUMMER-TIME UNBOXING AND SUMMER-TIME #ALLSPONSOREDCONTENT!
LINKS IN THE DESCRIPTION BELOW!
AND THEEENNN GO SUBSCRIBE TO MY NEW PODCAST, SUMMER-TIME SOCIAL!
MAKE SURE YOU LEAVE A FIVE-STAR REVIEW, IT REALLY HELPS!
IT'S A TOTALLY REAL AND HILARIOUS ADVICE-SLASH-TRUE CRIME-SLASH-MAKING FUN OF BAD MOVIES-SLASH-ALT-RIGHT CONSPIRACY SHOW WHERE I ASK TONS OF GREAT GUESTS ALL KINDS OF QUESTIONS--
--AND THEN WE POST THEIR ANSWERS EXCLUSIVELY FOR OUR PREMIUM BACKERS ON PAYMETRON!
SO! FIRST BIT OF HUGE NEWS?!
AD BREAK in :03

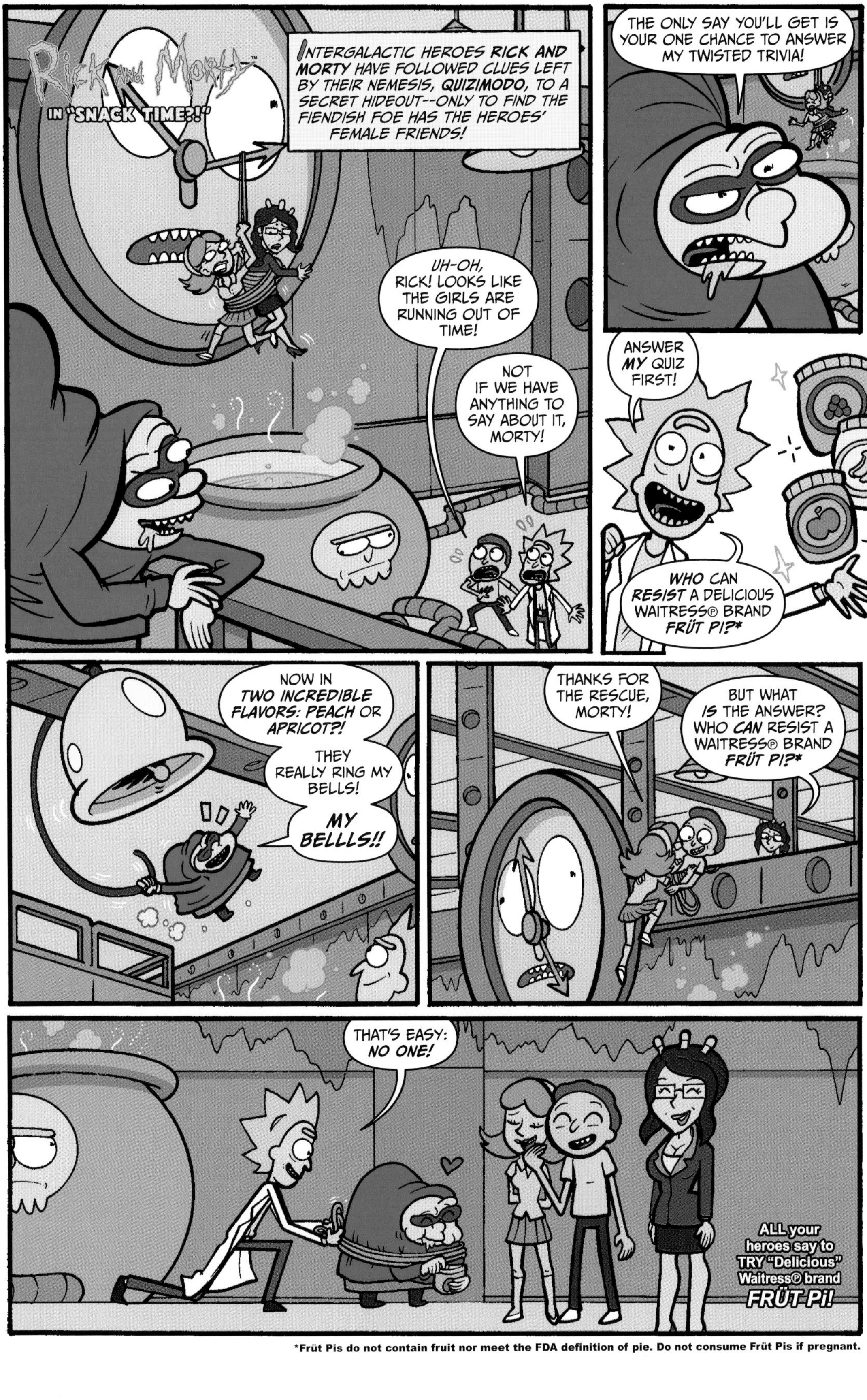

Rick and Morty™
IN "SNACK TIME?!"
INTERGALACTIC HEROES RICK AND MORTY HAVE FOLLOWED CLUES LEFT BY THEIR NEMESIS, QUIZIMODO, TO A SECRET HIDEOUT--ONLY TO FIND THE FIENDISH FOE HAS THE HEROES' FEMALE FRIENDS!
UH-OH, RICK! LOOKS LIKE THE GIRLS ARE RUNNING OUT OF TIME!
NOT IF WE HAVE ANYTHING TO SAY ABOUT IT, MORTY!
THE ONLY SAY YOU'LL GET IS YOUR ONE CHANCE TO ANSWER MY TWISTED TRIVIA!
ANSWER MY QUIZ FIRST!
WHO CAN RESIST A DELICIOUS WAITRESS® BRAND FRÜT PI?*
NOW IN TWO INCREDIBLE FLAVORS: PEACH OR APRICOT?!
THEY REALLY RING MY BELLS!
MY BELLLS!!
THANKS FOR THE RESCUE, MORTY!
BUT WHAT IS THE ANSWER? WHO CAN RESIST A WAITRESS® BRAND FRÜT PI?*
THAT'S EASY: NO ONE!
ALL your heroes say to TRY "Delicious" Waitress® brand FRÜT Pi!

*Früt Pis do not contain fruit nor meet the FDA definition of pie. Do not consume Früt Pis if pregnant.

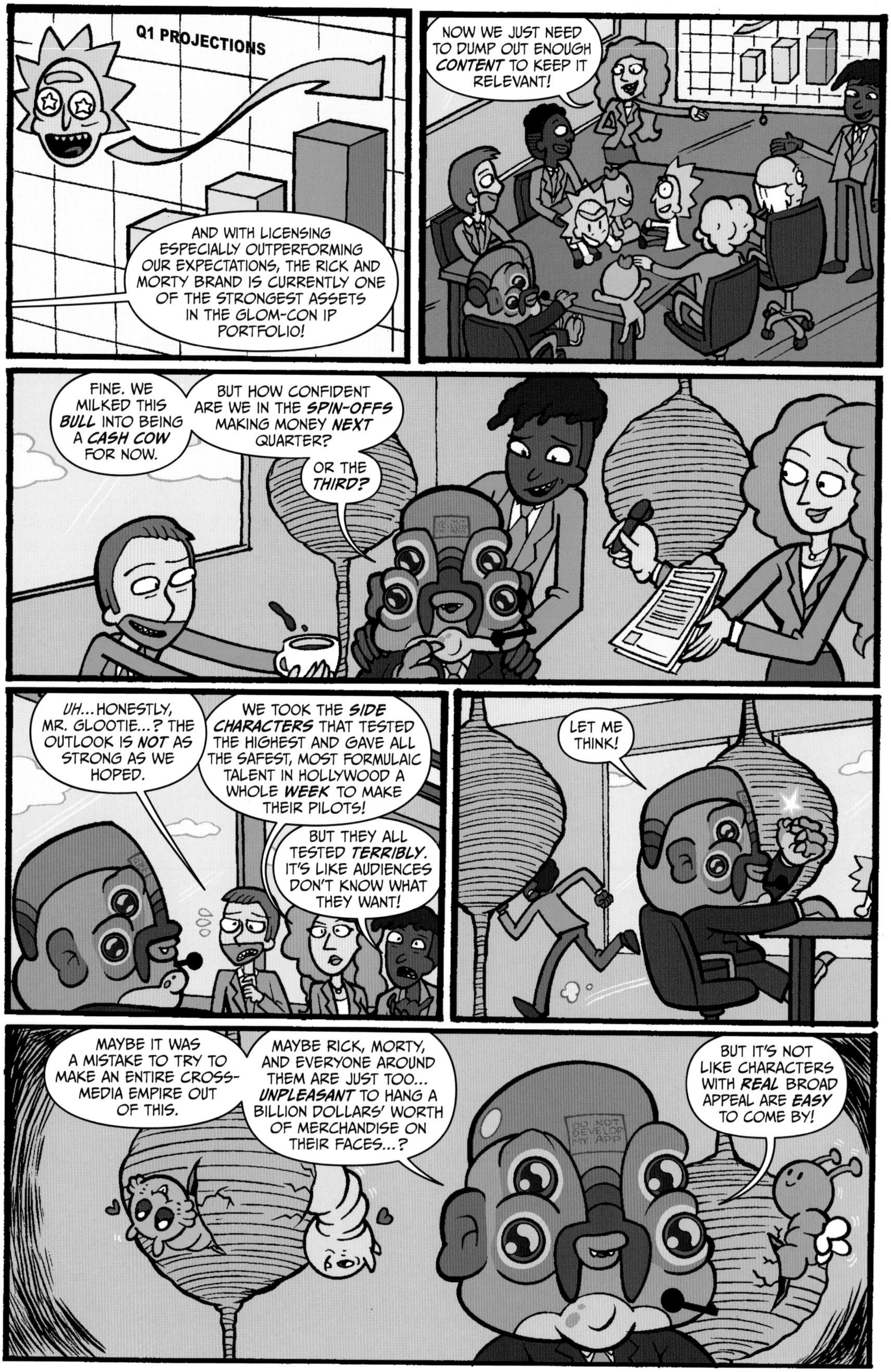
Q1 PROJECTIONS
AND WITH LICENSING ESPECIALLY OUTPERFORMING OUR EXPECTATIONS, THE RICK AND MORTY BRAND IS CURRENTLY ONE OF THE STRONGEST ASSETS IN THE GLOM-CON IP PORTFOLIO!
NOW WE JUST NEED TO DUMP OUT ENOUGH *CONTENT* TO KEEP IT RELEVANT!
FINE. WE MILKED THIS *BULL* INTO BEING A *CASH COW* FOR NOW.
BUT HOW CONFIDENT ARE WE IN THE *SPIN-OFFS* MAKING MONEY *NEXT* QUARTER?
OR THE *THIRD?*
UH... HONESTLY, MR. GLOOTIE...? THE OUTLOOK IS *NOT* AS STRONG AS WE HOPED.
WE TOOK THE *SIDE CHARACTERS* THAT TESTED THE HIGHEST AND GAVE ALL THE SAFEST, MOST FORMULAIC TALENT IN HOLLYWOOD A WHOLE *WEEK* TO MAKE THEIR PILOTS!
BUT THEY ALL TESTED *TERRIBLY*. IT'S LIKE AUDIENCES DON'T KNOW WHAT THEY WANT!
LET ME THINK!
MAYBE IT WAS A MISTAKE TO TRY TO MAKE AN ENTIRE CROSS-MEDIA EMPIRE OUT OF THIS.
MAYBE RICK, MORTY, AND EVERYONE AROUND THEM ARE JUST TOO... *UNPLEASANT* TO HANG A BILLION DOLLARS' WORTH OF MERCHANDISE ON THEIR FACES...?
DO NOT DEVELOP MY APP
BUT IT'S NOT LIKE CHARACTERS WITH *REAL* BROAD APPEAL ARE *EASY* TO COME BY!

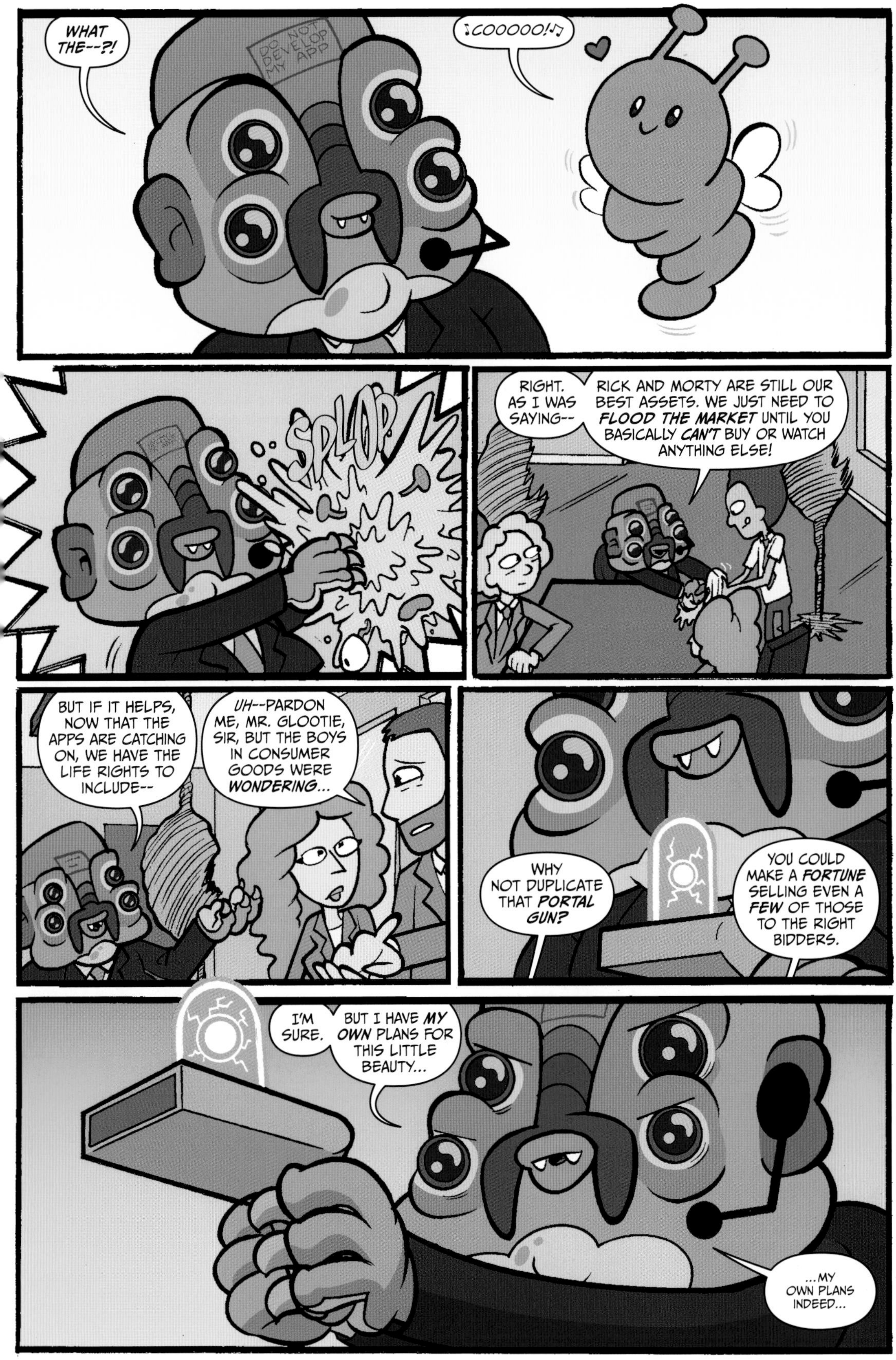
WHAT THE--?!
DO NOT DEVELOP MY APP
♪COOOOO!♪♫
SPLOP
RIGHT. AS I WAS SAYING--
RICK AND MORTY ARE STILL OUR BEST ASSETS. WE JUST NEED TO FLOOD THE MARKET UNTIL YOU BASICALLY CAN'T BUY OR WATCH ANYTHING ELSE!
BUT IF IT HELPS, NOW THAT THE APPS ARE CATCHING ON, WE HAVE THE LIFE RIGHTS TO INCLUDE--
UH--PARDON ME, MR. GLOOTIE, SIR, BUT THE BOYS IN CONSUMER GOODS WERE WONDERING...
WHY NOT DUPLICATE THAT PORTAL GUN?
YOU COULD MAKE A FORTUNE SELLING EVEN A FEW OF THOSE TO THE RIGHT BIDDERS.
I'M SURE.
BUT I HAVE MY OWN PLANS FOR THIS LITTLE BEAUTY...
...MY OWN PLANS INDEED...

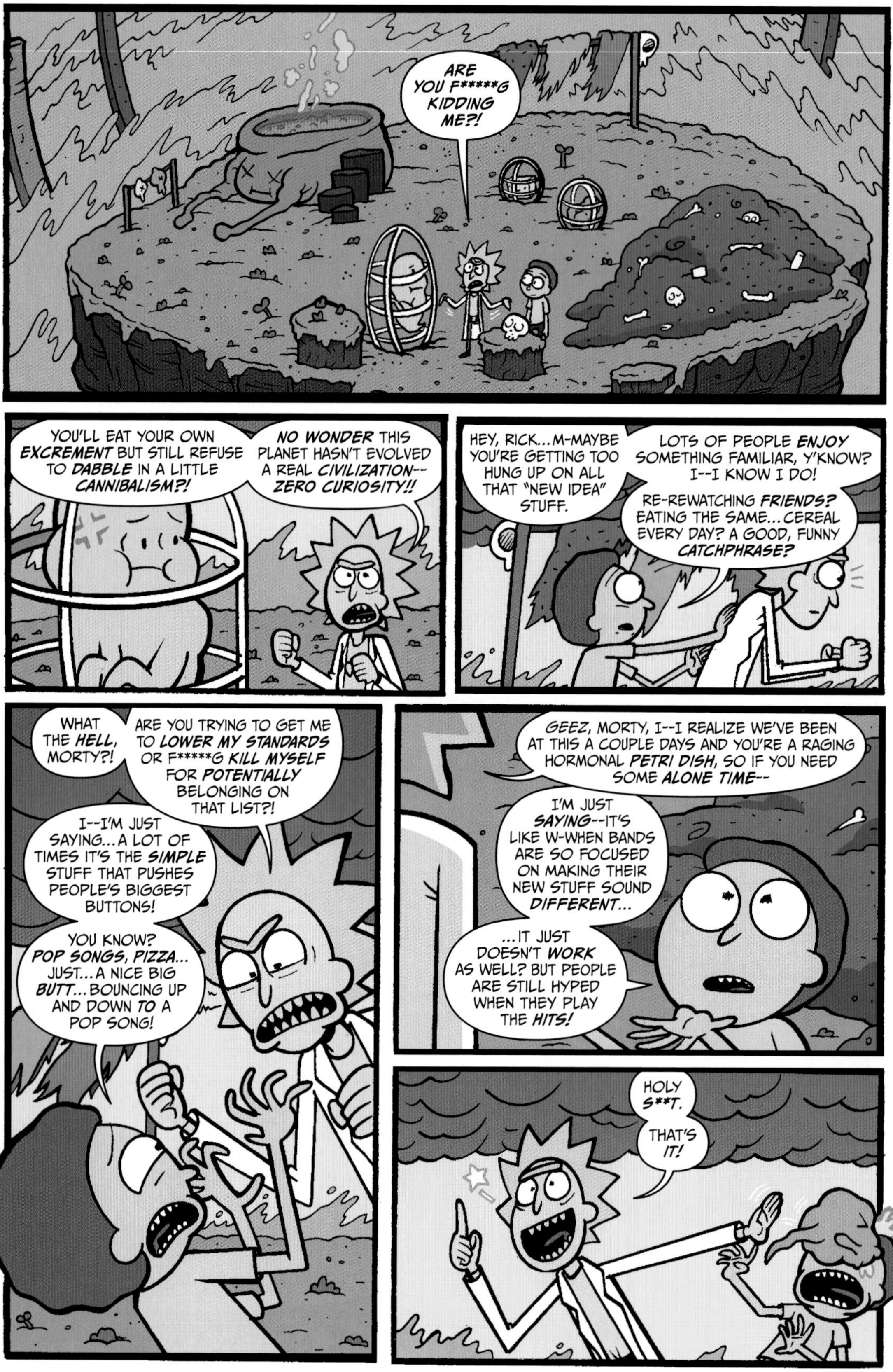
ARE YOU F*****G KIDDING ME?!
YOU'LL EAT YOUR OWN EXCREMENT BUT STILL REFUSE TO DABBLE IN A LITTLE CANNIBALISM?!
NO WONDER THIS PLANET HASN'T EVOLVED A REAL CIVILIZATION-- ZERO CURIOSITY!!
HEY, RICK... M-MAYBE YOU'RE GETTING TOO HUNG UP ON ALL THAT "NEW IDEA" STUFF.
LOTS OF PEOPLE ENJOY SOMETHING FAMILIAR, Y'KNOW? I--I KNOW I DO!
RE-REWATCHING FRIENDS? EATING THE SAME... CEREAL EVERY DAY? A GOOD, FUNNY CATCHPHRASE?
WHAT THE HELL, MORTY?!
ARE YOU TRYING TO GET ME TO LOWER MY STANDARDS OR F*****G KILL MYSELF FOR POTENTIALLY BELONGING ON THAT LIST?!
I--I'M JUST SAYING... A LOT OF TIMES IT'S THE SIMPLE STUFF THAT PUSHES PEOPLE'S BIGGEST BUTTONS!
YOU KNOW? POP SONGS, PIZZA... JUST... A NICE BIG BUTT... BOUNCING UP AND DOWN TO A POP SONG!
GEEZ, MORTY, I--I REALIZE WE'VE BEEN AT THIS A COUPLE DAYS AND YOU'RE A RAGING HORMONAL PETRI DISH, SO IF YOU NEED SOME ALONE TIME--
I'M JUST SAYING--IT'S LIKE W-WHEN BANDS ARE SO FOCUSED ON MAKING THEIR NEW STUFF SOUND DIFFERENT...
...IT JUST DOESN'T WORK AS WELL? BUT PEOPLE ARE STILL HYPED WHEN THEY PLAY THE HITS!
HOLY S**T.
THAT'S IT!

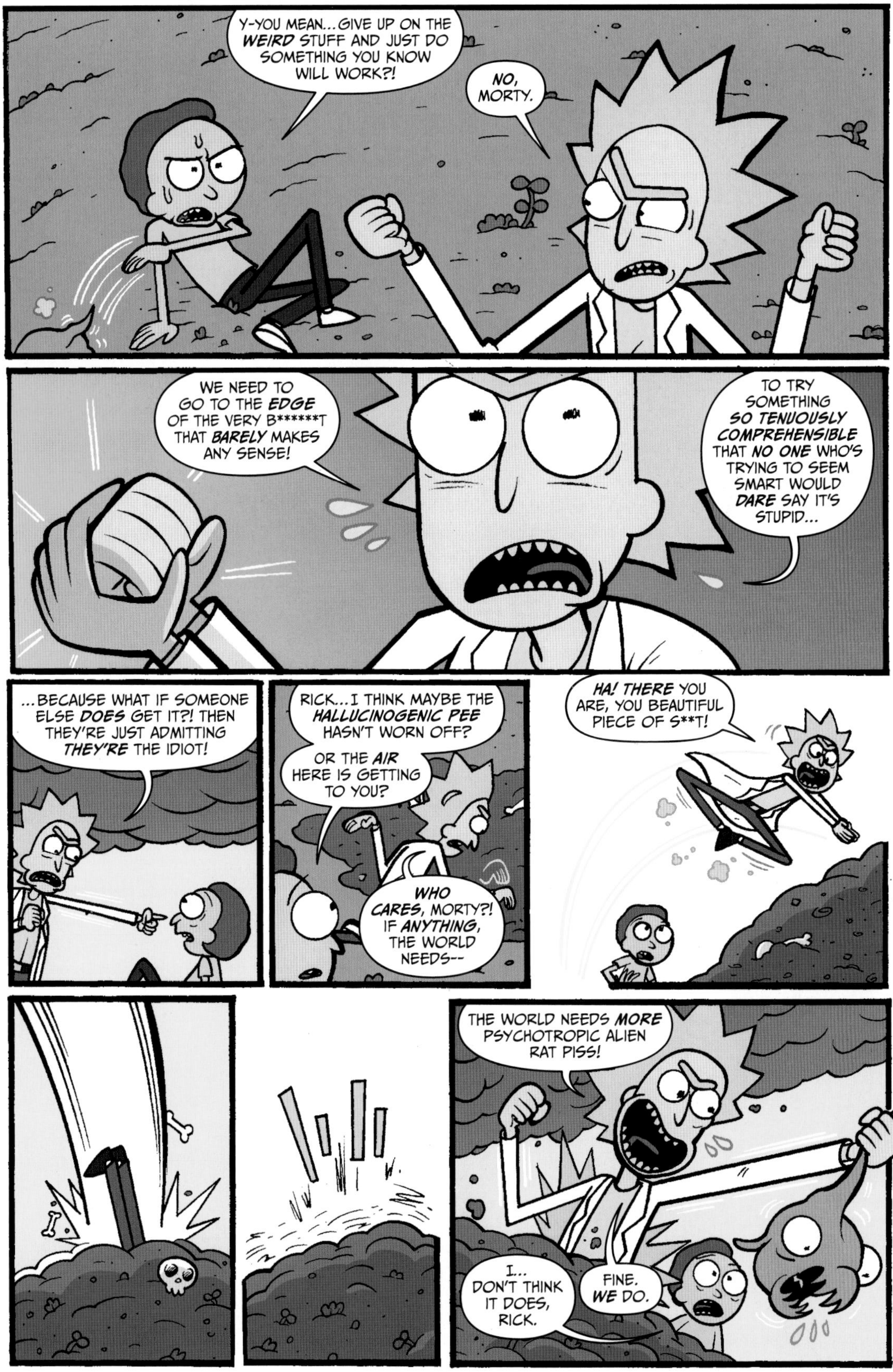
Y-YOU MEAN... GIVE UP ON THE WEIRD STUFF AND JUST DO SOMETHING YOU KNOW WILL WORK?!
NO, MORTY.
WE NEED TO GO TO THE EDGE OF THE VERY B******T THAT BARELY MAKES ANY SENSE!
TO TRY SOMETHING SO TENUOUSLY COMPREHENSIBLE THAT NO ONE WHO'S TRYING TO SEEM SMART WOULD DARE SAY IT'S STUPID...
...BECAUSE WHAT IF SOMEONE ELSE DOES GET IT?! THEN THEY'RE JUST ADMITTING THEY'RE THE IDIOT!
RICK... I THINK MAYBE THE HALLUCINOGENIC PEE HASN'T WORN OFF?
OR THE AIR HERE IS GETTING TO YOU?
WHO CARES, MORTY?! IF ANYTHING, THE WORLD NEEDS--
HA! THERE YOU ARE, YOU BEAUTIFUL PIECE OF S**T!
THE WORLD NEEDS MORE PSYCHOTROPIC ALIEN RAT PISS!
I... DON'T THINK IT DOES, RICK.
FINE. WE DO.

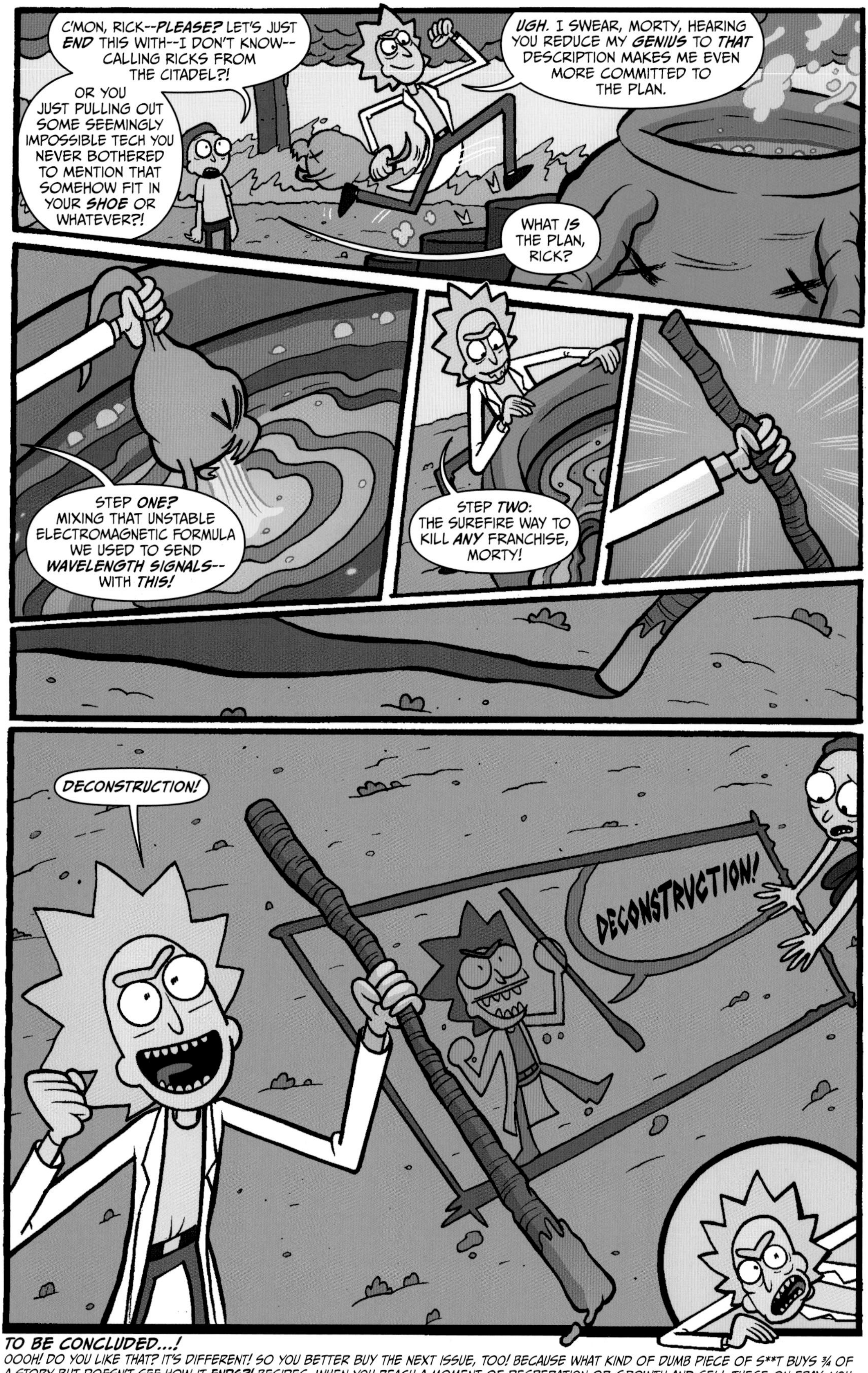
C'MON, RICK--PLEASE? LET'S JUST END THIS WITH--I DON'T KNOW--CALLING RICKS FROM THE CITADEL?!
OR YOU JUST PULLING OUT SOME SEEMINGLY IMPOSSIBLE TECH YOU NEVER BOTHERED TO MENTION THAT SOMEHOW FIT IN YOUR SHOE OR WHATEVER?!
UGH. I SWEAR, MORTY, HEARING YOU REDUCE MY GENIUS TO THAT DESCRIPTION MAKES ME EVEN MORE COMMITTED TO THE PLAN.
WHAT IS THE PLAN, RICK?
STEP ONE? MIXING THAT UNSTABLE ELECTROMAGNETIC FORMULA WE USED TO SEND WAVELENGTH SIGNALS--WITH THIS!
STEP TWO: THE SUREFIRE WAY TO KILL ANY FRANCHISE, MORTY!
DECONSTRUCTION!
DECONSTRUCTION!

TO BE CONCLUDED...!

*OOOH! DO YOU LIKE THAT? IT'S DIFFERENT! SO YOU BETTER BUY THE NEXT ISSUE, TOO! BECAUSE WHAT KIND OF DUMB PIECE OF S**T BUYS ¾ OF A STORY BUT DOESN'T SEE HOW IT **ENDS?!** BESIDES, WHEN YOU REACH A MOMENT OF DESPERATION OR GROWTH AND SELL THESE ON EBAY, YOU WON'T GET AS MUCH IF YOU DON'T HAVE THE FULL MINISERIES. (AND THEY ALWAYS **PRINT** FEWER OF THE LATER ISSUES, SO THOSE ARE THE ONES THAT ACTUALLY END UP BEING RARER AND WORTH MORE. **SO IT'LL BE AN **INVESTMENT**!**)*

CHAPTER 4

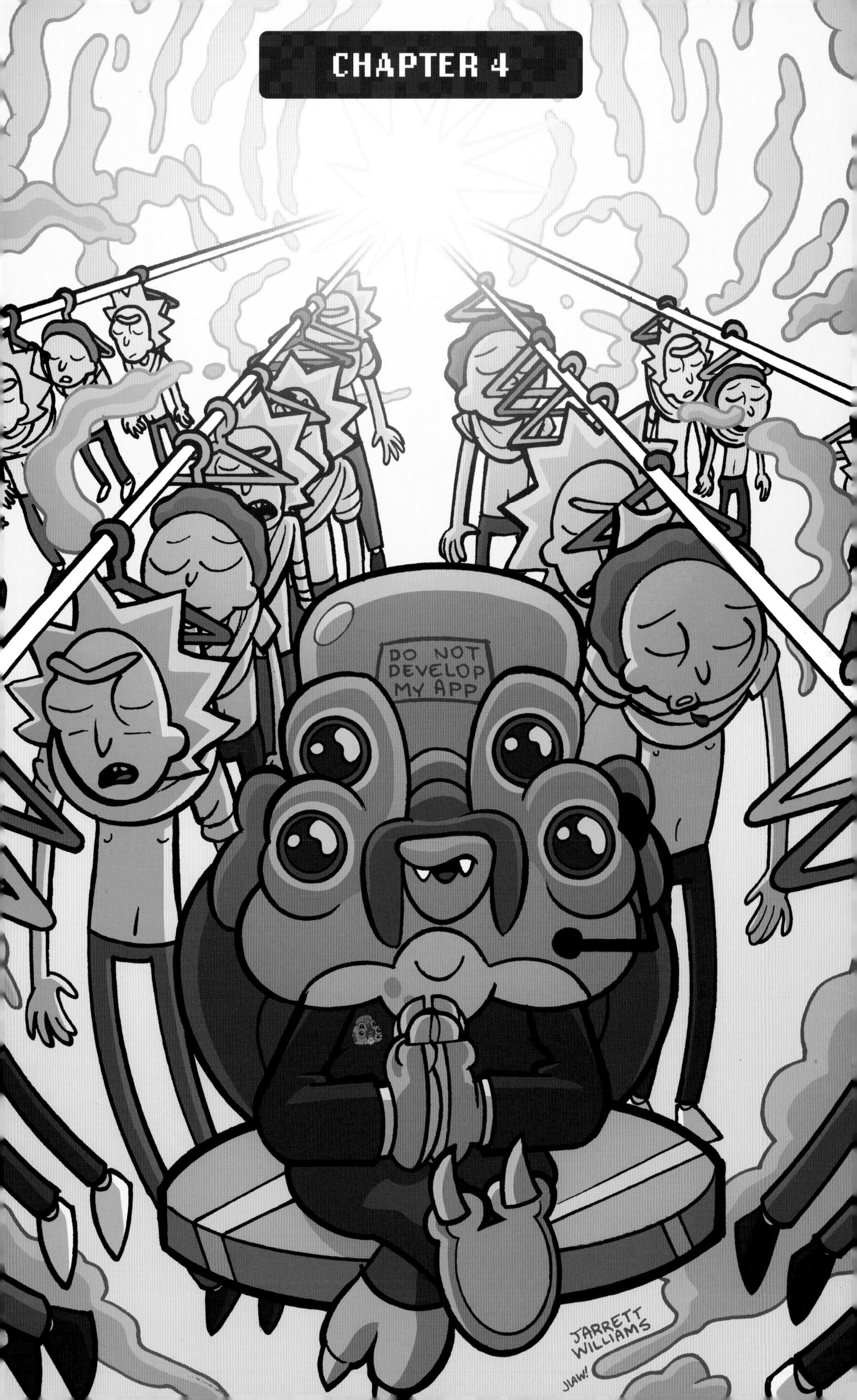
DO NOT DEVELOP MY APP
JARRETT WILLIAMS
JIAW!

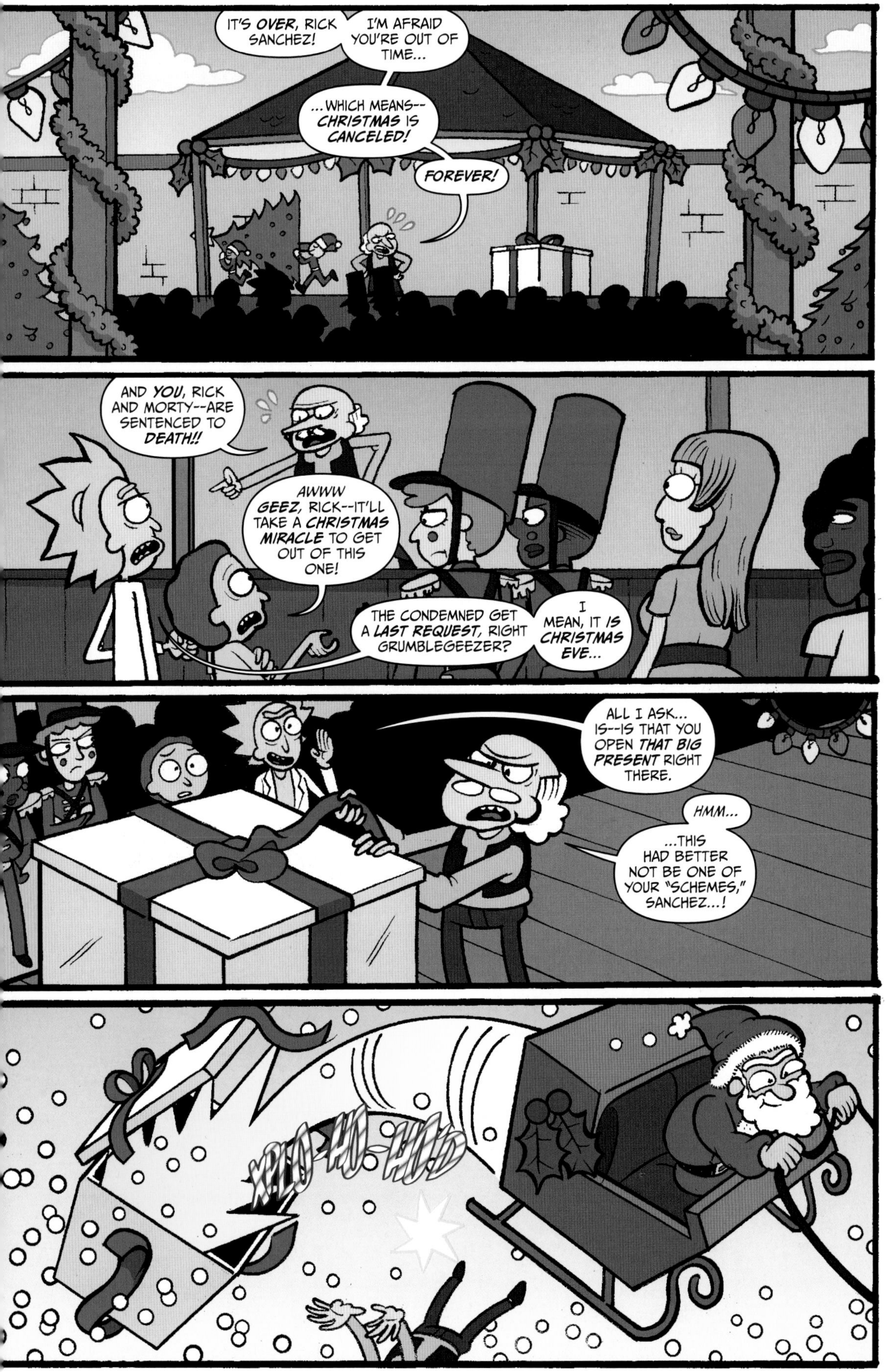
IT'S OVER, RICK SANCHEZ!
I'M AFRAID YOU'RE OUT OF TIME...
...WHICH MEANS-- CHRISTMAS IS CANCELED!
FOREVER!
AND YOU, RICK AND MORTY--ARE SENTENCED TO DEATH!!
AWWW GEEZ, RICK--IT'LL TAKE A CHRISTMAS MIRACLE TO GET OUT OF THIS ONE!
THE CONDEMNED GET A LAST REQUEST, RIGHT GRUMBLEGEEZER?
I MEAN, IT IS CHRISTMAS EVE...
ALL I ASK... IS--IS THAT YOU OPEN THAT BIG PRESENT RIGHT THERE.
HMM...
...THIS HAD BETTER NOT BE ONE OF YOUR "SCHEMES," SANCHEZ...!

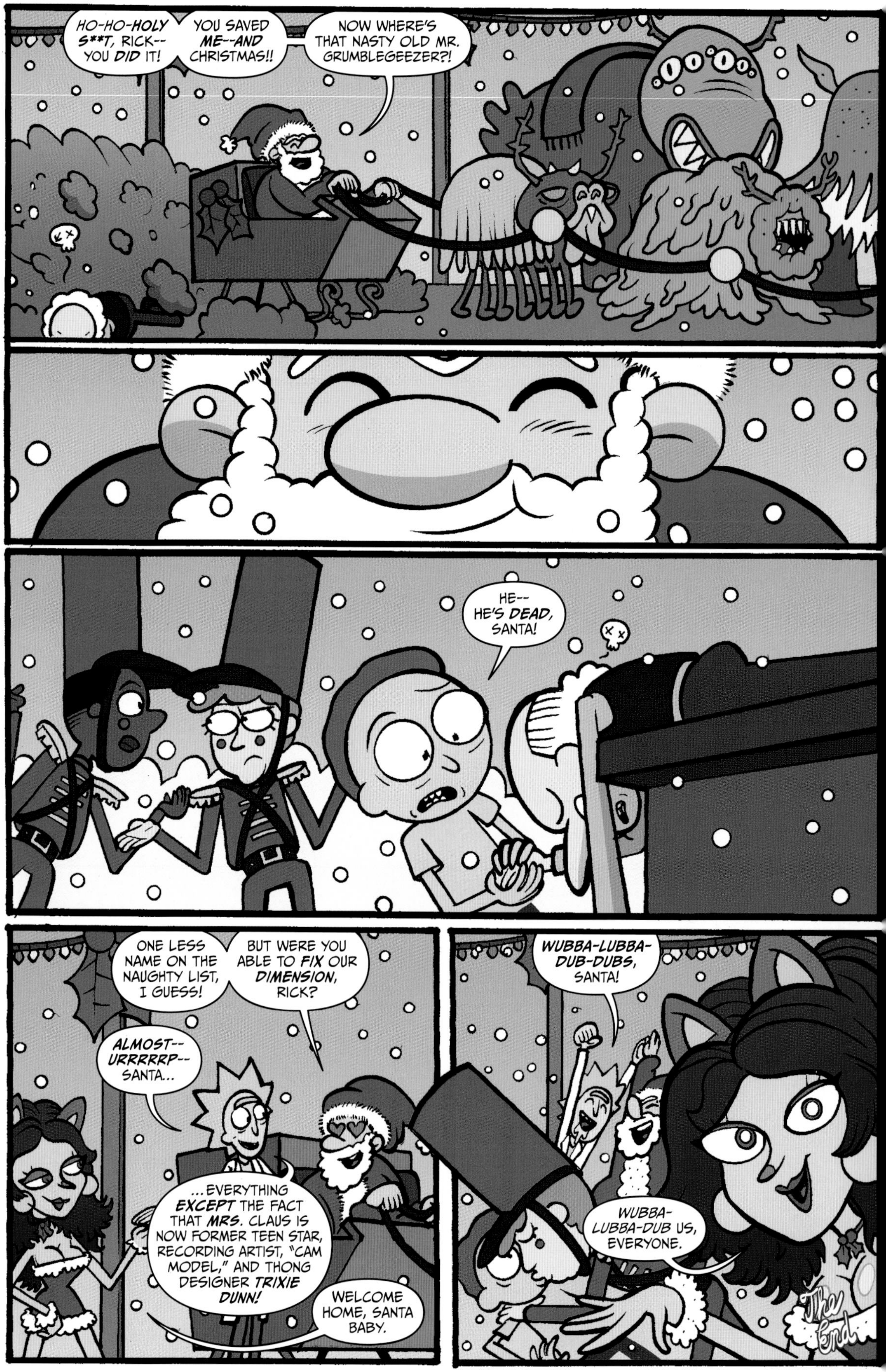

HO-HO-HOLY S**T, RICK-- YOU DID IT!
YOU SAVED ME--AND CHRISTMAS!!
NOW WHERE'S THAT NASTY OLD MR. GRUMBLEGEEZER?!
HE-- HE'S DEAD, SANTA!
ONE LESS NAME ON THE NAUGHTY LIST, I GUESS!
BUT WERE YOU ABLE TO FIX OUR DIMENSION, RICK?
ALMOST-- URRRRRP-- SANTA...
...EVERYTHING EXCEPT THE FACT THAT MRS. CLAUS IS NOW FORMER TEEN STAR, RECORDING ARTIST, "CAM MODEL," AND THONG DESIGNER TRIXIE DUNN!
WELCOME HOME, SANTA BABY.
WUBBA-LUBBA-DUB-DUBS, SANTA!
WUBBA-LUBBA-DUB US, EVERYONE.
The End

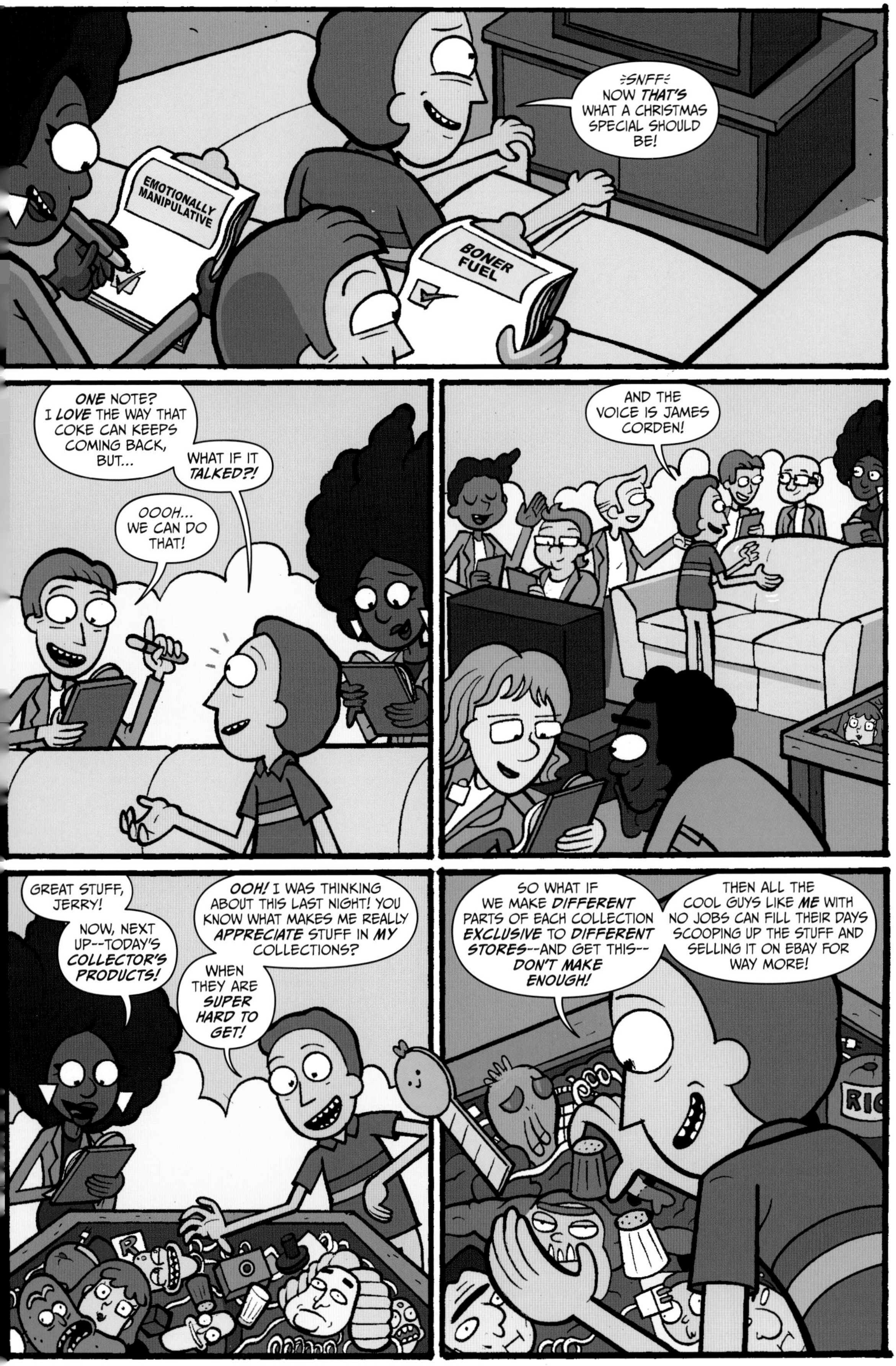

EMOTIONALLY MANIPULATIVE
BONER FUEL
≈SNFF≈ NOW THAT'S WHAT A CHRISTMAS SPECIAL SHOULD BE!
ONE NOTE? I LOVE THE WAY THAT COKE CAN KEEPS COMING BACK, BUT...
WHAT IF IT TALKED?!
OOOH... WE CAN DO THAT!
AND THE VOICE IS JAMES CORDEN!
GREAT STUFF, JERRY!
NOW, NEXT UP--TODAY'S COLLECTOR'S PRODUCTS!
OOH! I WAS THINKING ABOUT THIS LAST NIGHT! YOU KNOW WHAT MAKES ME REALLY APPRECIATE STUFF IN MY COLLECTIONS?
WHEN THEY ARE SUPER HARD TO GET!
SO WHAT IF WE MAKE DIFFERENT PARTS OF EACH COLLECTION EXCLUSIVE TO DIFFERENT STORES--AND GET THIS--DON'T MAKE ENOUGH!
THEN ALL THE COOL GUYS LIKE ME WITH NO JOBS CAN FILL THEIR DAYS SCOOPING UP THE STUFF AND SELLING IT ON EBAY FOR WAY MORE!

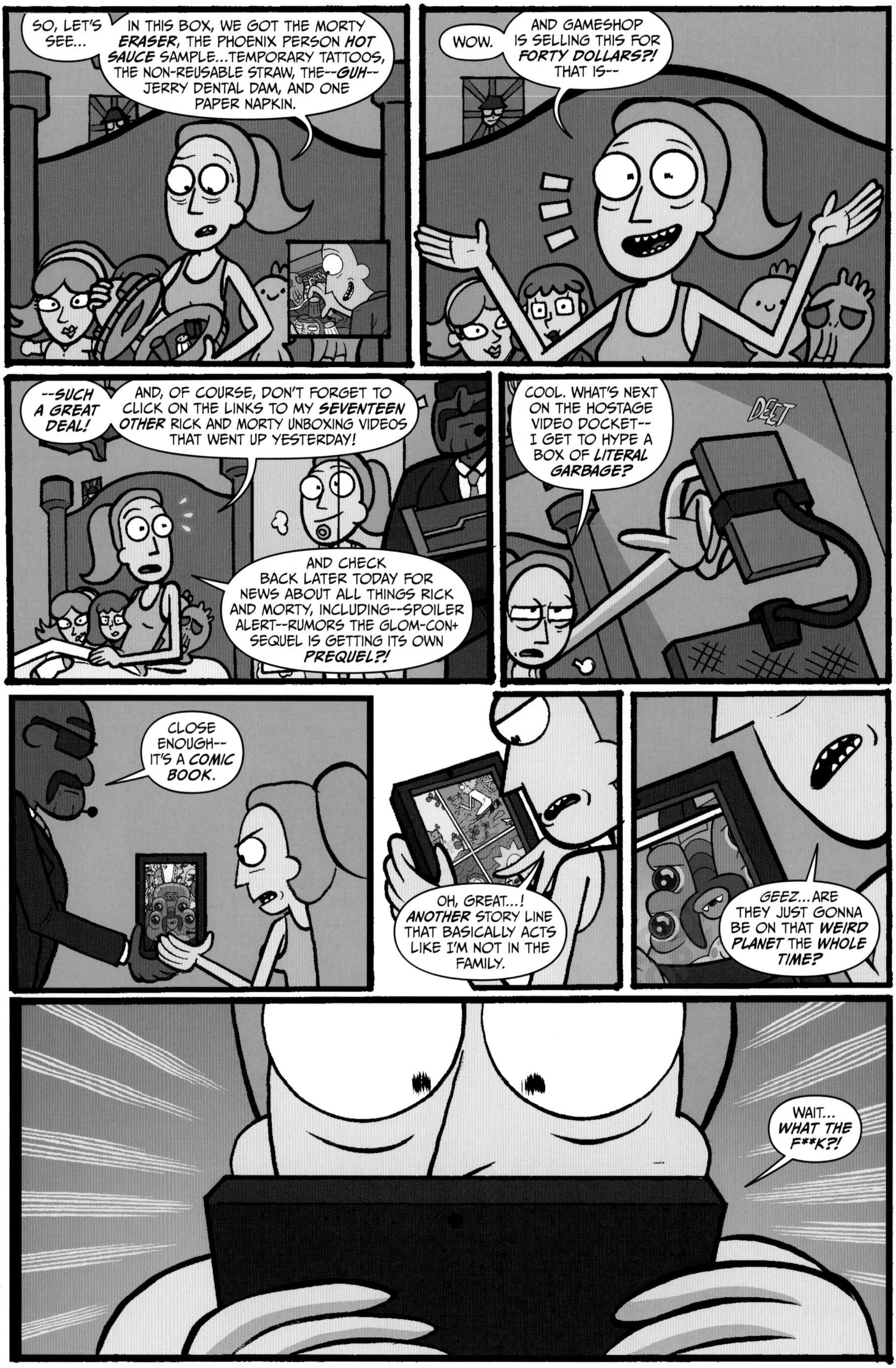
SO, LET'S SEE...
IN THIS BOX, WE GOT THE MORTY ERASER, THE PHOENIX PERSON HOT SAUCE SAMPLE...TEMPORARY TATTOOS, THE NON-REUSABLE STRAW, THE--GUH--JERRY DENTAL DAM, AND ONE PAPER NAPKIN.
WOW.
AND GAMESHOP IS SELLING THIS FOR FORTY DOLLARS?! THAT IS--
--SUCH A GREAT DEAL!
AND, OF COURSE, DON'T FORGET TO CLICK ON THE LINKS TO MY SEVENTEEN OTHER RICK AND MORTY UNBOXING VIDEOS THAT WENT UP YESTERDAY!
AND CHECK BACK LATER TODAY FOR NEWS ABOUT ALL THINGS RICK AND MORTY, INCLUDING--SPOILER ALERT--RUMORS THE GLOM-CON+ SEQUEL IS GETTING ITS OWN PREQUEL?!
COOL. WHAT'S NEXT ON THE HOSTAGE VIDEO DOCKET--I GET TO HYPE A BOX OF LITERAL GARBAGE?
DEET
CLOSE ENOUGH--IT'S A COMIC BOOK.
OH, GREAT...! ANOTHER STORY LINE THAT BASICALLY ACTS LIKE I'M NOT IN THE FAMILY.
GEEZ...ARE THEY JUST GONNA BE ON THAT WEIRD PLANET THE WHOLE TIME?
WAIT... WHAT THE F**K?!

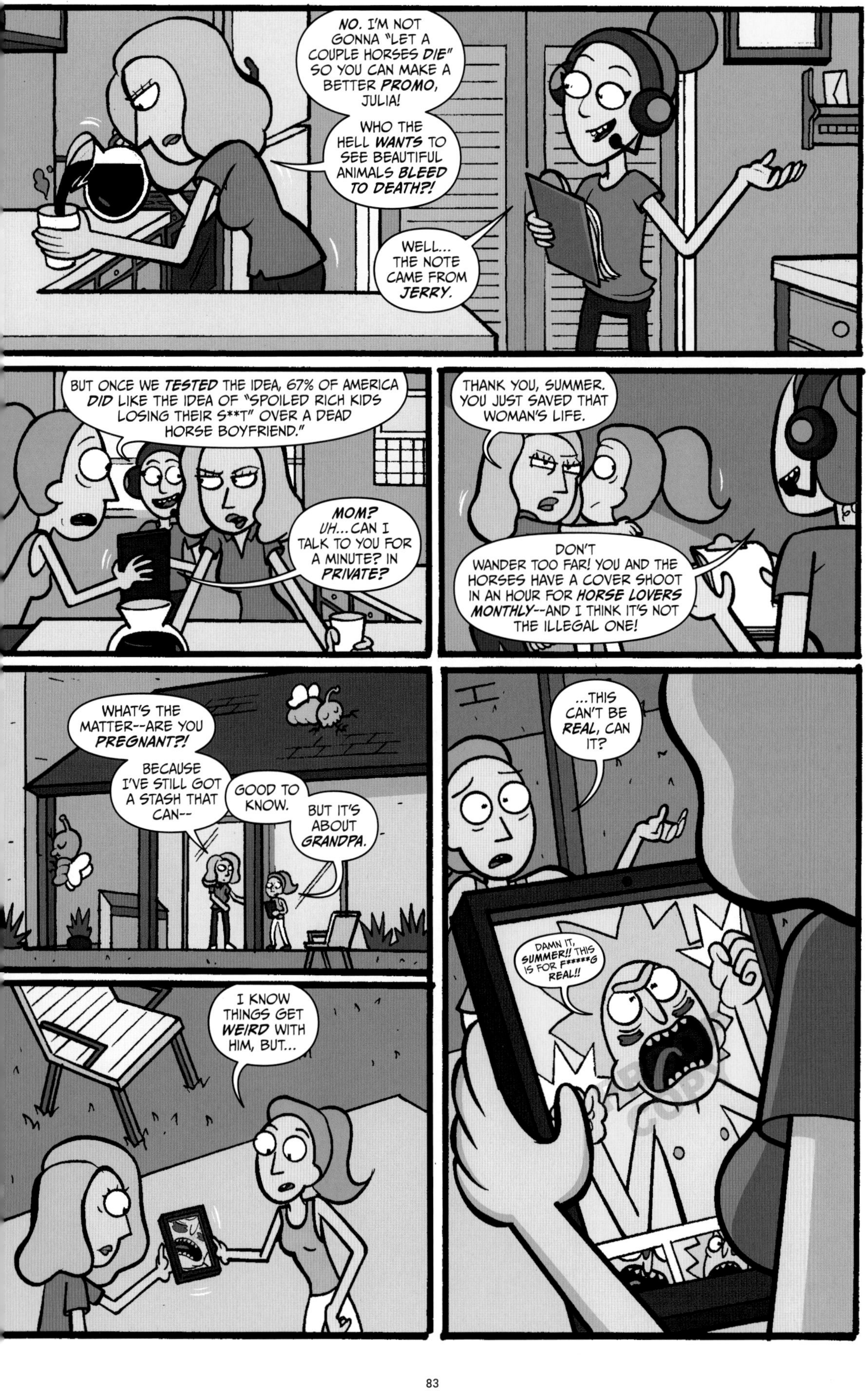
NO. I'M NOT GONNA "LET A COUPLE HORSES DIE" SO YOU CAN MAKE A BETTER PROMO, JULIA!
WHO THE HELL WANTS TO SEE BEAUTIFUL ANIMALS BLEED TO DEATH?!
WELL... THE NOTE CAME FROM JERRY.
BUT ONCE WE TESTED THE IDEA, 67% OF AMERICA DID LIKE THE IDEA OF "SPOILED RICH KIDS LOSING THEIR S**T" OVER A DEAD HORSE BOYFRIEND."
MOM? UH... CAN I TALK TO YOU FOR A MINUTE? IN PRIVATE?
THANK YOU, SUMMER. YOU JUST SAVED THAT WOMAN'S LIFE.
DON'T WANDER TOO FAR! YOU AND THE HORSES HAVE A COVER SHOOT IN AN HOUR FOR HORSE LOVERS MONTHLY--AND I THINK IT'S NOT THE ILLEGAL ONE!
WHAT'S THE MATTER--ARE YOU PREGNANT?!
BECAUSE I'VE STILL GOT A STASH THAT CAN--
GOOD TO KNOW.
BUT IT'S ABOUT GRANDPA.
I KNOW THINGS GET WEIRD WITH HIM, BUT...
...THIS CAN'T BE REAL, CAN IT?
DAMN IT, SUMMER!! THIS IS FOR F*****G REAL!!

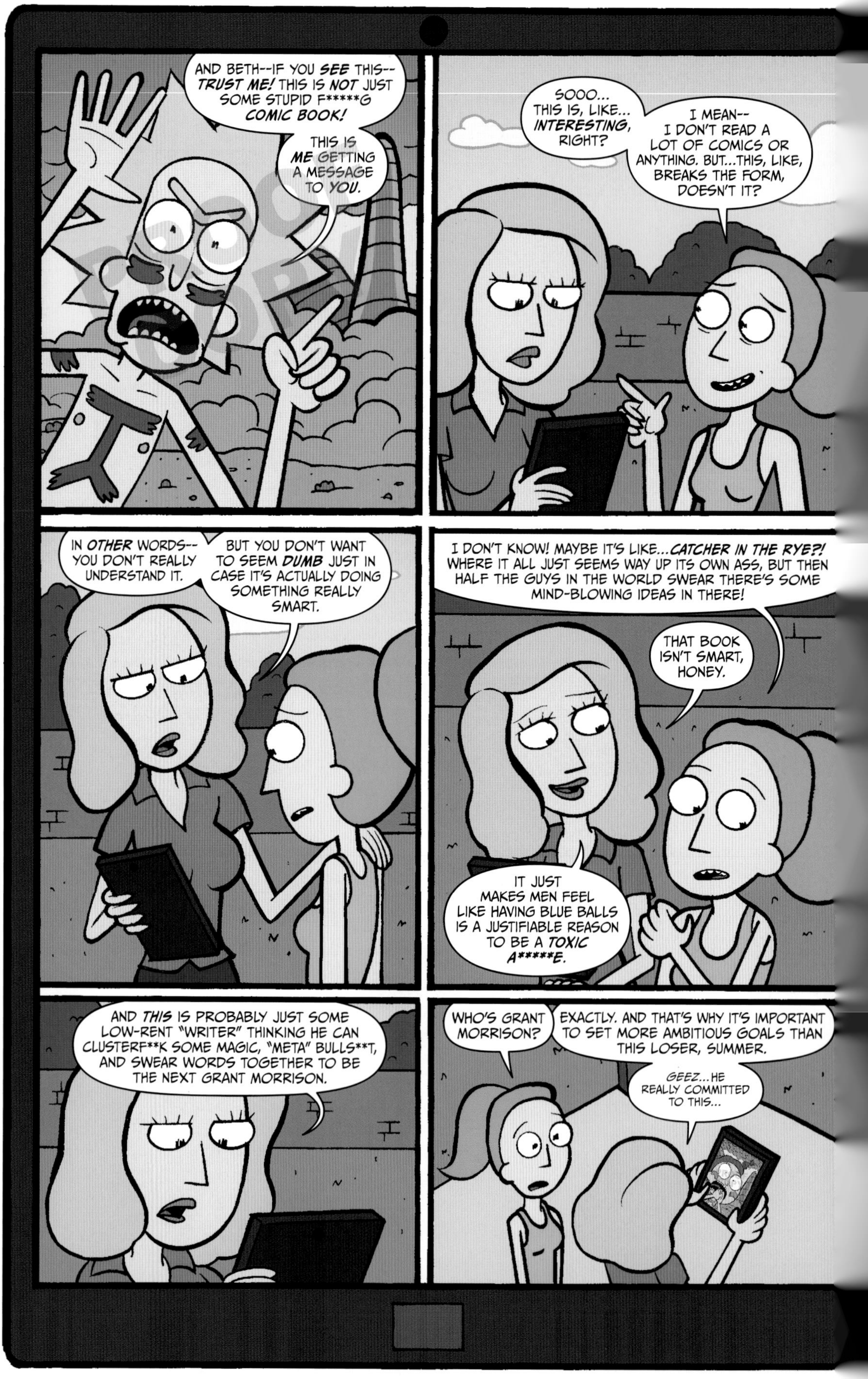
AND BETH--IF YOU SEE THIS--
TRUST ME! THIS IS NOT JUST SOME STUPID F*****G COMIC BOOK!
THIS IS ME GETTING A MESSAGE TO YOU.
SOOO... THIS IS, LIKE... INTERESTING, RIGHT?
I MEAN-- I DON'T READ A LOT OF COMICS OR ANYTHING. BUT...THIS, LIKE, BREAKS THE FORM, DOESN'T IT?
IN OTHER WORDS-- YOU DON'T REALLY UNDERSTAND IT.
BUT YOU DON'T WANT TO SEEM DUMB JUST IN CASE IT'S ACTUALLY DOING SOMETHING REALLY SMART.
I DON'T KNOW! MAYBE IT'S LIKE...CATCHER IN THE RYE?! WHERE IT ALL JUST SEEMS WAY UP ITS OWN ASS, BUT THEN HALF THE GUYS IN THE WORLD SWEAR THERE'S SOME MIND-BLOWING IDEAS IN THERE!
THAT BOOK ISN'T SMART, HONEY.
IT JUST MAKES MEN FEEL LIKE HAVING BLUE BALLS IS A JUSTIFIABLE REASON TO BE A TOXIC A*****E.
AND THIS IS PROBABLY JUST SOME LOW-RENT "WRITER" THINKING HE CAN CLUSTERF**K SOME MAGIC, "META" BULLS**T, AND SWEAR WORDS TOGETHER TO BE THE NEXT GRANT MORRISON.
WHO'S GRANT MORRISON?
EXACTLY. AND THAT'S WHY IT'S IMPORTANT TO SET MORE AMBITIOUS GOALS THAN THIS LOSER, SUMMER.
GEEZ...HE REALLY COMMITTED TO THIS...

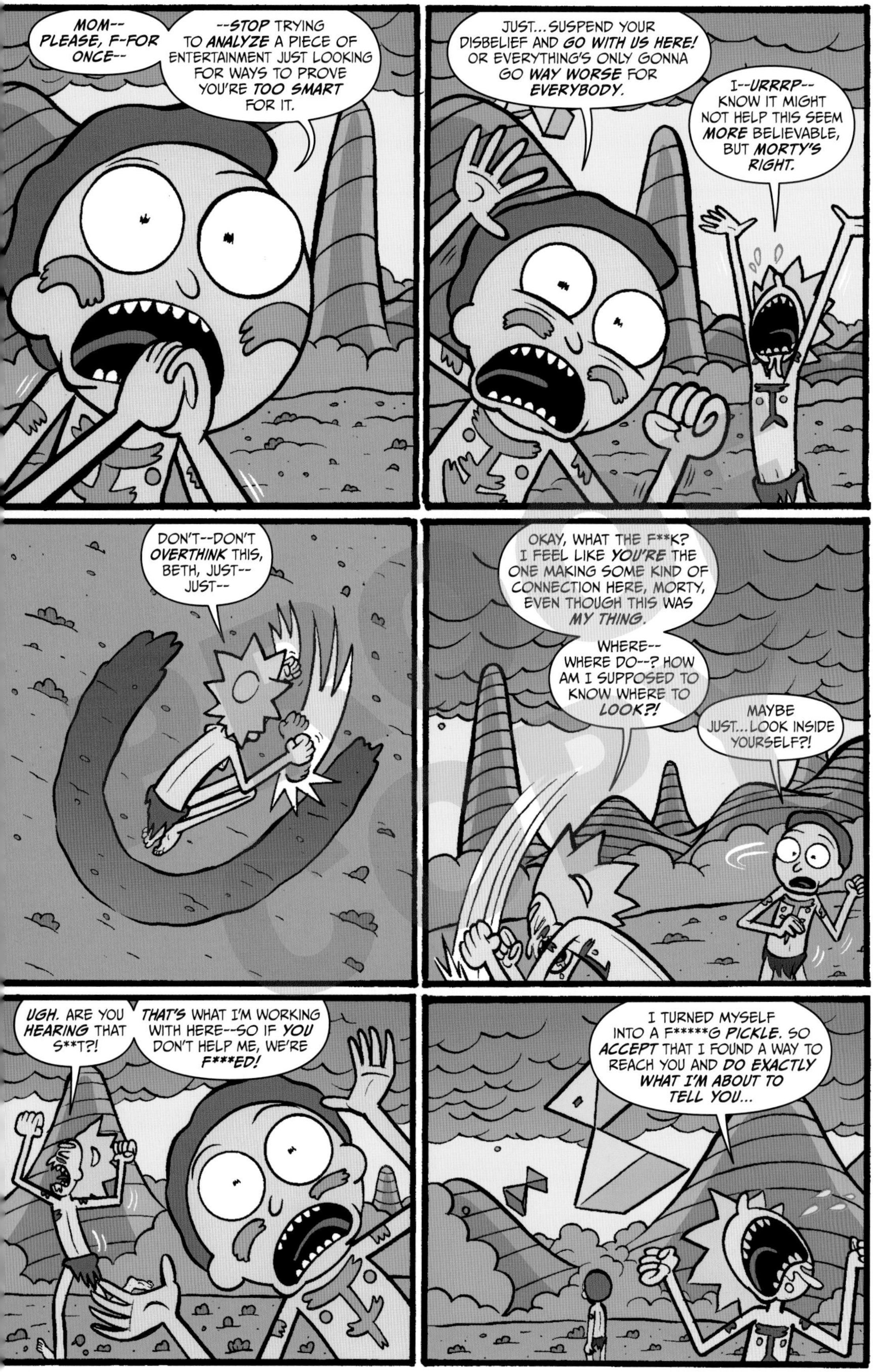
MOM--
PLEASE, F-FOR ONCE--
--STOP TRYING TO ANALYZE A PIECE OF ENTERTAINMENT JUST LOOKING FOR WAYS TO PROVE YOU'RE TOO SMART FOR IT.
JUST...SUSPEND YOUR DISBELIEF AND GO WITH US HERE! OR EVERYTHING'S ONLY GONNA GO WAY WORSE FOR EVERYBODY.
I--URRRP-- KNOW IT MIGHT NOT HELP THIS SEEM MORE BELIEVABLE, BUT MORTY'S RIGHT.
DON'T--DON'T OVERTHINK THIS, BETH, JUST-- JUST--
OKAY, WHAT THE F**K? I FEEL LIKE YOU'RE THE ONE MAKING SOME KIND OF CONNECTION HERE, MORTY, EVEN THOUGH THIS WAS MY THING.
WHERE-- WHERE DO--? HOW AM I SUPPOSED TO KNOW WHERE TO LOOK?!
MAYBE JUST...LOOK INSIDE YOURSELF?!
UGH. ARE YOU HEARING THAT S**T?!
THAT'S WHAT I'M WORKING WITH HERE--SO IF YOU DON'T HELP ME, WE'RE F***ED!
I TURNED MYSELF INTO A F*****G PICKLE. SO ACCEPT THAT I FOUND A WAY TO REACH YOU AND DO EXACTLY WHAT I'M ABOUT TO TELL YOU...

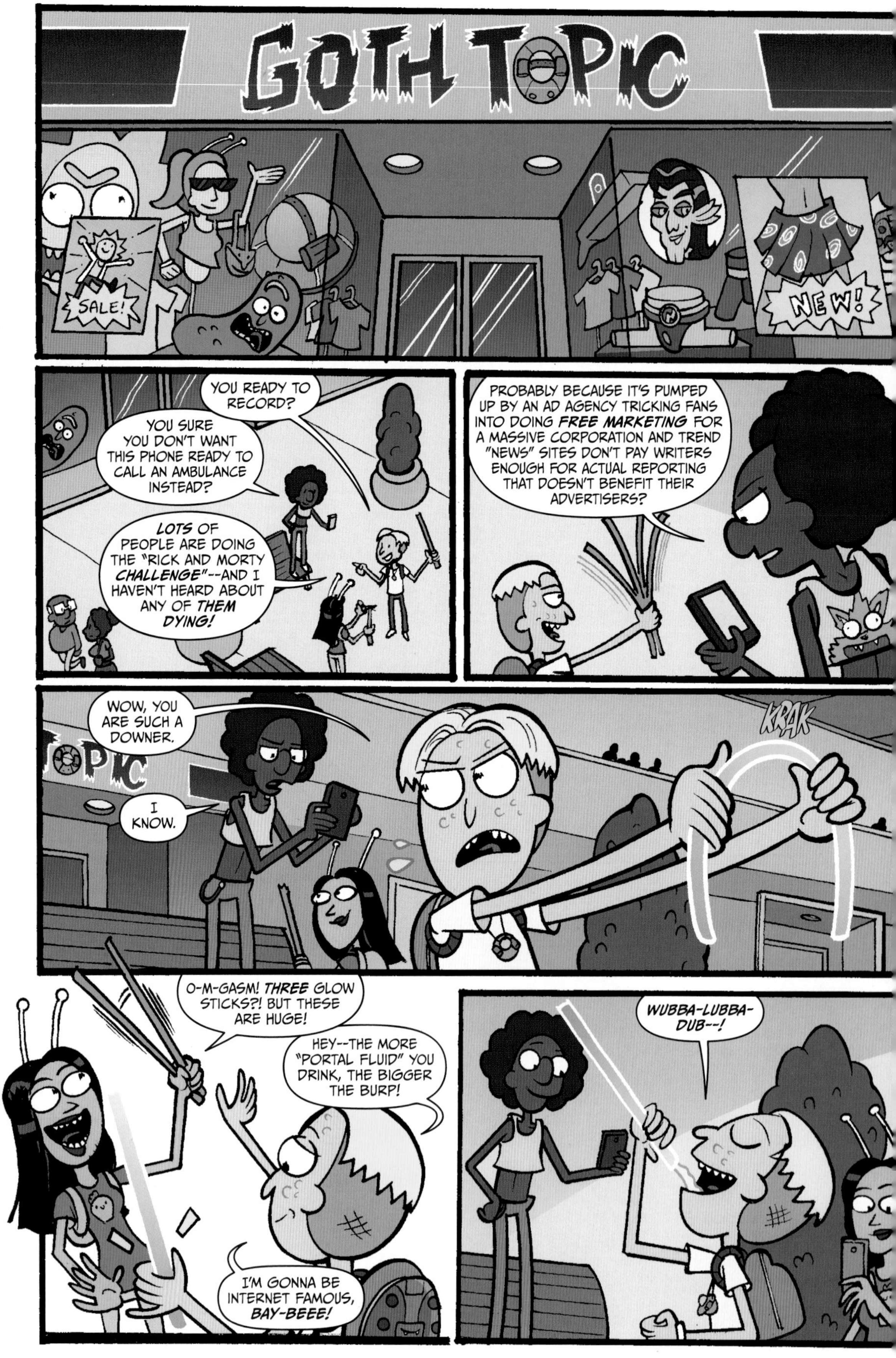
GOTH TOPIC
SALE!
NEW!
YOU READY TO RECORD?
YOU SURE YOU DON'T WANT THIS PHONE READY TO CALL AN AMBULANCE INSTEAD?
LOTS OF PEOPLE ARE DOING THE "RICK AND MORTY CHALLENGE"--AND I HAVEN'T HEARD ABOUT ANY OF THEM DYING!
PROBABLY BECAUSE IT'S PUMPED UP BY AN AD AGENCY TRICKING FANS INTO DOING FREE MARKETING FOR A MASSIVE CORPORATION AND TREND "NEWS" SITES DON'T PAY WRITERS ENOUGH FOR ACTUAL REPORTING THAT DOESN'T BENEFIT THEIR ADVERTISERS?
WOW, YOU ARE SUCH A DOWNER.
I KNOW.
KRAK
O-M-GASM! THREE GLOW STICKS?! BUT THESE ARE HUGE!
HEY--THE MORE "PORTAL FLUID" YOU DRINK, THE BIGGER THE BURP!
I'M GONNA BE INTERNET FAMOUS, BAY-BEEE!
WUBBA-LUBBA-DUB--!

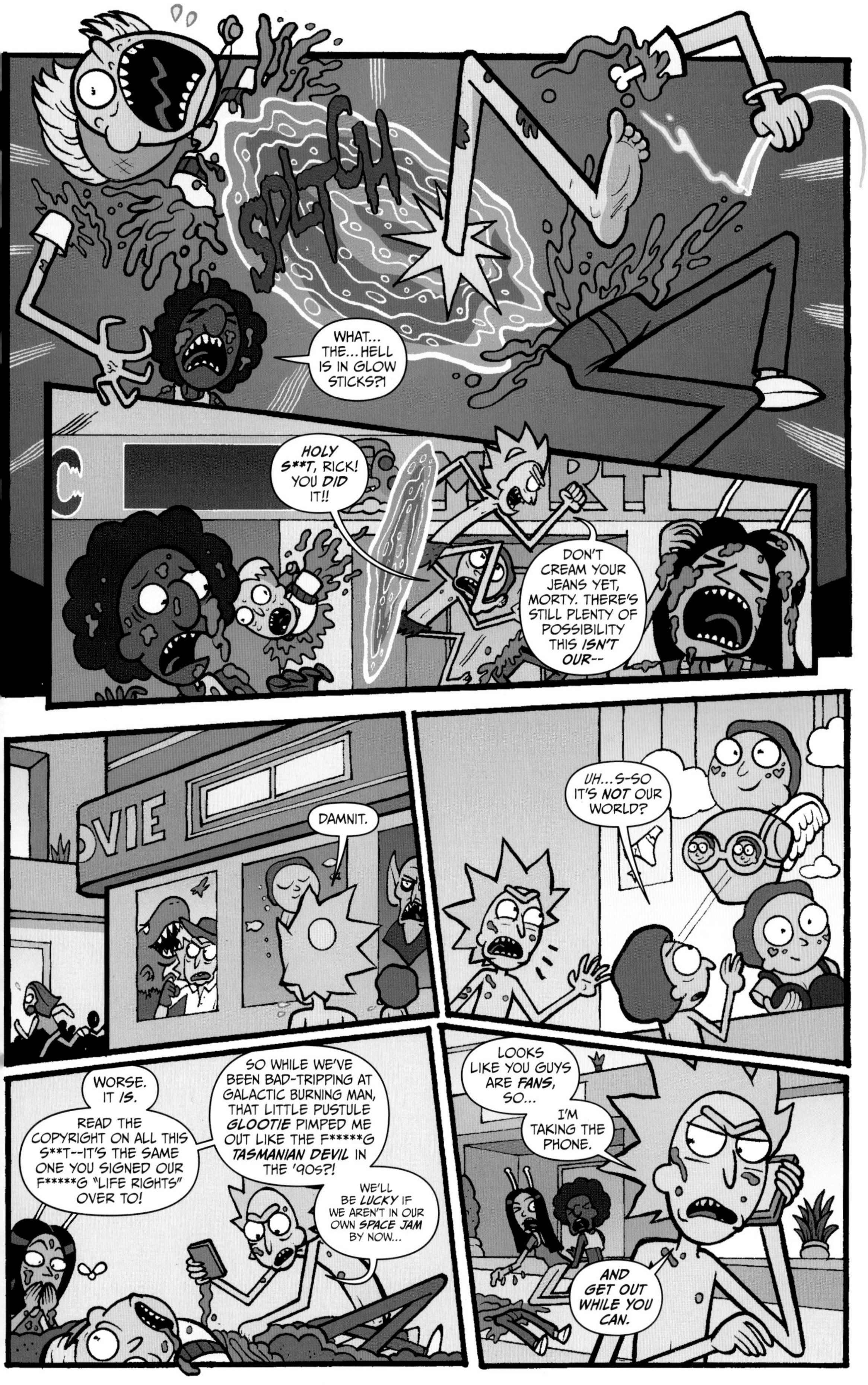
SPLTCH
WHAT... THE...HELL IS IN GLOW STICKS?!
HOLY S**T, RICK! YOU DID IT!!
DON'T CREAM YOUR JEANS YET, MORTY. THERE'S STILL PLENTY OF POSSIBILITY THIS ISN'T OUR--
DAMNIT.
UH...S-SO IT'S NOT OUR WORLD?
WORSE. IT IS.
READ THE COPYRIGHT ON ALL THIS S**T--IT'S THE SAME ONE YOU SIGNED OUR F*****G "LIFE RIGHTS" OVER TO!
SO WHILE WE'VE BEEN BAD-TRIPPING AT GALACTIC BURNING MAN, THAT LITTLE PUSTULE GLOOTIE PIMPED ME OUT LIKE THE F*****G TASMANIAN DEVIL IN THE '90S?!
WE'LL BE LUCKY IF WE AREN'T IN OUR OWN SPACE JAM BY NOW...
LOOKS LIKE YOU GUYS ARE FANS, SO...
I'M TAKING THE PHONE.
AND GET OUT WHILE YOU CAN.

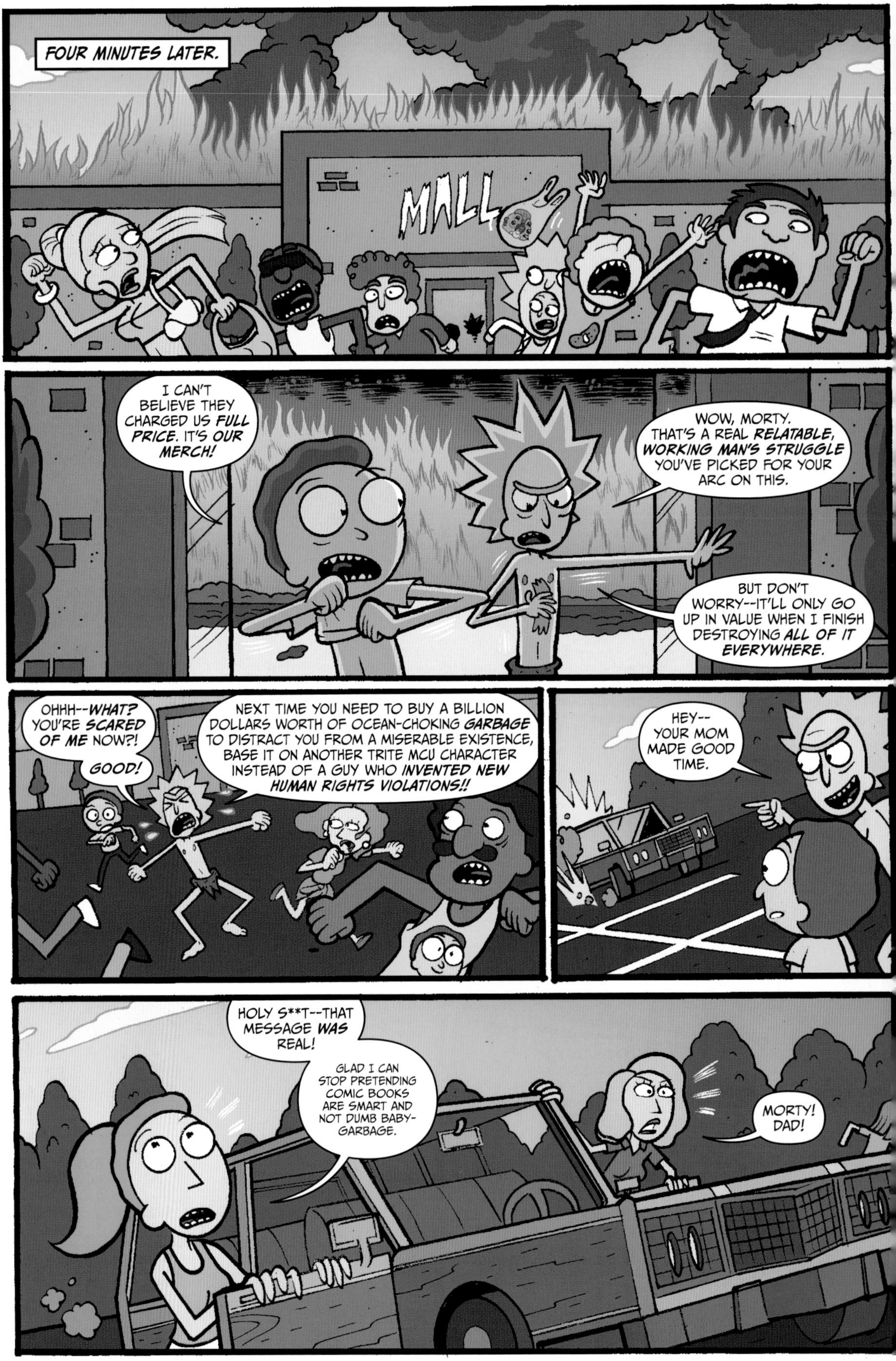
FOUR MINUTES LATER.
MALL
I CAN'T BELIEVE THEY CHARGED US FULL PRICE. IT'S OUR MERCH!
WOW, MORTY. THAT'S A REAL RELATABLE, WORKING MAN'S STRUGGLE YOU'VE PICKED FOR YOUR ARC ON THIS.
BUT DON'T WORRY--IT'LL ONLY GO UP IN VALUE WHEN I FINISH DESTROYING ALL OF IT EVERYWHERE.
OHHH--WHAT? YOU'RE SCARED OF ME NOW?!
GOOD!
NEXT TIME YOU NEED TO BUY A BILLION DOLLARS WORTH OF OCEAN-CHOKING GARBAGE TO DISTRACT YOU FROM A MISERABLE EXISTENCE, BASE IT ON ANOTHER TRITE MCU CHARACTER INSTEAD OF A GUY WHO INVENTED NEW HUMAN RIGHTS VIOLATIONS!!
HEY-- YOUR MOM MADE GOOD TIME.
HOLY S**T--THAT MESSAGE WAS REAL!
GLAD I CAN STOP PRETENDING COMIC BOOKS ARE SMART AND NOT DUMB BABY-GARBAGE.
MORTY! DAD!

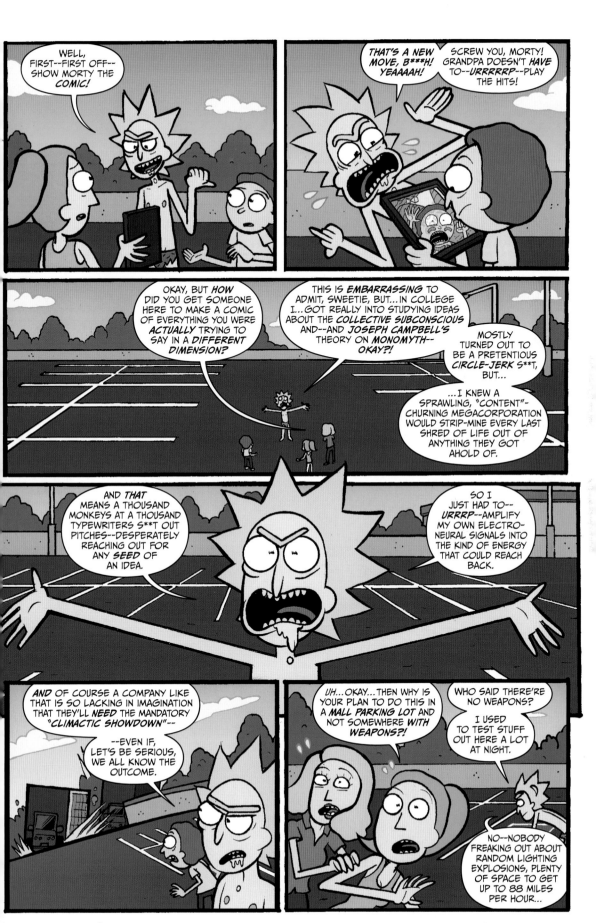

WELL, FIRST--FIRST OFF-- SHOW MORTY THE *COMIC!*

*THAT'S A NEW MOVE, B***H!* YEAAAAH!

SCREW YOU, MORTY! GRANDPA DOESN'T *HAVE* TO--URRRRRP--PLAY THE HITS!

OKAY, BUT *HOW* DID YOU GET SOMEONE HERE TO MAKE A COMIC OF EVERYTHING YOU WERE *ACTUALLY* TRYING TO SAY IN A *DIFFERENT DIMENSION?*

THIS IS *EMBARRASSING* TO ADMIT, SWEETIE, BUT...IN COLLEGE I...GOT REALLY INTO STUDYING IDEAS ABOUT THE *COLLECTIVE SUBCONSCIOUS* AND--AND *JOSEPH CAMPBELL'S* THEORY ON *MONOMYTH*-- OKAY?!

MOSTLY TURNED OUT TO BE A PRETENTIOUS *CIRCLE-JERK* S**T, BUT...

...I KNEW A SPRAWLING, "CONTENT"- CHURNING MEGACORPORATION WOULD STRIP-MINE EVERY LAST SHRED OF LIFE OUT OF ANYTHING THEY GOT AHOLD OF.

AND *THAT* MEANS A THOUSAND MONKEYS AT A THOUSAND TYPEWRITERS S**T OUT PITCHES--DESPERATELY REACHING OUT FOR ANY *SEED* OF AN IDEA.

SO I JUST HAD TO-- URRRP--AMPLIFY MY OWN ELECTRO- NEURAL SIGNALS INTO THE KIND OF ENERGY THAT COULD REACH BACK.

AND OF COURSE A COMPANY LIKE THAT IS SO LACKING IN IMAGINATION THAT THEY'LL *NEED* THE MANDATORY "CLIMACTIC SHOWDOWN"--

--EVEN IF, LET'S BE SERIOUS, WE ALL KNOW THE OUTCOME.

UH...OKAY...THEN WHY IS YOUR PLAN TO DO THIS IN A *MALL PARKING LOT* AND NOT SOMEWHERE *WITH WEAPONS?!*

WHO SAID THERE'RE NO WEAPONS? I USED TO TEST STUFF OUT HERE A LOT AT NIGHT.

NO--NOBODY FREAKING OUT ABOUT RANDOM LIGHTING EXPLOSIONS, PLENTY OF SPACE TO GET UP TO 88 MILES PER HOUR...

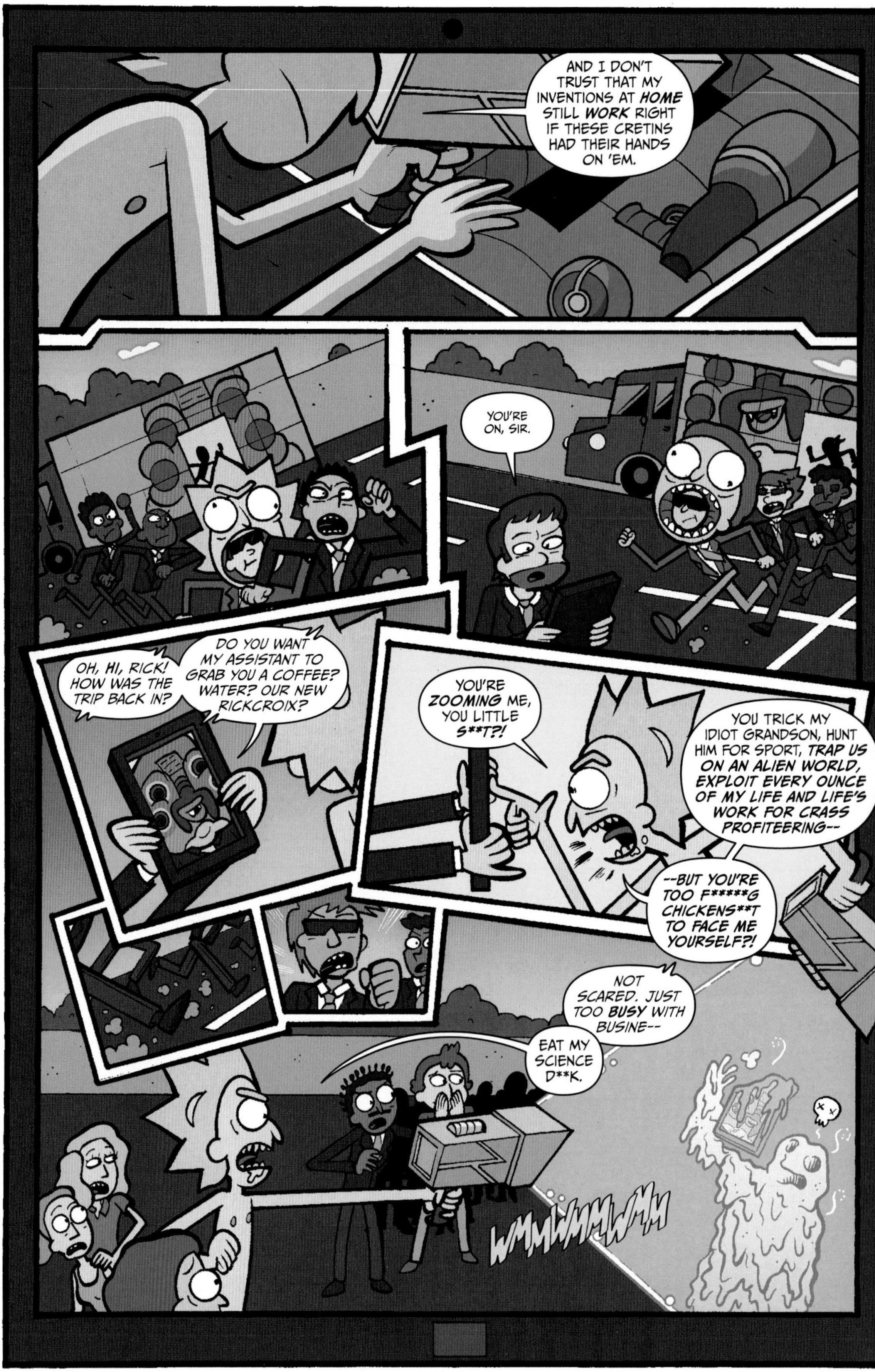
AND I DON'T TRUST THAT MY INVENTIONS AT HOME STILL WORK RIGHT IF THESE CRETINS HAD THEIR HANDS ON 'EM.
YOU'RE ON, SIR.
OH, HI, RICK! HOW WAS THE TRIP BACK IN?
DO YOU WANT MY ASSISTANT TO GRAB YOU A COFFEE? WATER? OUR NEW RICKCROIX?
YOU'RE ZOOMING ME, YOU LITTLE S**T?!
YOU TRICK MY IDIOT GRANDSON, HUNT HIM FOR SPORT, TRAP US ON AN ALIEN WORLD, EXPLOIT EVERY OUNCE OF MY LIFE AND LIFE'S WORK FOR CRASS PROFITEERING--
--BUT YOU'RE TOO F*****G CHICKENS**T TO FACE ME YOURSELF?!
NOT SCARED. JUST TOO BUSY WITH BUSINE--
EAT MY SCIENCE D**K.
WMMWMMWMM

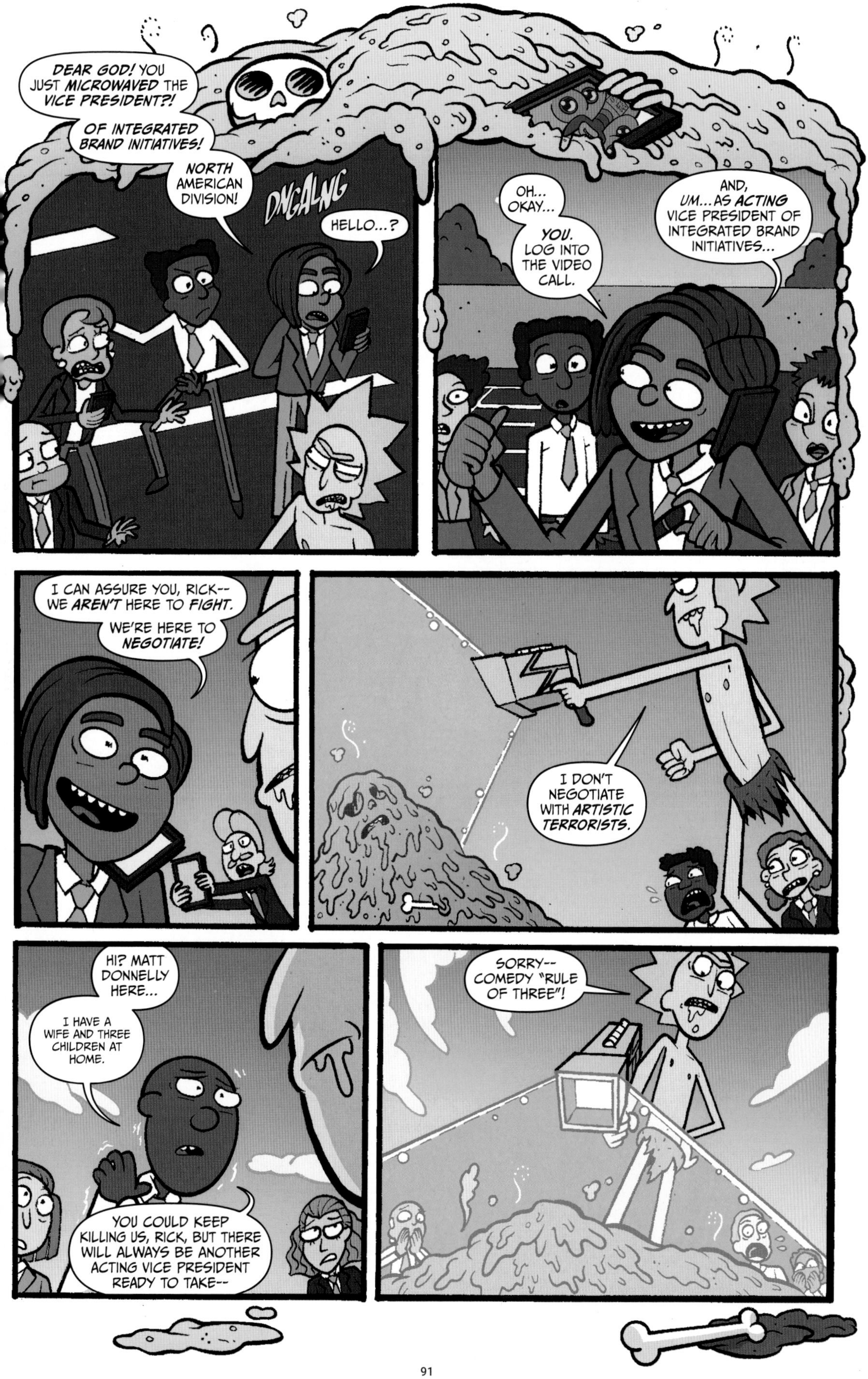
DEAR GOD! YOU JUST MICROWAVED THE VICE PRESIDENT?!
OF INTEGRATED BRAND INITIATIVES!
NORTH AMERICAN DIVISION!
DNGALNG
HELLO...?
OH... OKAY...
YOU. LOG INTO THE VIDEO CALL.
AND, UM...AS ACTING VICE PRESIDENT OF INTEGRATED BRAND INITIATIVES...
I CAN ASSURE YOU, RICK-- WE AREN'T HERE TO FIGHT.
WE'RE HERE TO NEGOTIATE!
I DON'T NEGOTIATE WITH ARTISTIC TERRORISTS.
HI? MATT DONNELLY HERE...
I HAVE A WIFE AND THREE CHILDREN AT HOME.
YOU COULD KEEP KILLING US, RICK, BUT THERE WILL ALWAYS BE ANOTHER ACTING VICE PRESIDENT READY TO TAKE--
SORRY-- COMEDY "RULE OF THREE"!

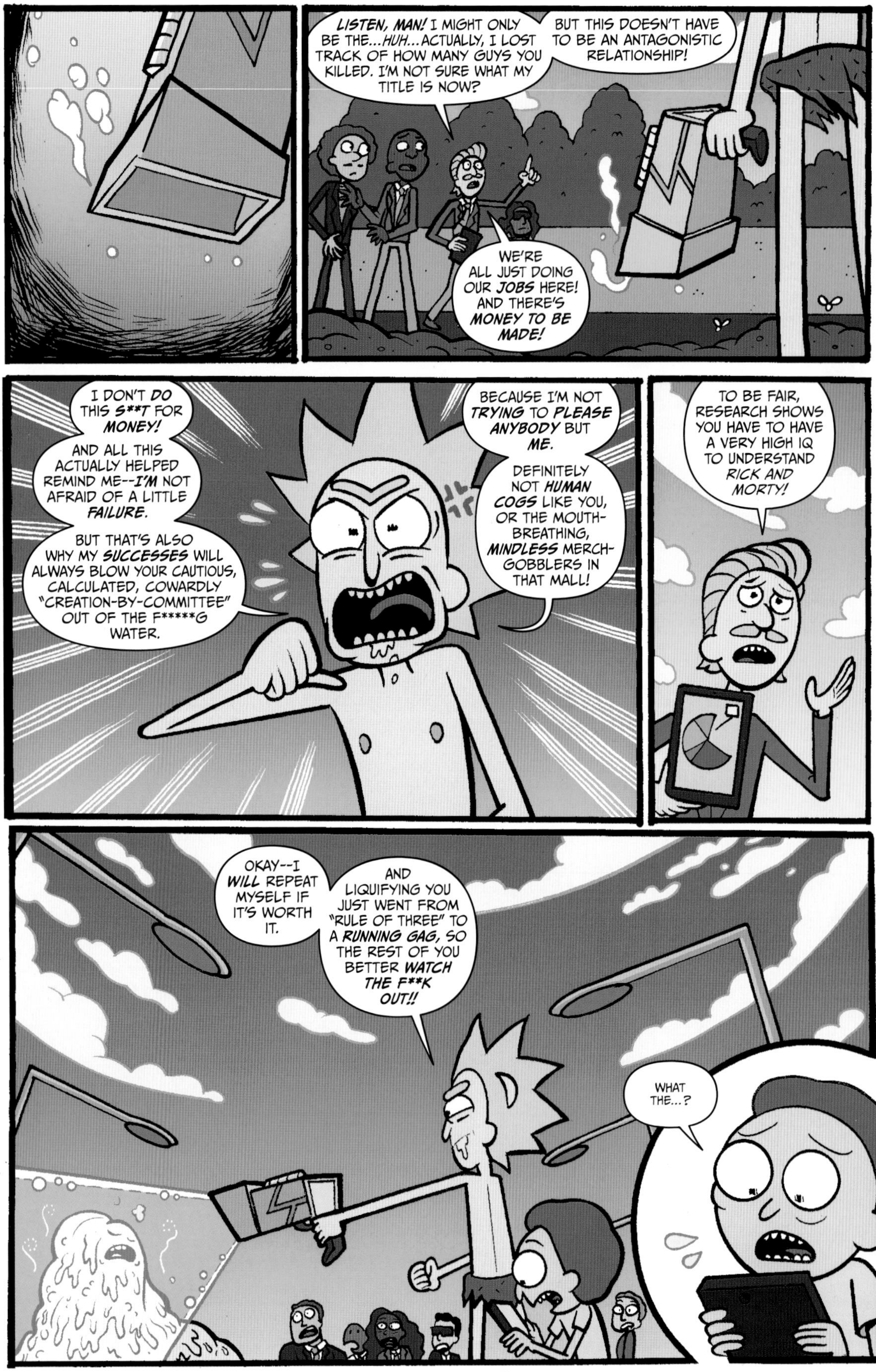
LISTEN, MAN! I MIGHT ONLY BE THE...HUH...ACTUALLY, I LOST TRACK OF HOW MANY GUYS YOU KILLED. I'M NOT SURE WHAT MY TITLE IS NOW?
BUT THIS DOESN'T HAVE TO BE AN ANTAGONISTIC RELATIONSHIP!
WE'RE ALL JUST DOING OUR JOBS HERE! AND THERE'S MONEY TO BE MADE!
I DON'T DO THIS S**T FOR MONEY!
AND ALL THIS ACTUALLY HELPED REMIND ME--I'M NOT AFRAID OF A LITTLE FAILURE.
BUT THAT'S ALSO WHY MY SUCCESSES WILL ALWAYS BLOW YOUR CAUTIOUS, CALCULATED, COWARDLY "CREATION-BY-COMMITTEE" OUT OF THE F*****G WATER.
BECAUSE I'M NOT TRYING TO PLEASE ANYBODY BUT ME.
DEFINITELY NOT HUMAN COGS LIKE YOU, OR THE MOUTH-BREATHING, MINDLESS MERCH-GOBBLERS IN THAT MALL!
TO BE FAIR, RESEARCH SHOWS YOU HAVE TO HAVE A VERY HIGH IQ TO UNDERSTAND RICK AND MORTY!
OKAY--I WILL REPEAT MYSELF IF IT'S WORTH IT.
AND LIQUIFYING YOU JUST WENT FROM "RULE OF THREE" TO A RUNNING GAG, SO THE REST OF YOU BETTER WATCH THE F**K OUT!!
WHAT THE...?

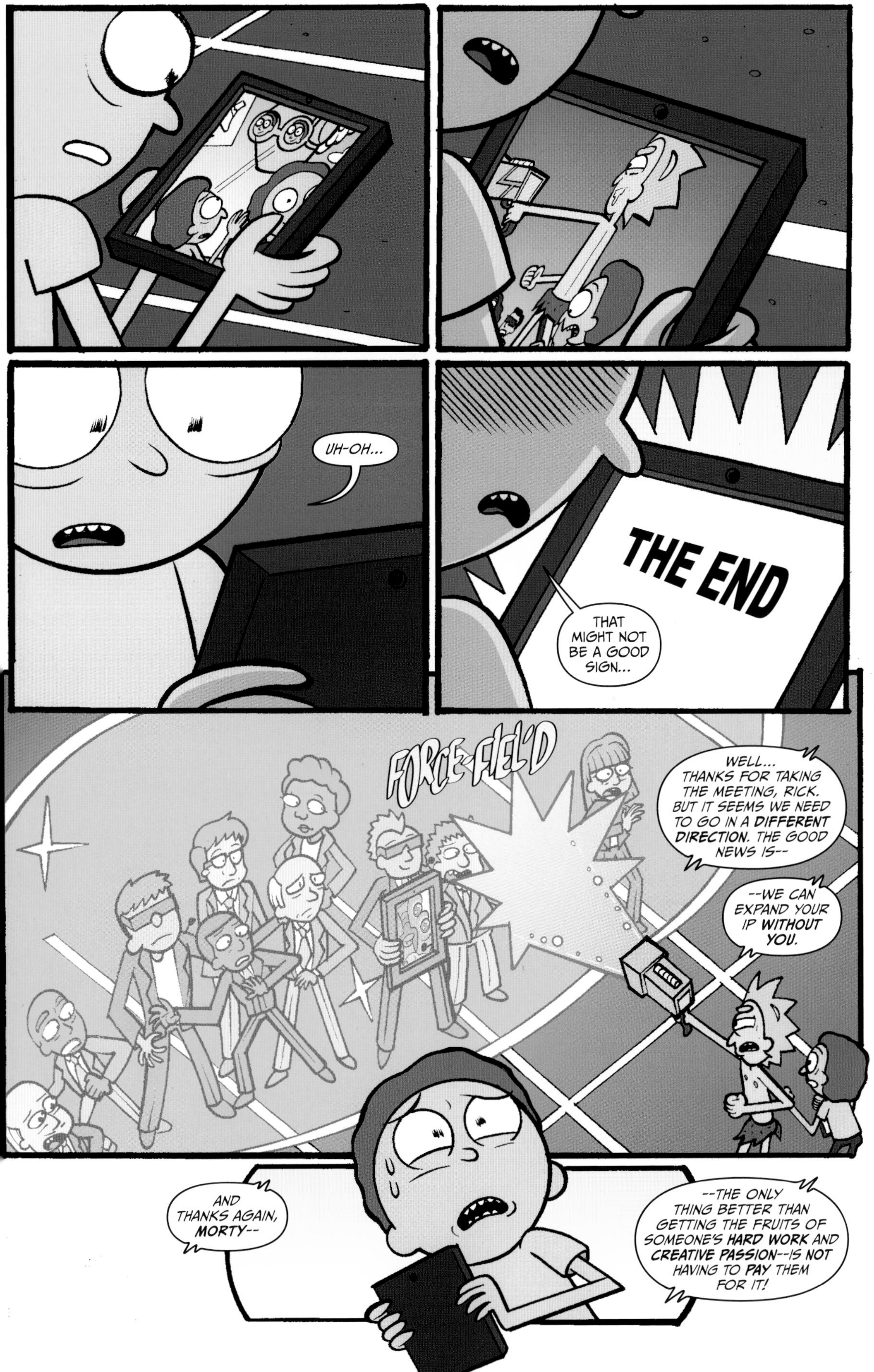
UH-OH...
THE END
THAT MIGHT NOT BE A GOOD SIGN...
FORCE-FIEL'D
WELL... THANKS FOR TAKING THE MEETING, RICK. BUT IT SEEMS WE NEED TO GO IN A DIFFERENT DIRECTION. THE GOOD NEWS IS--
--WE CAN EXPAND YOUR IP WITHOUT YOU.
AND THANKS AGAIN, MORTY--
--THE ONLY THING BETTER THAN GETTING THE FRUITS OF SOMEONE'S HARD WORK AND CREATIVE PASSION--IS NOT HAVING TO PAY THEM FOR IT!

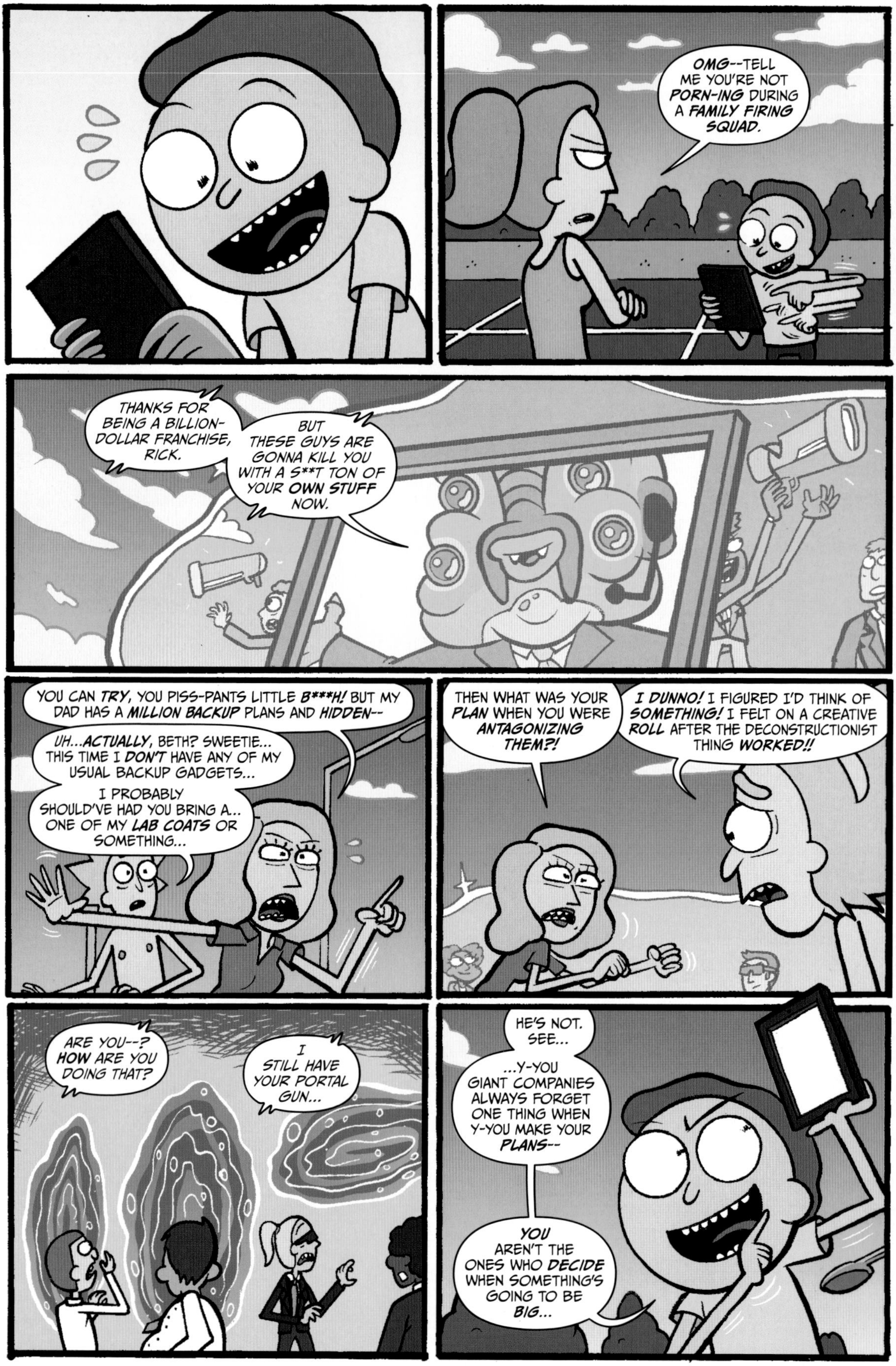
OMG--TELL ME YOU'RE NOT PORN-ING DURING A FAMILY FIRING SQUAD.
THANKS FOR BEING A BILLION-DOLLAR FRANCHISE, RICK.
BUT THESE GUYS ARE GONNA KILL YOU WITH A S**T TON OF YOUR OWN STUFF NOW.
YOU CAN TRY, YOU PISS-PANTS LITTLE B***H! BUT MY DAD HAS A MILLION BACKUP PLANS AND HIDDEN--
UH...ACTUALLY, BETH? SWEETIE... THIS TIME I DON'T HAVE ANY OF MY USUAL BACKUP GADGETS...
I PROBABLY SHOULD'VE HAD YOU BRING A... ONE OF MY LAB COATS OR SOMETHING...
THEN WHAT WAS YOUR PLAN WHEN YOU WERE ANTAGONIZING THEM?!
I DUNNO! I FIGURED I'D THINK OF SOMETHING! I FELT ON A CREATIVE ROLL AFTER THE DECONSTRUCTIONIST THING WORKED!!
ARE YOU--? HOW ARE YOU DOING THAT?
I STILL HAVE YOUR PORTAL GUN...
HE'S NOT. SEE...
...Y-YOU GIANT COMPANIES ALWAYS FORGET ONE THING WHEN Y-YOU MAKE YOUR PLANS--
YOU AREN'T THE ONES WHO DECIDE WHEN SOMETHING'S GOING TO BE BIG...

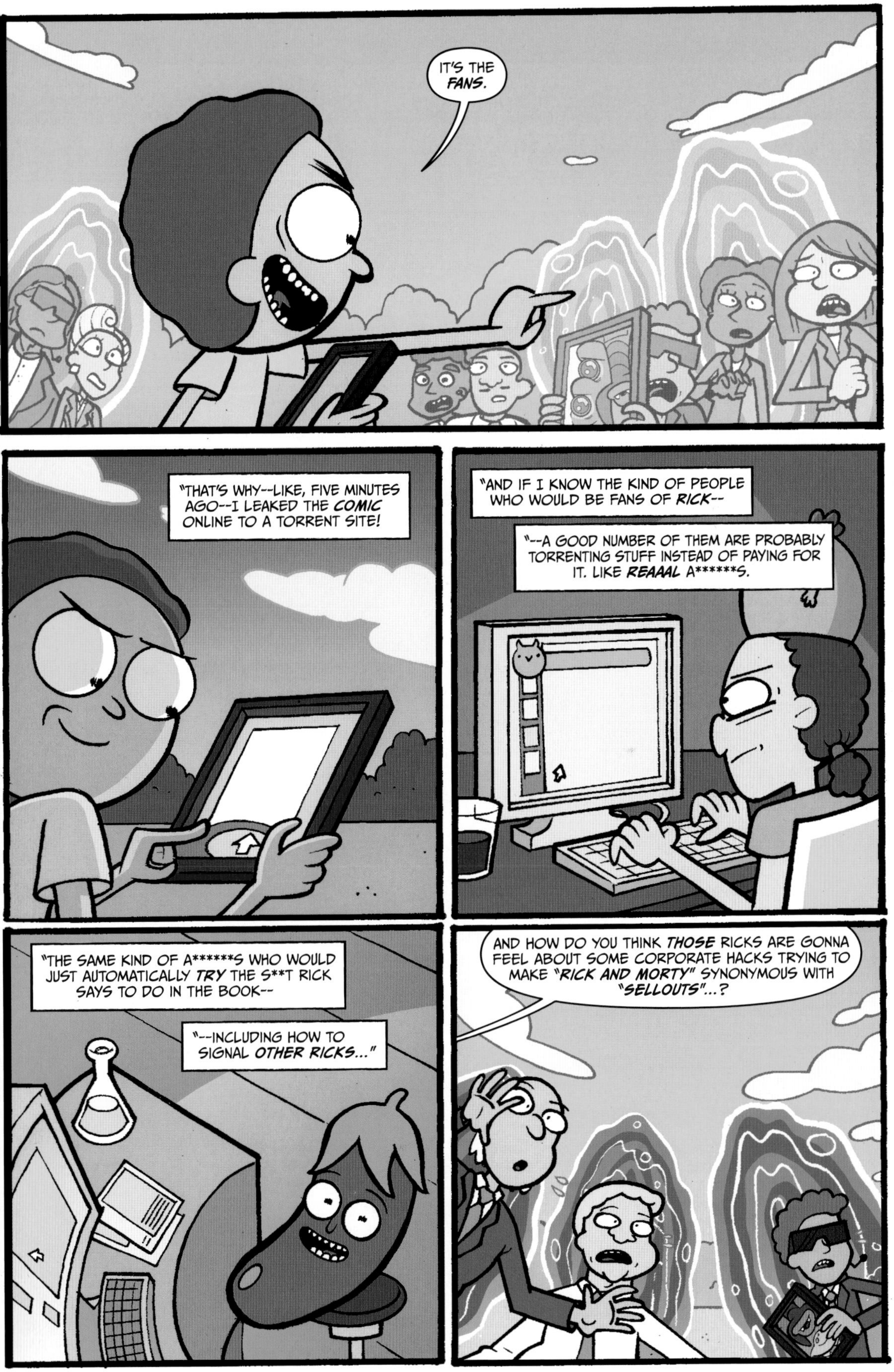
IT'S THE FANS.
"THAT'S WHY--LIKE, FIVE MINUTES AGO--I LEAKED THE COMIC ONLINE TO A TORRENT SITE!
"AND IF I KNOW THE KIND OF PEOPLE WHO WOULD BE FANS OF RICK--
"--A GOOD NUMBER OF THEM ARE PROBABLY TORRENTING STUFF INSTEAD OF PAYING FOR IT. LIKE REAAAL A******S.
"THE SAME KIND OF A******S WHO WOULD JUST AUTOMATICALLY TRY THE S**T RICK SAYS TO DO IN THE BOOK--
"--INCLUDING HOW TO SIGNAL OTHER RICKS..."
AND HOW DO YOU THINK THOSE RICKS ARE GONNA FEEL ABOUT SOME CORPORATE HACKS TRYING TO MAKE "RICK AND MORTY" SYNONYMOUS WITH "SELLOUTS"...?

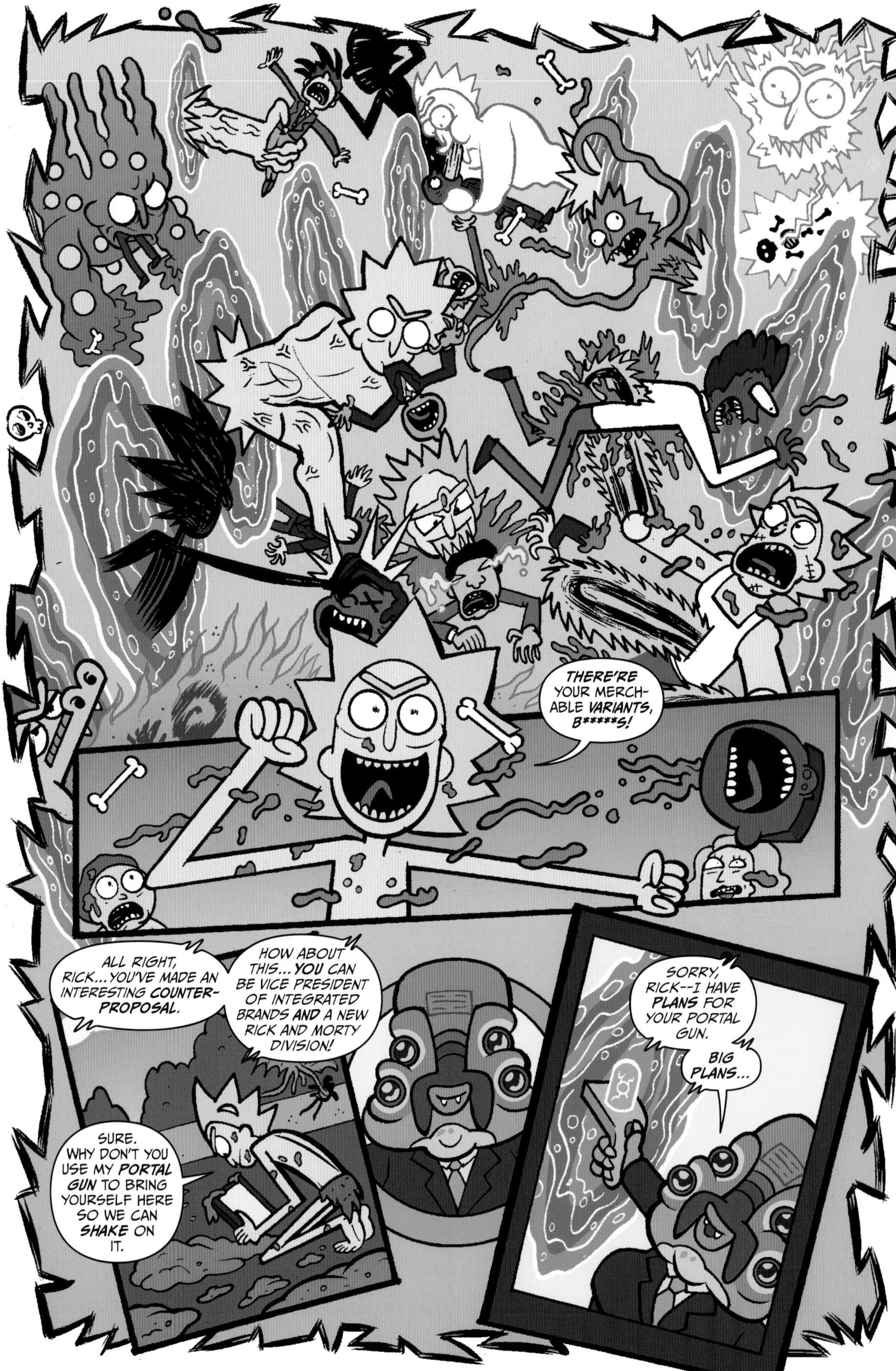
THERE'RE YOUR MERCH-ABLE VARIANTS, B*****S!
ALL RIGHT, RICK... YOU'VE MADE AN INTERESTING COUNTER-PROPOSAL.
HOW ABOUT THIS... YOU CAN BE VICE PRESIDENT OF INTEGRATED BRANDS AND A NEW RICK AND MORTY DIVISION!
SURE. WHY DON'T YOU USE MY PORTAL GUN TO BRING YOURSELF HERE SO WE CAN SHAKE ON IT.
SORRY, RICK--I HAVE PLANS FOR YOUR PORTAL GUN.
BIG PLANS...

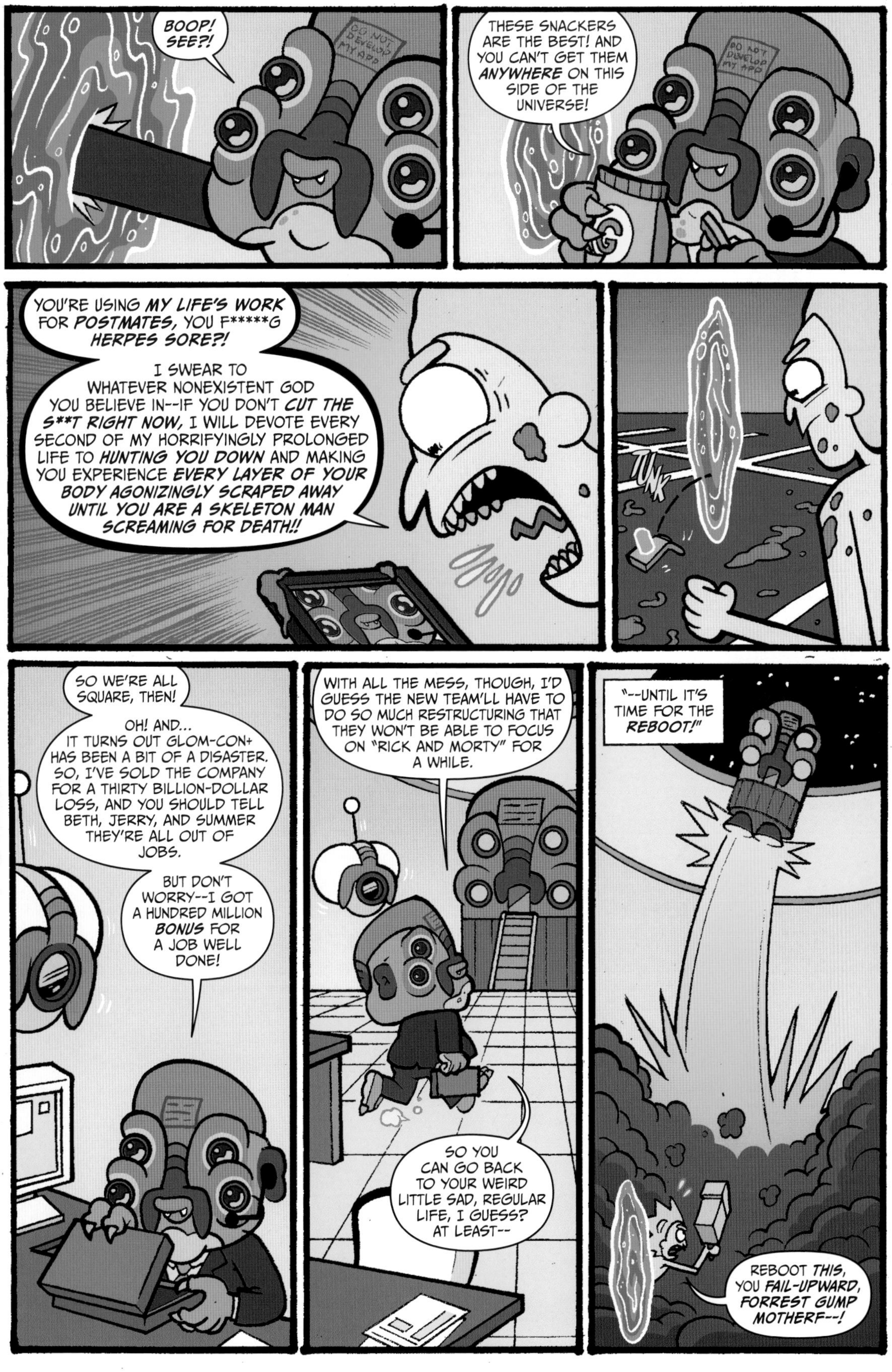
BOOP! SEE?!
DO NOT DEVELOP MY APP
THESE SNACKERS ARE THE BEST! AND YOU CAN'T GET THEM ANYWHERE ON THIS SIDE OF THE UNIVERSE!
DO NOT DEVELOP MY APP
YOU'RE USING MY LIFE'S WORK FOR POSTMATES, YOU F*****G HERPES SORE?!
I SWEAR TO WHATEVER NONEXISTENT GOD YOU BELIEVE IN--IF YOU DON'T CUT THE S**T RIGHT NOW, I WILL DEVOTE EVERY SECOND OF MY HORRIFYINGLY PROLONGED LIFE TO HUNTING YOU DOWN AND MAKING YOU EXPERIENCE EVERY LAYER OF YOUR BODY AGONIZINGLY SCRAPED AWAY UNTIL YOU ARE A SKELETON MAN SCREAMING FOR DEATH!!
TUNK
SO WE'RE ALL SQUARE, THEN!
OH! AND... IT TURNS OUT GLOM-CON+ HAS BEEN A BIT OF A DISASTER. SO, I'VE SOLD THE COMPANY FOR A THIRTY BILLION-DOLLAR LOSS, AND YOU SHOULD TELL BETH, JERRY, AND SUMMER THEY'RE ALL OUT OF JOBS.
BUT DON'T WORRY--I GOT A HUNDRED MILLION BONUS FOR A JOB WELL DONE!
WITH ALL THE MESS, THOUGH, I'D GUESS THE NEW TEAM'LL HAVE TO DO SO MUCH RESTRUCTURING THAT THEY WON'T BE ABLE TO FOCUS ON "RICK AND MORTY" FOR A WHILE.
SO YOU CAN GO BACK TO YOUR WEIRD LITTLE SAD, REGULAR LIFE, I GUESS? AT LEAST--
"--UNTIL IT'S TIME FOR THE REBOOT!"
REBOOT THIS, YOU FAIL-UPWARD, FORREST GUMP MOTHERF--!

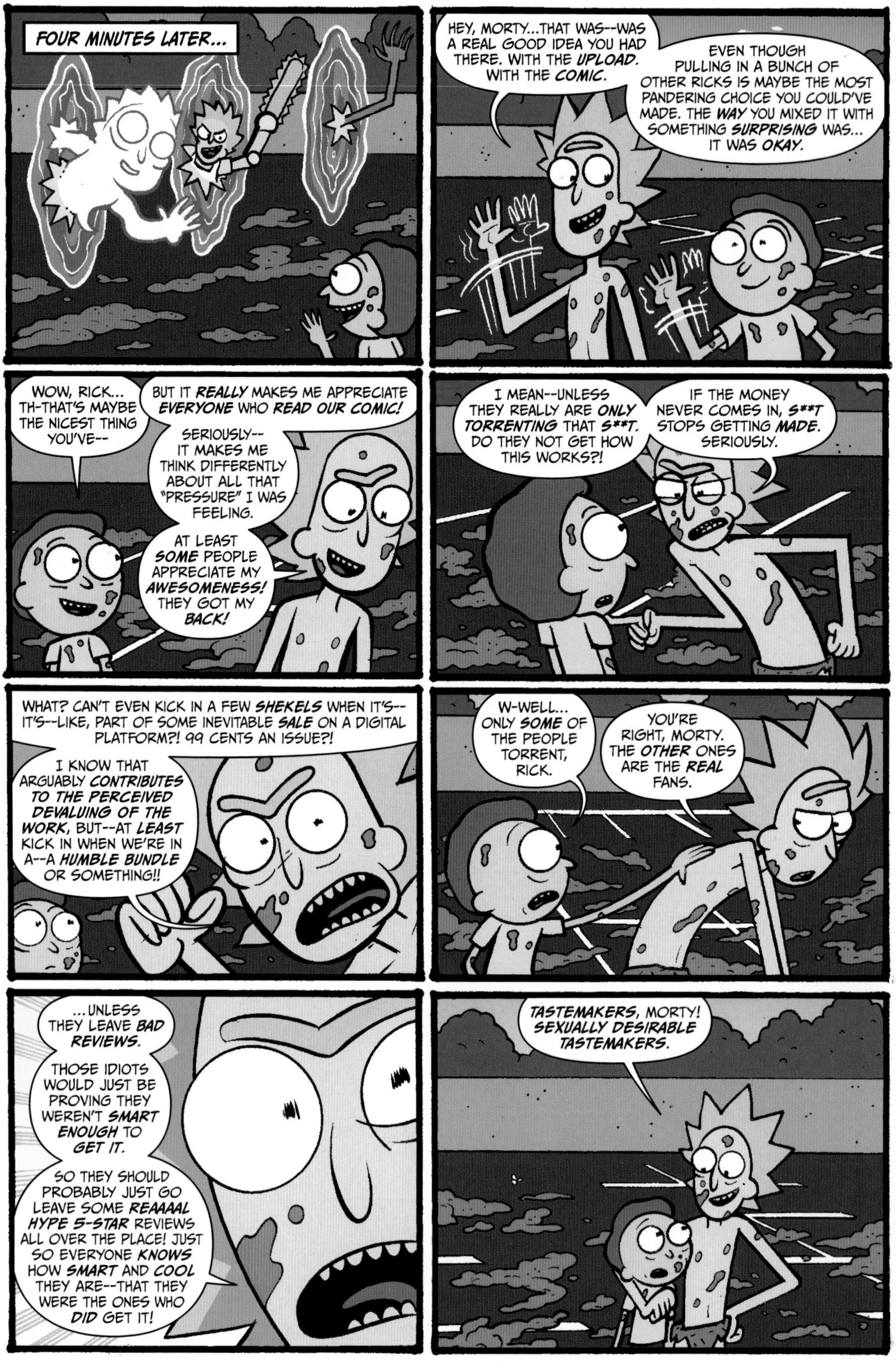
FOUR MINUTES LATER...
HEY, MORTY...THAT WAS--WAS A REAL GOOD IDEA YOU HAD THERE. WITH THE UPLOAD. WITH THE COMIC.
EVEN THOUGH PULLING IN A BUNCH OF OTHER RICKS IS MAYBE THE MOST PANDERING CHOICE YOU COULD'VE MADE. THE WAY YOU MIXED IT WITH SOMETHING SURPRISING WAS... IT WAS OKAY.
WOW, RICK... TH-THAT'S MAYBE THE NICEST THING YOU'VE--
BUT IT REALLY MAKES ME APPRECIATE EVERYONE WHO READ OUR COMIC!
SERIOUSLY-- IT MAKES ME THINK DIFFERENTLY ABOUT ALL THAT "PRESSURE" I WAS FEELING.
AT LEAST SOME PEOPLE APPRECIATE MY AWESOMENESS! THEY GOT MY BACK!
I MEAN--UNLESS THEY REALLY ARE ONLY TORRENTING THAT S**T. DO THEY NOT GET HOW THIS WORKS?!
IF THE MONEY NEVER COMES IN, S**T STOPS GETTING MADE. SERIOUSLY.
WHAT? CAN'T EVEN KICK IN A FEW SHEKELS WHEN IT'S--IT'S--LIKE, PART OF SOME INEVITABLE SALE ON A DIGITAL PLATFORM?! 99 CENTS AN ISSUE?!
I KNOW THAT ARGUABLY CONTRIBUTES TO THE PERCEIVED DEVALUING OF THE WORK, BUT--AT LEAST KICK IN WHEN WE'RE IN A--A HUMBLE BUNDLE OR SOMETHING!!
W-WELL... ONLY SOME OF THE PEOPLE TORRENT, RICK.
YOU'RE RIGHT, MORTY. THE OTHER ONES ARE THE REAL FANS.
...UNLESS THEY LEAVE BAD REVIEWS.
THOSE IDIOTS WOULD JUST BE PROVING THEY WEREN'T SMART ENOUGH TO GET IT.
SO THEY SHOULD PROBABLY JUST GO LEAVE SOME REAAAAL HYPE 5-STAR REVIEWS ALL OVER THE PLACE! JUST SO EVERYONE KNOWS HOW SMART AND COOL THEY ARE--THAT THEY WERE THE ONES WHO DID GET IT!
TASTEMAKERS, MORTY! SEXUALLY DESIRABLE TASTEMAKERS.

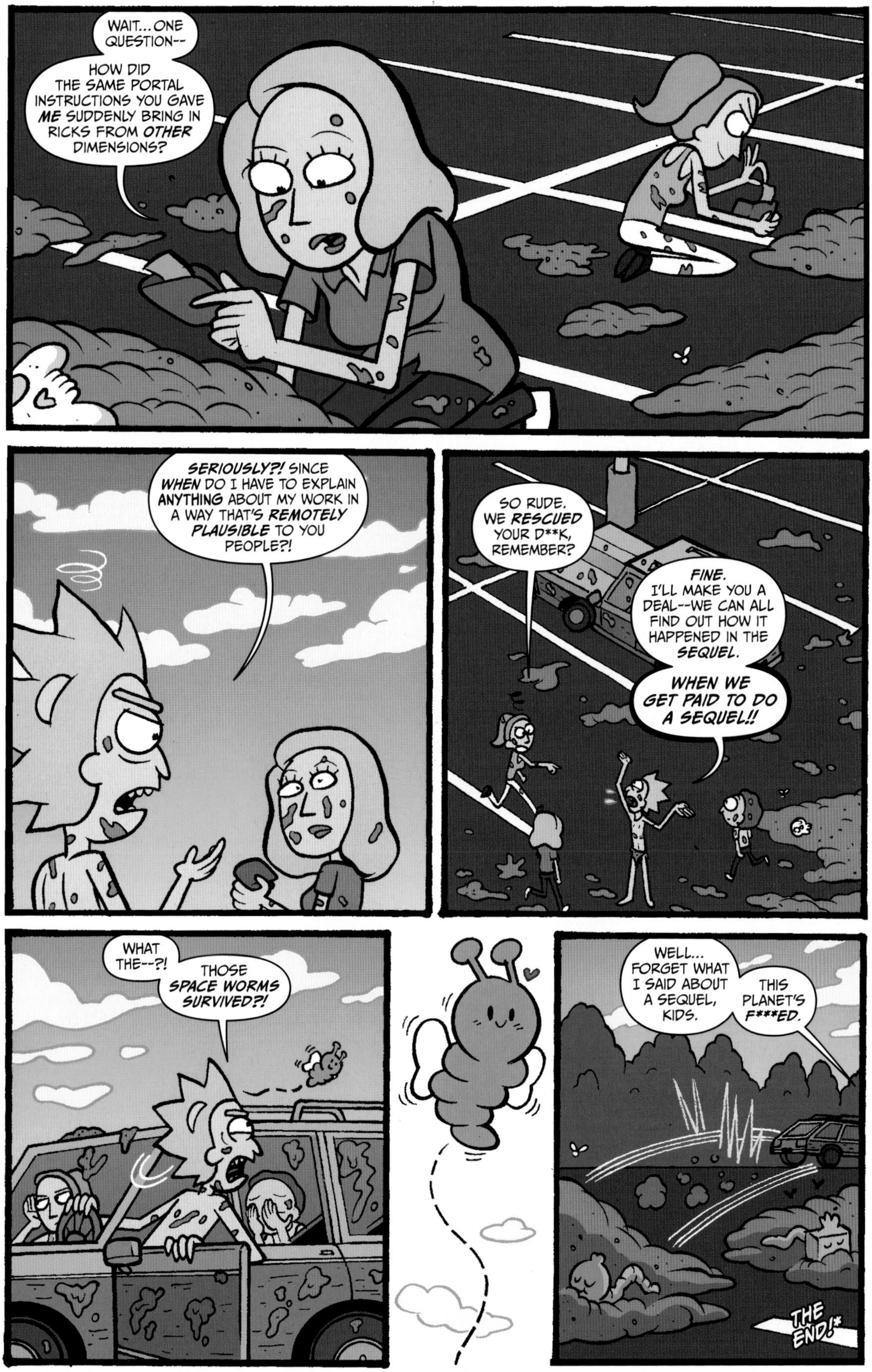
WAIT... ONE QUESTION--
HOW DID THE SAME PORTAL INSTRUCTIONS YOU GAVE ME SUDDENLY BRING IN RICKS FROM OTHER DIMENSIONS?
SERIOUSLY?! SINCE WHEN DO I HAVE TO EXPLAIN ANYTHING ABOUT MY WORK IN A WAY THAT'S REMOTELY PLAUSIBLE TO YOU PEOPLE?!
SO RUDE. WE RESCUED YOUR D**K, REMEMBER?
FINE. I'LL MAKE YOU A DEAL--WE CAN ALL FIND OUT HOW IT HAPPENED IN THE SEQUEL.
WHEN WE GET PAID TO DO A SEQUEL!!
WHAT THE--?!
THOSE SPACE WORMS SURVIVED?!
WELL... FORGET WHAT I SAID ABOUT A SEQUEL, KIDS.
THIS PLANET'S F***ED.
THE END!*

*UNLESS A CORPORATE FUNCTIONARY DECIDES THIS PARTICULAR INSTALLMENT HAS ENOUGH PROFIT POTENTIAL TO EXPLOIT FURTHER! **YOU ARE A CUSTOMER DEMOGRAPHIC, AND WE HAVE YOU WHERE WE WANT YOU!!** USE CODE **"RICKANDMORTY"** FOR A FREE MONTH TRIAL OF GLOM-CON+!

EPILOGUE

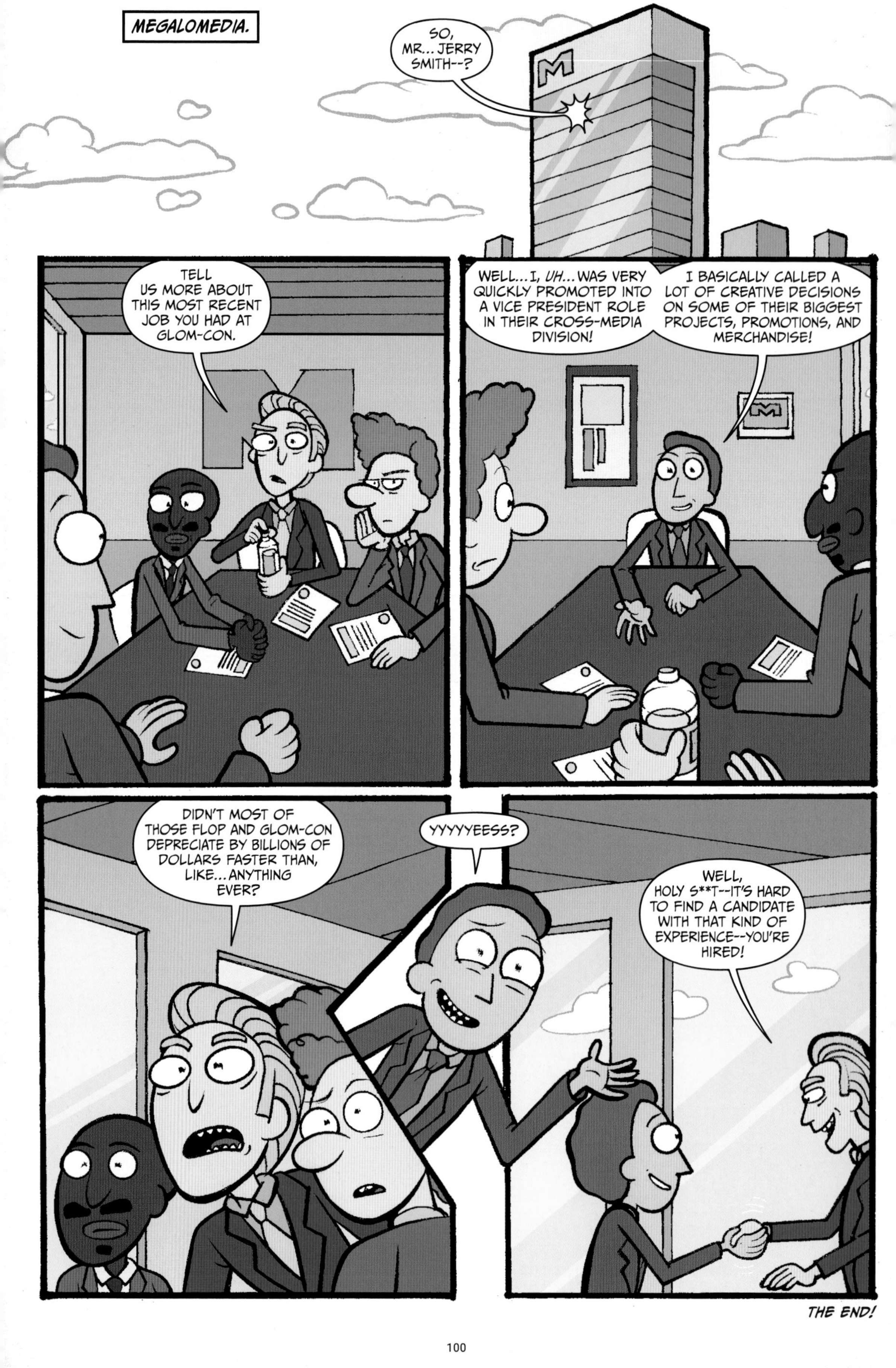
MEGALOMEDIA.
SO, MR... JERRY SMITH--?
TELL US MORE ABOUT THIS MOST RECENT JOB YOU HAD AT GLOM-CON.
WELL... I, UH... WAS VERY QUICKLY PROMOTED INTO A VICE PRESIDENT ROLE IN THEIR CROSS-MEDIA DIVISION!
I BASICALLY CALLED A LOT OF CREATIVE DECISIONS ON SOME OF THEIR BIGGEST PROJECTS, PROMOTIONS, AND MERCHANDISE!
DIDN'T MOST OF THOSE FLOP AND GLOM-CON DEPRECIATE BY BILLIONS OF DOLLARS FASTER THAN, LIKE... ANYTHING EVER?
YYYYYEESS?
WELL, HOLY S**T--IT'S HARD TO FIND A CANDIDATE WITH THAT KIND OF EXPERIENCE--YOU'RE HIRED!
THE END!

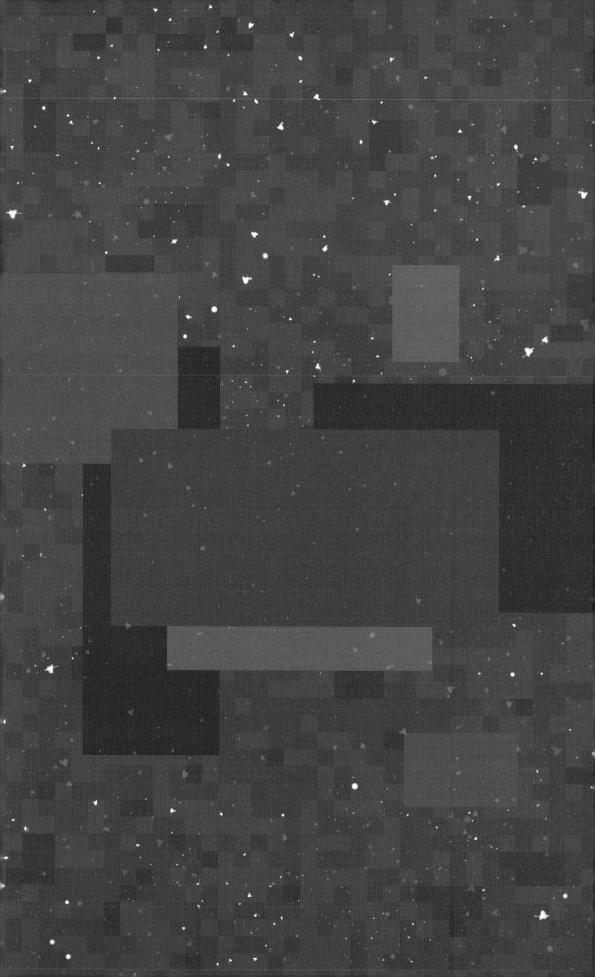

COVER GALLERY

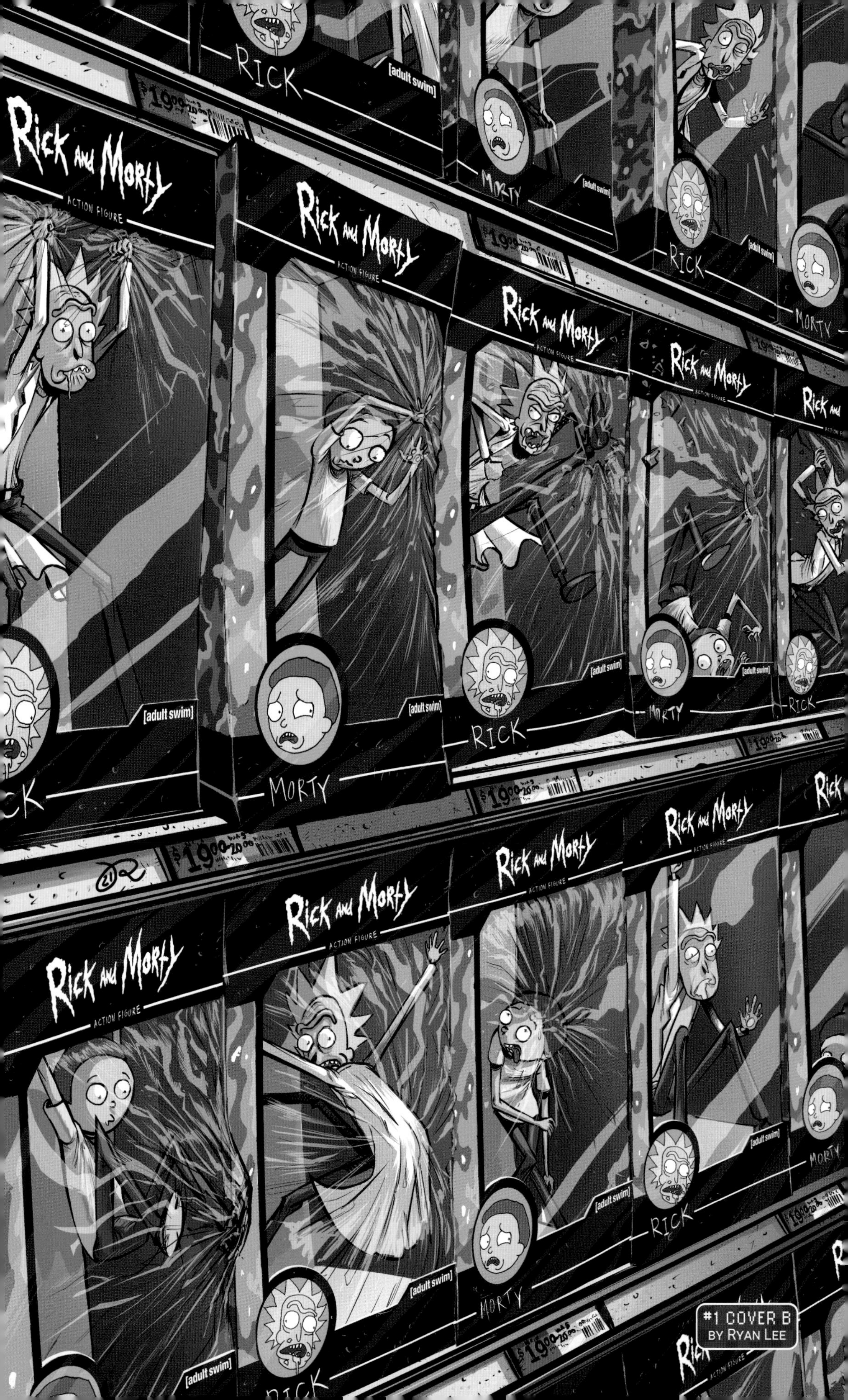
RICK
[adult swim]
MORTY
[adult swim]
RICK
[adult swim]
Rick and Morty
ACTION FIGURE
[adult swim]
RICK
Rick and Morty
ACTION FIGURE
[adult swim]
MORTY
Rick and Morty
ACTION FIGURE
[adult swim]
RICK
Rick and Morty
ACTION FIGURE
[adult swim]
MORTY
Rick and Morty
ACTION FIGURE
Rick and Morty
ACTION FIGURE
[adult swim]
RICK
Rick and Morty
ACTION FIGURE
[adult swim]
Rick and Morty
ACTION FIGURE
[adult swim]
MORTY
Rick and Morty
ACTION FIGURE
[adult swim]
RICK
[adult swim]
MORTY
#1 COVER B
BY RYAN LEE

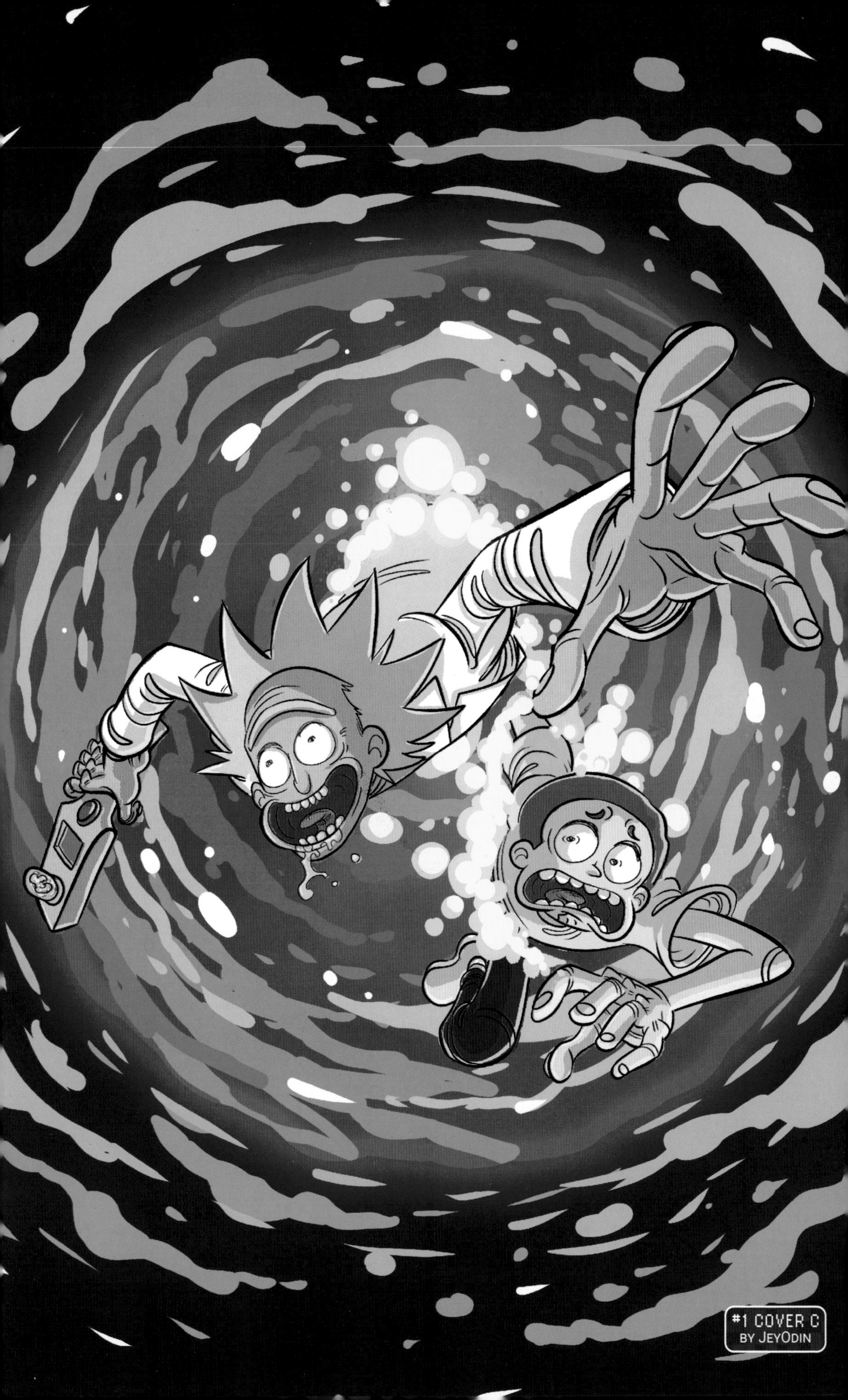
#1 COVER C
BY JEYODIN

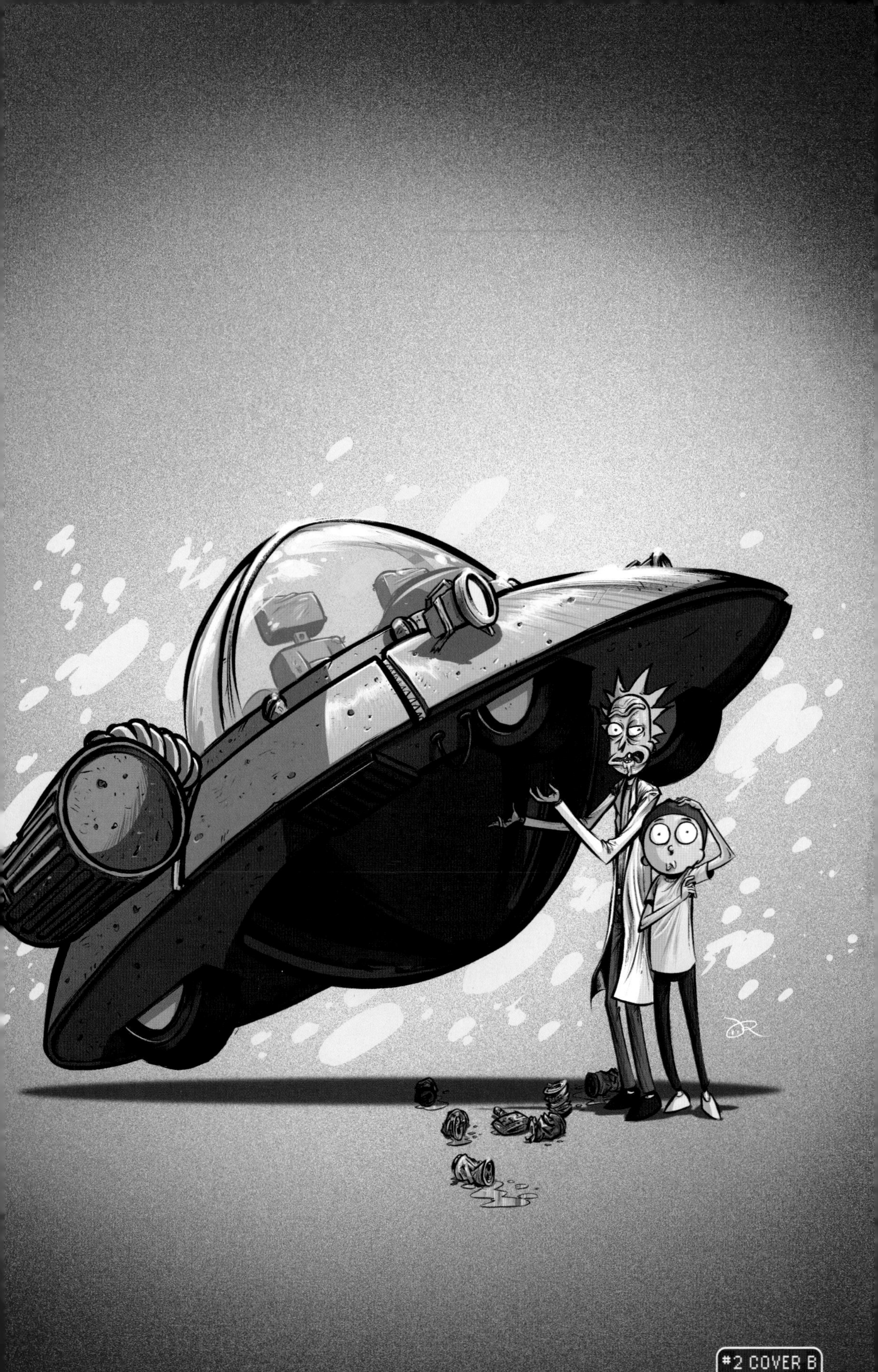

#2 COVER B
BY RYAN LEE

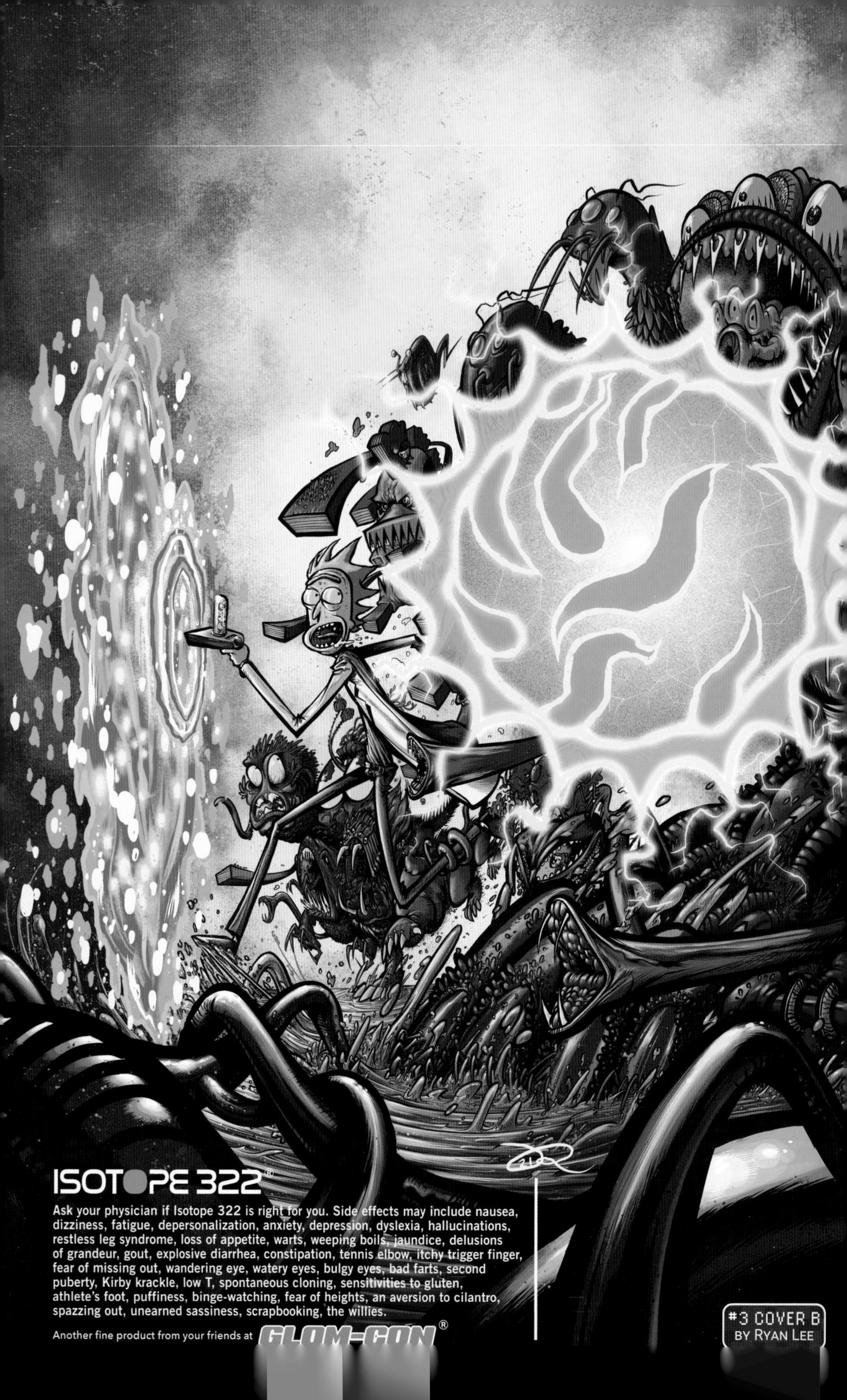
ISOTOPE 322®
Ask your physician if Isotope 322 is right for you. Side effects may include nausea, dizziness, fatigue, depersonalization, anxiety, depression, dyslexia, hallucinations, restless leg syndrome, loss of appetite, warts, weeping boils, jaundice, delusions of grandeur, gout, explosive diarrhea, constipation, tennis elbow, itchy trigger finger, fear of missing out, wandering eye, watery eyes, bulgy eyes, bad farts, second puberty, Kirby krackle, low T, spontaneous cloning, sensitivities to gluten, athlete's foot, puffiness, binge-watching, fear of heights, an aversion to cilantro, spazzing out, unearned sassiness, scrapbooking, the willies.
Another fine product from your friends at GLOM-CON®
#3 COVER B
BY RYAN LEE